A classical dictionary of the vulgar tongue. The second edition, corrected and enlarged.

Francis Grose

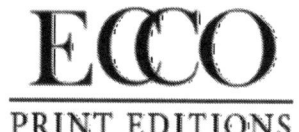

A classical dictionary of the vulgar tongue. The second edition, corrected and enlarged.
Grose, Francis
ESTCID: T006268
Reproduction from British Library
Anonymous. By Francis Grose.
London : printed for S. Hooper, 1788.
xv,[249]p. ; 8°

Eighteenth Century
Collections Online
Print Editions

Gale ECCO Print Editions

Relive history with *Eighteenth Century Collections Online*, now available in print for the independent historian and collector. This series includes the most significant English-language and foreign-language works printed in Great Britain during the eighteenth century, and is organized in seven different subject areas including literature and language; medicine, science, and technology; and religion and philosophy. The collection also includes thousands of important works from the Americas.

The eighteenth century has been called "The Age of Enlightenment." It was a period of rapid advance in print culture and publishing, in world exploration, and in the rapid growth of science and technology – all of which had a profound impact on the political and cultural landscape. At the end of the century the American Revolution, French Revolution and Industrial Revolution, perhaps three of the most significant events in modern history, set in motion developments that eventually dominated world political, economic, and social life.

In a groundbreaking effort, Gale initiated a revolution of its own: digitization of epic proportions to preserve these invaluable works in the largest online archive of its kind. Contributions from major world libraries constitute over 175,000 original printed works. Scanned images of the actual pages, rather than transcriptions, recreate the works *as they first appeared.*

Now for the first time, these high-quality digital scans of original works are available via print-on-demand, making them readily accessible to libraries, students, independent scholars, and readers of all ages.

For our initial release we have created seven robust collections to form one the world's most comprehensive catalogs of 18th century works.

Initial Gale ECCO Print Editions collections include:

> ### History and Geography
> Rich in titles on English life and social history, this collection spans the world as it was known to eighteenth-century historians and explorers. Titles include a wealth of travel accounts and diaries, histories of nations from throughout the world, and maps and charts of a world that was still being discovered. Students of the War of American Independence will find fascinating accounts from the British side of conflict.

Social Science
Delve into what it was like to live during the eighteenth century by reading the first-hand accounts of everyday people, including city dwellers and farmers, businessmen and bankers, artisans and merchants, artists and their patrons, politicians and their constituents. Original texts make the American, French, and Industrial revolutions vividly contemporary.

Medicine, Science and Technology
Medical theory and practice of the 1700s developed rapidly, as is evidenced by the extensive collection, which includes descriptions of diseases, their conditions, and treatments. Books on science and technology, agriculture, military technology, natural philosophy, even cookbooks, are all contained here.

Literature and Language
Western literary study flows out of eighteenth-century works by Alexander Pope, Daniel Defoe, Henry Fielding, Frances Burney, Denis Diderot, Johann Gottfried Herder, Johann Wolfgang von Goethe, and others. Experience the birth of the modern novel, or compare the development of language using dictionaries and grammar discourses.

Religion and Philosophy
The Age of Enlightenment profoundly enriched religious and philosophical understanding and continues to influence present-day thinking. Works collected here include masterpieces by David Hume, Immanuel Kant, and Jean-Jacques Rousseau, as well as religious sermons and moral debates on the issues of the day, such as the slave trade. The Age of Reason saw conflict between Protestantism and Catholicism transformed into one between faith and logic -- a debate that continues in the twenty-first century.

Law and Reference
This collection reveals the history of English common law and Empire law in a vastly changing world of British expansion. Dominating the legal field is the *Commentaries of the Law of England* by Sir William Blackstone, which first appeared in 1765. Reference works such as almanacs and catalogues continue to educate us by revealing the day-to-day workings of society.

Fine Arts
The eighteenth-century fascination with Greek and Roman antiquity followed the systematic excavation of the ruins at Pompeii and Herculaneum in southern Italy; and after 1750 a neoclassical style dominated all artistic fields. The titles here trace developments in mostly English-language works on painting, sculpture, architecture, music, theater, and other disciplines. Instructional works on musical instruments, catalogs of art objects, comic operas, and more are also included.

The BiblioLife Network

This project was made possible in part by the BiblioLife Network (BLN), a project aimed at addressing some of the huge challenges facing book preservationists around the world. The BLN includes libraries, library networks, archives, subject matter experts, online communities and library service providers. We believe every book ever published should be available as a high-quality print reproduction; printed on-demand anywhere in the world. This insures the ongoing accessibility of the content and helps generate sustainable revenue for the libraries and organizations that work to preserve these important materials.

The following book is in the "public domain" and represents an authentic reproduction of the text as printed by the original publisher. While we have attempted to accurately maintain the integrity of the original work, there are sometimes problems with the original work or the micro-film from which the books were digitized. This can result in minor errors in reproduction. Possible imperfections include missing and blurred pages, poor pictures, markings and other reproduction issues beyond our control. Because this work is culturally important, we have made it available as part of our commitment to protecting, preserving, and promoting the world's literature.

GUIDE TO FOLD-OUTS MAPS and OVERSIZED IMAGES

The book you are reading was digitized from microfilm captured over the past thirty to forty years. Years after the creation of the original microfilm, the book was converted to digital files and made available in an online database.

In an online database, page images do not need to conform to the size restrictions found in a printed book. When converting these images back into a printed bound book, the page sizes are standardized in ways that maintain the detail of the original. For large images, such as fold-out maps, the original page image is split into two or more pages

Guidelines used to determine how to split the page image follows:

- Some images are split vertically; large images require vertical and horizontal splits.
- For horizontal splits, the content is split left to right.
- For vertical splits, the content is split from top to bottom.
- For both vertical and horizontal splits, the image is processed from top left to bottom right.

DICTIONARIES — VOCABULARIES
&
ETC. — ENGLISH
SLANG

1560/1923

A

CLASSICAL

DICTIONARY

OF THE

VULGAR TONGUE.

THE SECOND EDITION,

CORRECTED AND ENLARGED.

LONDON.

PRINTED FOR S. HOOPER, N°. 212, HIGH HOLBORN,
FACING BLOOMSBURY SQUARE.

M.DCC.LXXXVIII.

PREFACE

TO THE

SECOND EDITION.

THE favourable reception with which this Book was honoured by the Public, has encouraged the Editor to present a second edition, more correctly arranged, and very considerably enlarged. Some words and explanations in the former edition having been pointed out as rather indecent or indelicate, though to be found in Le Roux, and other Glossaries of the like kind, these have been either omitted, softened, or their explanations taken from books long sanctioned with general approbation, and admitted into the seminaries for the education of youth—such as Bailey's, Miege's, or Philips's Dictionaries; so that it is hoped this work will now be found as little offensive to delicacy as the nature of it would admit.

A list is here added of such books as have been consulted for the additions.

PREFACE TO THE

A

CAVEAT

FOR

COMMON CURSETORS,

VULGARLY CALLED

VAGABONES;

SET FORTH BY

THOMAS HARMAN, Esquier,

FOR THE

Utilitie and Proffit of hys Naturall Countrey.

Newly Augmented and Imprinted, Anno Domini
M.D.LXVII.

Viewed, Examined, and Allowed according unto the Queen's Majeſtye's Injunctions.

Imprinted at London, in Flete-ſtreet, at the Signe of the Faulcon, by William Gryffith; and are to be folde at his Shoppe in Saynt Dunſtone's Churche Yarde, in the Weſt.

SECOND EDITION. v

THE
CANTING ACADEMY;
OR,
VILLANIES DISCOVERED:

WHEREIN ARE SHEWN

The Mysterious and Villanous Practices of that Wicked Crew, commonly known by the Names of

HECTORS, TRAPANNERS, GILTS, &c.

With several NEW CATCHES and SONGS.

ALSO A

COMPLEAT CANTING DICTIONARY,

BOTH OF

Old Words, and such as are *now most in Use*.

A Book very useful and necessary (to be known, but not practised) for all People.

THE SECOND EDITION.

LONDON:

Printed by F. LEACH, for MAT. DRUW, and are to be sold by the Booksellers.

N. B. *The Dedication is signed*, R. HEAD.

HELL upon EARTH;

OR THE MOST PLEASANT AND DELECTABLE

HISTORY

OF

WHITTINGTON's COLLEDGE,

OTHERWISE (VULGARLY) CALLED

NEWGATE.

Giving an Account of the Humours of thofe Collegians who are ftrictly examined at the Old Baily, and take their higheft Degrees near Hyde Park Corner.

Being very ufeful to all Perfons, either Gentle or Simple, in fhewing them the Manner of the Robberies and Cheats committed by Villains on the Nation; whereby they may be the more careful of being wronged by them for the future.

LONDON:

PRINTED IN THE YEAR 1703.

SECOND EDITION.

THE
SCOUNDRELS DICTIONARY;
OR, AN
EXPLANATION
OF THE
CANT WORDS used by THIEVES, HOUSE-BREAKERS, STREET ROBBERS, and PICKPOCKETS about Town.

TO WHICH ARE PREFIXED

Some CURIOUS DISSERTATIONS on the ART of WHEEDLING,

AND A

Collection of their FLASH SONGS, with a PROPER GLOSSARY.

The whole printed from a *Copy taken on one of their Gang*, in the late Scuffle between the Watchmen and a Party of them on Clerkenwell Green, which Copy is now in the Custody of one of the Constables of that Parish.

LONDON:
Printed for J. BROWNNELL, in Pater-noster-row.
M.DCC.LIV.
[Price Sixpence.]

PREFACE

TO THE

FIRST EDITION.

THE great approbation with which so polite a nation as France has received the Satirical and Burlesque Dictionary of Monsieur Le Roux, testified by the several editions it has gone through, will, it is hoped, apologize for an attempt to compile an English Dictionary on a similar plan; our language being at least as copious as the French, and as capable of the witty equivoque: besides which, the freedom of thought and speech arising from, and privileged by, our constitution, gives a force and poignancy to the expressions of our common people, not to be found under arbitrary governments, where the ebullitions of vulgar wit are checked by the fear of the bastinado, or of a lodging during pleasure in some gaol or castle.

The many vulgar allusions and cant expressions that so frequently occur in our com-

mon

mon conversation and periodical publications, make a work of this kind extremely useful, if not absolutely necessary, not only to foreigners, but even to natives resident at a distance from the Metropolis, or who do not mix in the busy world: without some such help, they might hunt through all the ordinary Dictionaries, from Alpha to Omega, in search of the words, " black legs, lame duck, a plumb, malingeror, nip cheese, darbies, and the new drop," although these are all terms of well-known import at Newmarket, Exchange-alley, the City, the Parade, Wapping, and Newgate.

The fashionable words, or favourite expressions of the day, also find their way into our political and theatrical compositions: these, as they generally originate from some trifling event, or temporary circumstance, on falling into disuse, or being superseded by new ones, vanish without leaving a trace behind. Such were the late fashionable words, *a bore* and *a twaddle*, among the great vulgar; *maccaroni* and *the barber*, among the small: these, too, are here carefully registered.

The

The Vulgar Tongue confifts of two parts: the firft is the Cant Language, called fometimes Pedlars French, or St. Giles's Greek; the fecond, thofe burlefque phrafes, quaint allufions, and nick-names for perfons, things, and places, which, from long uninterrupted ufage, are made claffical by prefcription.

Refpecting the firft, that is, the canting language, take the account given of its origin, and the cataftrophe of its inftitutor, from Mr. Harrifon's Defcription of England, prefixed to Hollingfhead's Chronicle; where, treating of beggars, gypfies, &c. he fays, " It is not yet fifty years fith this trade be-
" gan: but how it hath profpered fithens
" that time, it is eafy to judge; for they are
" now fuppofed, of one fexe and another,
" to amount unto above ten thoufand per-
" fons, as I have harde reported. More-
" over, in counterfeiting the Egyptian roges,
" they have devifed a language among them-
" felves, which they name Canting, but
" others Pedlars French, a fpeache compact
" thirty yeares fince of Englifh, and a great
" number of odde wordes of their own de-
" vifing, without all order or reafon; and
" yet fuch it is, as none but themfelves are
" able

" able to underftand. The firft devifer
" thereof was hanged by the neck, as a juft
" reward, no doubt, for his defartes, and a
" common end to all of that profeffion.

" A gentleman (Mr. Thomas Harman)
" alfo of late hath taken great paines to
" fearch out the fecret practizes of this un-
" gracious rabble; and, among other things,
" he fetteth down and defcribeth twenty-two
" forts of them, whofe names it fhall not
" be amiffe to remember, whereby each one
" may gather what wicked people they are,
" and what vi'lany remaineth in them."

For this lift fee the word CREW.—This was the origin of the cant language; its terms have been collected from the following Treatifes.

The Bellman of London, bringing to light the moft notorious villanies that are now practifed in the kingdom. Profitable for gentlemen, lawyers, merchants, citizens, farmers, mafters of houfeholds, and all forts of fervants, to marke, and delightfull for men to reade.—Lege, Perlege, Relege.— 1608.

Thieves falling out, true men come by their goods.—1615.

English Villanies, seven severall times preſt to death by the printers; but (ſtill reviving againe) are now the eighth time (as the firſt) diſcovered by lanthorne and candle-light: and the helpe of a new cryer, called O-per-ſe O; whoſe loud voyce proclaimes, to all that will heare him, another conſpiracy of abuſes lately plotting together, to hurt the peace of the kingdom; which the bell-man (becauſe he ther went ſtumbling i'th' dark) could never ſee till now; and becauſe a company of rogues, cunning canting gypſies, and all the ſcumme of our nation, fight under their tattered colours. At the end is a canting dictionary to teach their language, with canting ſongs. A booke to make gentlemen merry, citizens warie, countrymen carefull; fit for juſtices to reade over, becauſe it is a pilot by whom they may make ſtrange diſcoveries.—London, 1638.

Bailey's, and the new Canting Dictionary, have alſo been conſulted, with the Hiſtory of Bamfield More Carew, the Seſſions Papers, and other modern authorities. As many

many of thefe terms are ftill profeffionally ufed by our prefent race of free-booters of different denominations, who feem to have eftablifhed a fyftematical manner of carrying on their bufinefs, a knowledge of them may therefore be ufeful to gentlemen in the commiffion of the peace.

The fecond part, or burlefque terms, have been drawn from the moft claffical authorities; fuch as foldiers on the long march, feamen at the capftern, ladies difpofing of their fifh, and the colloquies of a Gravefend boat.

Many heroic fentences, expreffing and inculcating a contempt of death, have been caught from the mouths of the applauding populace, attending thofe triumphant proceffions up Holborn-hill, with which many an unfortunate hero till lately finifhed his courfe: and various choice flowers have been collected at executions, as well thofe authorized by the fentence of the law, and performed under the direction of the fheriff, as thofe inflicted under the authority and infpection of that impartial and fummary tribunal, called the Mob, upon the pickpockets,

pockets, informers, or other unpopular criminals.

In the courfe of this work many ludicrous games and cuftoms are explained, which are not to be met with in any other book: the fucceffion of the finifhers of the law, the abolition of the triumph or ovation of Holborn Hill, with the introduction of the prefent mode of execution at Newgate, are chronologically afcertained; points of great importance to both the prefent and future compilers of the Tyburn Chronicle.

To prevent any charge of immorality being brought againft this work, the Editor begs leave to obferve, that when an indelicate or immodeft word has obtruded itfelf for explanation, he has endeavoured to get rid of it in the moft decent manner poffible; and none have been admitted but fuch as either could not be left out without rendering the work incomplete, or in fome meafure compenfate by their wit for the trefpafs committed on decorum. Indeed, refpecting this matter, he can with great truth make the fame defence that Falftaff ludicroufly urges in behalf of one engaged in rebellion,

VIZ.

viz. that he did not seek them, but that, like rebellion in the case instanced, they lay in his way, and he found them.

The Editor likewise begs leave to add, that if he has had the misfortune to run foul of the dignity of any body of men, profession, or trade, it is totally contrary to his intention; and he hopes the interpretations given to any particular terms that may seem to bear hard upon them, will not be considered as his sentiments, but as the sentiments of the persons by whom such terms were first invented, or those by whom they are used.

A CLASSICAL DICTIONARY OF THE VULGAR TONGUE.

A.

ACA

ABBESS, or LADY ABBESS. A bawd, the mistress of a brothel.

ABEL-WACKETS. Blows given on the palm of the hand with a twisted handkerchief, instead of a ferula; a jocular punishment among seamen, who sometimes play at cards for wackets, the loser suffering as many strokes as he has lost games.

ABIGAIL. A lady's waiting maid.

ABRAM. Naked. *Cant.*

ABRAM COVE. A cant word among thieves, signifying a naked or poor man, also a lusty, strong rogue.

ABRAM MEN. Pretended mad men.

TO SHAM ABRAM. To pretend sickness.

ACADEMY, or PUSHING SCHOOL. A brothel.—The Floating Academy, the lighters on board of which those persons are confined, who by a late regulation are condemned to hard labour, instead of transportation.—Campbell's Academy; the same,

same, from a gentleman of that name, who had the contract for finding and victualling the hulks or lighters.

ACCOUNTS. To cast up one's accounts, to vomit.

ACORN. You will ride a horse foaled by an acorn, i. e. the gallows, called also the Wooden and Three-legged Mare. You will be hanged.—See THREE LEGGED MARE.

ACT OF PARLIAMENT. A military term for small beer, five pints of which, by an act of parliament, a landlord was formerly obliged to give to each soldier gratis

ACTEON. A cuckold, from the horns planted on the head of Acteon by Diana

ADAM'S ALE. Water.

ADAM TILER. A pickpocket's associate, who receives the stolen goods, and runs off with them. *Cant.*

ADAMS. The most ancient, honourable, and venerable society of the name of Adams, A. D. 1750, held their meetings at the Royal Swan, Kingsland Road, kept by George Adams.

ADDLE PATE. An inconsiderate foolish fellow.

ADDLE PLOT. A spoil-sport, a mar-all.

ADMIRAL OF THE BLUE, who carries his flag on the mainmast. A landlord or publican wearing a blue apron, as was formerly the custom among gentlemen of that vocation.

ADMIRAL OF THE NARROW SEAS. One who from drunkenness vomits into the lap of the person sitting opposite to him. *Sea phrase.*

ADRIFT Loose, turned adrift, discharged. *Sea phrase.*

AFFIDAVIT MEN Knights of the post, or false witnesses, said to attend Westminster Hall, and other courts of justice, ready to swear any thing for hire, distinguished by having straw stuck in the heels of their shoes.

AFTER-CLAP. A demand after the first given-in has been discharged, a charge for pretended omissions.

AGAINST THE GRAIN. Unwilling It went much against the grain with him, i. e, it was much against his inclination, or against his pluck.

AGOG, ALL-A-GOG. Anxious, eager, impatient from the Italian *agogare*, to desire eagerly.

AGROUND. Stuck fast, stopped, at a loss, ruined, like a boat or vessel aground,

AIR AND EXERCISE. He has had air and exercise, i. e. he has been whipped at the cart's tail, or, as it is generally, though more vulgarly, expressed, at the cart's a—se.

ALDERMAN. A roasted turkey garnished with sausages, the latter are supposed to represent the gold chain worn by those magistrates.

ALE DRAPER An alehouse keeper.

ALE POST A may-pole.

ALL-A-MORT Struck dumb, confounded.

ALGATE. A draught on the pump at Algate, a bad bill of exchange, drawn on persons who have no effects of the drawer.

ALL HOLIDAY. It is all holiday at Peckham, or it is all holiday with him; a saying signifying that it is all over with the business or person spoken of or alluded to.

ALL HOLLOW He was beat all hollow, i e. he had no chance of conquering, it was all hollow, or a hollow thing, it was a decided thing from the beginning. See HOLLOW.

ALL NATIONS. A composition of all the different spirits sold in a dram shop, collected in a vessel, into which the drainings of the bottles and quartern pots are emptied.

ALLS. The five alls is a country sign, representing five human figures, each having a motto under him The first is a king in his regalia; his motto, I govern all the second a bishop in pontificals, motto, I pray for all third, a lawyer in his gown; motto, I plead for all fourth, a soldier in his regimentals, fully accoutred, motto, I fight for all fifth, a poor countryman with his scythe and rake, motto, I pay for all.

ALSASIA THE HIGHER. White Friars, once a place privileged from arrests for debt, as was also the Mint, but suppressed on account of the notorious abuses committed there.

ALSASIA THE LOWER. The Mint in Southwark.

ALSASIANS The inhabitants of White Fryers or the Mint.

ALTAMEL. A verbal or lump account, without particulars, such as is commonly produced at bawdy houses, spunging houses, &c. Vide DUTCH RECKONING.

ALTITUDES. The man is in his altitudes, i e he is drunk.

AMBASSADOR. A trick to duck some ignorant fellow or landsman, frequently played on board ships in the warm latitudes. It is thus managed. a large tub is filled with water, and two stools placed on each side of it. Over the whole is thrown a tarpawlin, or old sail. this is kept tight by two persons, who are to represent the king and queen of a foreign country, and are seated on the stools. The person intended to be ducked plays the ambassador, and after repeating a ridiculous speech dictated to him, is led in great form up to the throne, and seated between the king and queen, who rising suddenly as soon as he is seated, he falls backwards into the tub of water.

AMBIDEXTER. A lawyer who takes fees from both, plaintiff and defendant, or that goes snacks with both parties in gaming.

AMEN CURLER. A parish clerk.

AMEN. He said Yes and Amen to every thing, he agreed to every thing.

AMINIDAB. A jeering name for a quaker.

AMES ACE. Within ames ace; nearly, very near.

TO AMUSE. To fling dust or snuff in the eyes of the person intended to be robbed; also to invent some plausible tale, to delude shopkeepers and others, thereby to put them off their guard. *Cant.*

AMUSERS. Rogues who carried snuff or dust in their pockets, which they threw into the eyes of any person they intended to rob, and running away (their accomplices pretending to assist and pity the half-blinded person), took that opportunity of plundering him.

ANABAPTIST. A pickpocket caught in the fact, and punished with the discipline of the pump or horse-pond.

ANCHOR. Bring your a-se to an anchor, i. e. sit down. To let go an anchor to the windward of the law, to keep within the letter of the law. *Sea Wit.*

ANGLERS. Pilferers, or petty thieves, who, with a stick having a hook at the end, steal goods out of shop windows, grates, &c; also those who draw in or entice unwary persons to prick at the belt, or such like devices.

ANGLING FOR FARTHINGS. Begging out of a prison window with a cap, or box, let down at the end of a long string.

ANKLE. A girl who is got with child, is said to have sprained her ankle.

ANODYNE NECKLACE. A halter.

ANTPONY or TANTONY PIG. The favourite or smallest pig

in the litter —To follow like a tantony pig, i. e. St Anthony's pig, to follow close at one's heels. St. Anthony the hermit was a swine herd, and is always represented with a swine's bell and a pig. Some derive this saying from a privilege enjoyed by the friars of certain convents in England and France (sons of St. Anthony) whose swine were permitted to feed in the streets. These swine would follow any one having greens or other provisions, till they obtained some of them.

To knock Anthony. Said of an inkneed person, or one whose knees knock together, to cuff Jonas. See Jonas.

Ape Leader. An old maid; their punishment after death, for neglecting to increase and multiply, will be, it is said, leading apes in hell.

Apostles. To manœuvre the apostles, i. e. rob Peter to pay Paul, that is, to borrow money of one man to pay another.

Apothecary. To talk like an apothecary, to talk nonsense; from the assumed gravity and affectation of knowledge generally put on by the gentlemen of that profession, who are commonly but superficial in their learning.

Apothecary's Bill. A long bill.

Apothecary's or Law Latin. Barbarous Latin, vulgarly called Dog Latin, in Ireland Bog Latin.

Apple Cart. Down with his apple-cart, knock or throw him down.

Apple Dumplin Shop. A woman's bosom.

Apple-pye Bed. A bed made apple-pye fashion, like what is called a turnover apple-pye, where the sheets are so doubled as to prevent any one from getting at his length between them: a common trick played by frolicsome country lasses on their sweethearts, male relations, or visitors.

April Fool. Any one imposed on, or sent on a bootless errand, on the first of April, on which day it is the custom among the lower people, children, and servants, by dropping empty papers carefully doubled up, sending persons on absurd messages, and such like contrivances, to impose on every one they can, and then to salute them with the title of April Fool.

Apron String Hold. An estate held by a man during his wife's life.

AQUA PUMPAGINIS. Pump water. *Apothecaries Latin.*

ARRBOR VITÆ. A man's penis.

ARCH DUKE. A comical or eccentric fellow.

ARCH ROGUE, or DIMBER DAMBER UPRIGHT MAN. The chief of a gang of thieves or gypsies.

ARCH DELL, or ARCH DOXY, signifies the same in rank among the female canters or gypsies.

ARD. Hot *Cant.*

ARISTIPPUS. A diet drink, or decoction of sarsaparilla, china, &c. sold at certain coffee-houses, and drank as tea.

ARMOUR. In his armour, pot valiant; to fight in armour, to make use of Mrs. Philips's ware. See C--D--M.

ARK. A boat or wherry. Let us take an Ark and winns, let us take a sculler. *Cant.*

ARK RUFFIANS Rogues who, in conjunction with watermen, robbed, and sometimes murdered, on the water, by picking a quarrel with the passengers in a boat, boarding it, plundering, stripping, and throwing them overboard, &c. A species of badgers. *Cant*

ARRAH NOW. An unmeaning expletive, frequently used by the vulgar Irish

ARS MUSICA. A bum-fiddle.

ARSE To hang an arse; to hang back, to be afraid to advance. He would lend his a--e, and sh-te through his ribs, a saying of any one who lends his money inconsiderately He would lose his a--e if it was loose; said of a careless person. A--e about, turn round.

ARSY VARSEY. To fall arsy varsey, i. e. head over heels.

ARTHUR, KING ARTHUR. A game used at sea, when near the line, or in a hot latitude. It is performed thus a man who is to represent king Arthur, ridiculously dressed, having a large wig made out of oakum, or some old swabs, is seated on the side, or over a large vessel of water. Every person in his turn is to be ceremoniously introduced to him, and to pour a bucket of water over him, crying, Hail, king Arthur! If during this ceremony the person introduced laughs or smiles (to which his majesty endeavours to excite him, by all sorts of ridiculous gesticulations), he changes place with, and then

becomes,

AUT

becomes, king Arthur, till relieved by some brother tar, who has as little command over his muscles as himself.

ARTICLES. Breeches, coat, waistcoat, and articles.

ASK or AX MY A--E. A common reply to any question; still deemed wit at sea, and formerly at court, under the denomination of selling bargains. See BARGAIN.

ASSIG. An assignation.

ATHANASIAN WENCH, or QUICUNQUE VULT A forward girl, ready to oblige every man that shall ask her.

AUNT. Mine aunt, a bawd or procuress, a title of eminence for the senior dells, who serve for instructresses, midwives, &c. for the dells. *Cant.*—See DELLS.

AVOIR DU POIS LAY. Stealing brass weights off the counters of shops. *Cant.*

AUTEM. A church.

AUTEM BAWLER. A parson. *Cant.*

AUTEM CACKLERS. } Dissenters of every denomination *Cant.*
AUTEM PRICKEARS.

AUTEM CACKLE TUB. A conventicle or meeting house for dissenters. *Cant.*

AUTEM DIPPERS. Anabaptists. *Cant.*

AUTEM DIVERS. Pickpockets who practise in churches; also churchwardens and overseers of the poor *Cant*

AUTEM GOGLERS. Pretended French prophets *Cant.*

AUTEM MORT. A married woman, also a female beggar with several children hired or borrowed to excite charity. *Cant.*

AUTEM QUAVERS. Quakers.

AUTEM QUAVER TUB. A Quakers meeting-house. *Cant.*

B.

BAC.

BABES IN THE WOOD. Rogues in the stocks, or pillory.

BABBLE Confused, unintelligible talk, such as was used at the building the Tower of Bable.

BACK BITER One who slanders another behind his back, i. e. in his absence. His bosom friends are become his back biterss said of a lousy man.

BACKED. Dead. He wishes to have the senior, or old squaretoes, backed he longs to have his father on six men's shoulders, that is, carrying to the grave.

BACK UP. His back is up, i. e he is offended or angry. an expression or idea taken from a cat; that animal, when angry, always raising its back. An allusion also sometimes used to jeer a crooked man; as, So, Sir, I see somebody has offended you, for your back is up.

BACON. He has saved his bacon, he has escaped. He has a good voice to beg bacon, a saying in ridicule of a bad voice.

BACON FACED. Full faced.

BACON FED. Fat, greasy.

BACK GAMMON PLAYER. A sodomite.

BACK DOOR (USHER or GENTLEMAN OF THE). The same.

BAD BARGAIN. One of his majesty's bad bargains, a worthless soldier, a malingeror. See MALINGEROR.

BADGE. A term used for one burned in the hand. He has got his badge, and piked, he was burned in the hand, and is at liberty. *Cant.*

BADGE COVES. Parish pensioners. *Cant.*

BADGERS A crew of desperate villains who robbed near rivers, into which they threw the bodies of those they murdered. *Cant.*

TO BADGER. To confound, perplex, or teize.

BAG. He gave them the bag, i e. left them.

BAG OF NAILS. He squints like a bag of nails, i. e. his eyes are directed as many ways as the points of a bag of nails. The old BAG OF NAILS at Pimlico, originally the BACCHANALS.

BAGGAGE. Heavy baggage, women and children. Also a familiar epithet for a woman, as, cunning baggage, wanton baggage, &c.

BAKERS DOZEN. Fourteen, that number of rolls being allowed to the purchasers of a dozen.

BAKER-KNEE'D. One whose knees knock together in walking, as if kneading dough.

BALDERDASH. Adulterated wine.

BALLOCKS. The testicles of a man or beast; also a vulgar nick name for a parson.

BALLUM RANCUM. A hop or dance, where the women are all prostitutes. N. B. The company dance in their birthday suits.

BALSAM. Money.

BAM. A jocular imposition, the same as a humbug. See HUMBUG.

TO BAM. To impose on any one by a falsity; also to jeer or make fun of any one.

TO BAMBOOZLE. To make a fool of any one, to humbug or impose on him.

BANAGHAN. He beats Banaghan, an Irish saying of one who tells wonderful stories. Perhaps Banaghan was a minstrel famous for dealing in the marvellous.

BANDBOX. Mine a—se on a bandbox, an answer to the offer of any thing inadequate to the purpose for which it is proffered, like offering a bandbox for a seat.

BANBURY STORY OF A COCK AND A BULL. A roundabout, nonsensical story.

BANDOG. A bailiff or his follower, also a very fierce mastiff; likewise, a bandbox. *Cant*

BANDORE. A widow's mourning peak, also a musical instrument.

TO BANG. To beat.

BANGING. Great. a fine banging boy.

BAR

BANG STRAW. A nick name for a thresher, but applied to all the servants of a farmer.

BANKRUPT CART. A one-horse chaise, said to be so called by a Lord Chief Justice, from their being so frequently used on Sunday jaunts by extravagant shopkeepers and tradesmen.

BANKS's HORSE. A horse famous for playing tricks, the property of one Banks It is mentioned in Sir Walter Raleigh's Hist. of the World, p 178, also by Sir Kenelm Digby and Ben Jonson.

BANTLING A young child

BANYAN DAY A sea term for those days on which no meat is allowed to the sailors the term is borrowed from the Banyans in the East Indies, a cast that eat nothing that had life.

BAPTISED, or CHRISTENED Rum, brandy, or any other spirits, that have been lowered with water.

BARBER That's the barber, a ridiculous and unmeaning phrase, in the mouths of the common people about the year 1760, signifying their approbation of any action, measure, or thing

BARBER's CHAIR She is as common as a barber's chair, in which a whole parish sit to be trimmed; said of a prostitute.

BARBER's SIGN A standing pole and two wash-balls

BARGAIN To sell a bargain, a species of wit, much in vogue about the latter end of the reign of Queen Anne, and frequently alluded to by Dean Swift, who says the maids of honour often amused themselves with it. It consisted in the seller naming his or her hinder parts, in answer to the question, What? which the buyer was artfully led to ask. As a specimen, take the following instance. A lady would come into a room full of company, apparently in a fright, crying out, It is white, and follows me! On any of the company asking, What? she sold him the bargain, by saying, Mine a—e

BARKER The shopman of a bow-wow shop, or dealer in second-hand clothes, particularly about Monmouth-street,

who

who walks before his master's door, and deafens every passenger with his cries of—Clothes, coats, or gowns—what d'ye want, gemmen?—what d'ye buy? See Bow-wow Shop

BARKSHIRE A member or candidate for Barkshire; said of one troubled with a cough, vulgarly styled barking

BARKING IRONS. Pistols, from their explosion resembling the bow-wow or barking of a dog *Irish*

BARN. A parson's barn, never so full but there is still room for more Bit by a barn mouse, tipsey, probably from an allusion to barley

BARNABY An old dance to a quick movement. See Cotton, in his Virgil Travesti, where, speaking of Eolus, he has these lines

Bounce cry the port holes, out they fly,
And make the world dance Barnaby

BARNACLE. A good job, or snack easily got, also shell fish growing at the bottoms of ships, a bird of the goose kind; an instrument like a pair of pincers, to fix on the noses of vicious horses whilst shoeing, a nick name for spectacles, and also for the gratuity given to grooms by the buyers and sellers of horses

BARTHOLOMEW BABY. A person dressed up in a tawdry manner, like the dolls or babies sold at Bartholomew fair.

BAR WIG. A wig between a Dalmahoy and a double cauliflower or full bottom. See DALMAHOY.

BASKET An exclamation frequently made use of in cock pits, at cock fightings, where persons refusing or unable to pay their losings, are adjudged by that respectable assembly to be put into a basket suspended over the pit, there to remain during that day's diversion . on the least demur to pay a bet, Basket ! is vociferated in terrorem He grins like a basket of chips, a saying of one who is on the broad grin.

BASKET-MAKING. The good old trade of basket-making, copulation, or making feet for children's stockings.

BASTARD. The child of an unmarried woman.

BASTARDLY GULLION. A bastard's bastard.

To BASTE. To beat. I'll give him his bastings, I'll beat him heartily.

BASTING. A beating.

BASTONADING. Beating any one with a stick, from baton, a stick, formerly spelt baston.

BATCH. We had a pretty batch of it last night, we had a hearty dose of liquor. Batch originally means the whole quantity of bread baked at one time in an oven.

BATTNER. An ox, beef being apt to batten or fatten those that eat it. The cove has hushed the battner, i. e. has killed the ox.

BATCHELORS FARE. Bread and cheese and kisses.

BATCHELOR's SON. A bastard.

BATTLE-ROYAL. A battle or bout at cudgels or fisty-cuffs, wherein more than two persons are engaged; perhaps from its resemblance, in that particular, to more serious engagements fought to settle royal disputes.

BAUDRANS. A cat. *Scotch.*

BAWBEE. A halfpenny. *Scotch.*

BAWBELS or BAWBLES. Trinkets, a man's testicles.

BAWD. A female procuress.

BAWDY BASKET. The twenty-third rank of canters, who carry pins, tape, ballads, and obscene books to sell, but live mostly by stealing. *Cant.*

BAWDY-HOUSE BOTTLE. A very small bottle, short measure being among the many means used by the keepers of those houses, to gain what they call an honest livelihood; indeed this is one of the least reprehensible, the less they give a man of their infernal beverages for his money, the kinder they behave to him.

BAY WINDOWS. Old projecting windows.

BAYARD OF TEN TOES. To ride bayard of ten toes, is to walk on foot. Bayard was a horse famous in old romances.

BEAR. One who contracts to deliver a certain quantity or sum of stock in the public funds, on a future day, and at a stated price, or, in other words, sells what he has not got, like the huntsman in the fable, who sold the bear's skin before

fore the bear was killed As the bear fells the stock he is not possessed of, so the bull purchases what he has not money to pay for, but in case of any alteration in the price agreed on, either party pays or receives the difference. *Exchange Alley*

BEAR-GARDEN JAW or DISCOURSE. Rude, vulgar language, such as was used at the bear gardens

BEAR LEADER A travelling tutor

BEARD SPLITTER A man much given to wenching.

BEARINGS. I'll bring him to his bearings, I'll bring him to reason. *Sea term.*

BEAST. To drink like a beast, i. e. only when thirsty.

BEAST WITH TWO BACKS A man and woman in the act of copulation *Shakespeare in Othello.*

BEATER CASES Boots. *Cant*

BEAU-NASTY. A slovenly fop, one finely dressed, but dirty.

BEAU TRAP A loose stone in a pavement, under which water lodges, and, on being trod upon, squirts it up, to the great damage of white stockings, also a sharper neatly dressed, lying in wait for raw country squires, or ignorant fops.

BECALMED A piece of sea wit, sported in hot weather. I am becalmed, the sail sticks to the mast; that is, my shirt sticks to my back.

BECK. A beadle See HERMANBECK

BED. Put to bed with a mattock, and tucked up with a spade, said of one that is dead and buried. You will go up a ladder to bed, i. e you will be hanged. In many country places, persons hanged are made to mount up a ladder, which is afterwards turned round or taken away; whence the term, "Turned off"

BEDAWBED ALL OVER WITH LACE Vulgar saying of any one dressed in clothes richly laced

BEDFORDSHIRE I am for Bedfordshire, i. e. for going to bed.

BEDIZENED Dressed out, over dressed, or aukwardly ornamented

BEEF To cry beef, to give the alarm They have cried beef on us. *Cant.*—To be in a man's beef, to wound him
with

with a sword To be in a woman's beef, to have carnal knowledge of her. Say you bought your beef of me, a jocular request from a butcher to a fat man, implying that he credits the butcher who serves him

BEEF EATER. A yeoman of the guards, instituted by Henry VII. Their office was to stand near the bouffet, or cupboard, thence called Bouffetiers, since corrupted to Beef Eaters Others suppose they obtained this name from the size of their persons, and the easiness of their duty, as having scarce more to do than to eat the king's beef.

BEETLE-BROWED One having thick projecting eyebrows.

BEETLE-HEADED Dull, stupid.

BEGGAR MAKER A publican, or ale-house keeper

BEGGARS BULLETS. Stones. The beggars bullets began to fly, i. e they began to throw stones

BEILBY'S BALL He will dance at Beilby's ball, where the sheriff pays the musick; he will be hanged. Who Mr. Beilby was, or why that ceremony was so called, remains with the quadrature of the circle, the discovery of the philosopher's stone, and divers other desiderata yet undiscovered.

BELCH. All sorts of beer; that liquor being apt to cause eructation.

BELL, BOOK, AND CANDLE They cursed him with bell, book, and candle; an allusion to the popish form of excommunicating and anathematizing persons who had offended the church.

TO BEAR THE BELL. To excel or surpass all competitors, to be the principal in a body or society; an allusion to the fore horse or leader of a team, whose harness is commonly ornamented with a bell or bells. Some suppose it a term borrowed from an ancient tournament, where the victorious knight bore away the *belle* or *fair lady*. Others derive it from a horse race, or other rural contentions, where bells where frequently given as prizes.

BELLOWS. The lungs.

BELLOWER. The town crier

BELLY. His eye was bigger than his belly; a saying of a person at a table, who takes more on his plate than he can eat.

BELLY-

BELLYFULL. A hearty beating, sufficient to make a man yield or give out. A woman with child is also said to have got her belly full.

BELLY CHEAT. An apron.

BELLY PLEA. The plea of pregnancy, generally adduced by female felons capitally convicted, which they take care to provide for, previous to their trials; every gaol having, as the Beggar's Opera informs us, one or more child getters, who qualify the ladies for that expedient to procure a respite.

BELLY TIMBER. Food of all sorts.

BELL SWAGGER. A noisy bullying fellow.

BELL WETHER. The chief or leader of a mob, an idea taken from a flock of sheep, where the wether has a bell about his neck.

BENE. Good.—BENAR. Better. *Cant.*

BENE BOWSE. Good beer, or other strong liquor. *Cant.*

BENE COVE. A good fellow. *Cant.*

BENE DARKMANS. Good night. *Cant.*

BENE FEAKERS. Counterfeiters of bills. *Cant.*

BENE FEAKERS OF GYBES. Counterfeiters of passes. *Cant.*

BENESHIPLY. Worshipfully. *Cant.*

BEN. A fool. *Cant.*

BENISH. Foolish.

BENISON. The beggar's benison, May your ***** and purse never fail you.

BERMUDAS. A cant name for certain places in London, privileged against arrests, like the Mint in Southwark. *Ben Jonson.*

BESS, or BETTY. A small instrument used by house-breakers to force open doors. Bring bess and glym, bring the instrument to force the door, and the dark lanthorn. Small flasks like those for Florence wine, are also called betties.

BESS. See BROWN BESS.

BETHLEHEMITES. Christmas carol singers. *Cant.*

BEST. To the best in Christendom, i. e. the best **** in Christendom, a health formerly much in vogue.

BET. A wager.—TO BET. To lay a wager.

BETTY MARTIN. That's my eye, Betty Martin, an answer to any one that attempts to impose or humbug.

BETWAT-

BETWATTLED. Surprised, confounded, out of one's senses, also bewrayed.

BEVER. An afternoon's luncheon, also a fine hat, bevers fur making the best hats.

BEVERAGE. Garnish money, or money for drink, demanded of any one having a new suit of clothes.

BIBLE. A boatswain's great axe. *Sea term*

BIBLE OATH Supposed by the vulgar to be more binding than an oath taken on the Testament only, as being the bigger book, and generally containing both the Old and New Testaments

BIDDY, or CHICK-A-BIDDY A chicken, and figuratively a young wench

BIDET, commonly pronounced BIDDY. A kind of tub, contrived for ladies to wash themselves, for which purpose they bestride it like a little French poney, or post-horse, called in France bidets.

BIENLY Excellently. She wheedled so bienly, she coaxed or flattered so cleverly. *French*

BILBOA A sword. Bilboa in Spain was once famous for well-tempered blades, these are quoted by Falstaff, where he describes the manner in which he lay in the buck basket The Bilboas, the stocks. *Cant.*

TO BILK To cheat Let us bilk the rattling cove, let us cheat the hackney coachman of his fare *Cant.*—Bilking a coachman, a box keeper, and a poor whore, were formerly, among men of the town, thought gallant actions.

BILL OF SALE. A widow's weeds See HOUSE TO LET.

BILLINGSGATE LANGUAGE Foul language, or abuse. Billingsgate is the market where the fish women assemble to purchase fish, and where, in their dealings and disputes, they are somewhat apt to leave decency and good manners a little on the left hand

BING To go. *Cant* —Bing avast; get you gone Binged avast in a darkmans, stole away in the night. Bing we to Rumeville? shall we go to London?

BINGO. Brandy or other spirituous liquor. *Cant.*

BINGO BOY. A dram drinker. *Cant*

BINGO MORT. A female dram drinker. *Cant.*

BINNACLE

BIT

BINNACLE WORD. A fine or affected word, which sailors jeeringly offer to chalk up on the binnacle

BIRD AND BABY   The sign of the eagle and child

BIRD-WITTED. Inconsiderate, thoughtless, easily imposed on.

BIRDS OF A FEATHER.   Rogues of the same gang

BIRTH-DAY SUIT.   He was in his birth-day suit, that is, stark naked

BISHOP.   A mixture of wine and water, into which is put a roasted orange. Also one of the largest of Mrs Phillips's purses, used to contain the others

BISHOPPED, or TO BISHOP. A term among horse dealers, for burning the mark into a horse's tooth, after he has lost it by age, by bishopping, a horse is made to appear younger than he is   It is a common saying of milk that is burnt to, that the bishop has set his foot in it   Formerly, when a bishop passed through a village, all the inhabitants ran out of their houses to solicit his blessing, even leaving their milk, &c. on the fire, to take its chance; which, when burnt to, was said to be bishopped.

BIT.   Money.   He grappled the cull's bit, he seized the man's money.   A bit is also the smallest current coin in Jamaica, equal to about sixpence sterling.

BITCH. A she dog, or doggess, the most offensive appellation that can be given to an English woman, even more provoking than that of whore, as may be gathered from the regular Billingsgate or St Giles's answer—" I may be " a whore, but can't be a bitch "

TO BITCH   To yield, or give up an attempt through fear. To stand bitch, to make tea, or do the honours of the tea table, performing a female part   bitch there standing for woman, species for genus

BITCH BOOBY   A country wench   *Military term*

BITER   A wench whose **** is ready to bite her a—se; a lascivious, rampant wench.

BITE. A cheat, also a woman's privities   The cull wapt the mort's bite; the fellow enjoyed the wench heartily. *Cant*

TO BITE   To over-reach, or impose, also to steal   *Cant.* —Biting was once esteemed a kind of wit, similar to the humbug.

humbug. An instance of it is given in the Spectator. A man under sentence of death having sold his body to a surgeon rather below the market price, on receiving the money, cried, A bite! I am to be hanged in chains.—To bite the roger, to steal a portmanteau. To bite the wiper, to steal a handkerchief. To bite on the bridle, to be pinched or reduced to difficulties. Hark ye, friend, whether do they bite in the collar or the cod-piece? *Water cant to anglers.*

BLAB. A tell-tale, or one incapable of keeping a secret.

BLACK AND WHITE. In writing. I have it in black and white, I have written evidence.

BLACK ART. The art of picking a lock. *Cant.*

BLACK A-SE. A copper or kettle. The pot calls the kettle black a-se. *Cant.*

BLACK BOOK. He is down in the black book, i. e. has a stain in his character. A black book is kept in most regiments, wherein the names of all persons sentenced to punishment are recorded.

BLACK BOX. A lawyer. *Cant.*

BLACK EYE. We gave the bottle a black eye, i. e. drank it almost up. He cannot say black is the white of my eye, he cannot point out a blot in my character.

BLACK FLY. The greatest drawback on the farmer is the black fly, i. e. the parson who takes tythe of the harvest.

BLACK-GUARD. A shabby, dirty fellow, a term said to be derived from a number of dirty, tattered, and roguish boys, who attended at the Horse Guards, and Parade in St James's Park, to black the boots and shoes of the soldiers, or to do any other dirty offices. These, from their constant attendance about the time of guard mounting, were nick-named the black-guards.

BLACK JACK. A jug to drink out of, made of jacked leather.

BLACK JOKE. A popular tune to a song, having for the burthen, "Her black joke and belly so white" figuratively the black joke signifies the monosyllable. See MONOSYLLABLE.

BLACK

BLACK INDIES. Newcastle in Northumberland, whose rich coal mines prove an Indies to the proprietors.

BLACK LEGS. A gambler or sharper on the turf or in the cock-pit: so called, perhaps, from their appearing generally in boots, or else from game cocks, whose legs are always black.

BLACK MONDAY. The first Monday after the school-boys holidays, or breaking up, when they are to go to school, and produce or repeat the tasks set them.

BLACK MUNS. Hoods and scarves of alamode lutestring.

BLACK PSALM. To sing the black psalm, to cry: a saying used to children.

BLACK SPY. The Devil.

BLACK STRAP. Bene Carlo wine; also port. A task of labour imposed on soldiers at Gibraltar, as a punishment for small offences.

BLANK. To look blank, to appear disappointed or confounded.

BLARNEY. He has licked the Blarney stone, he deals in the wonderful, or tips us the traveller. The blarney stone is a triangular stone on the very top of an ancient castle of that name, in the county of Cork in Ireland, extremely difficult of access, so that to have ascended to it, was considered as a proof of perseverance, courage, and agility, whereof many are supposed to claim the honour, who never achieved the adventure: and to tip the blarney, is figuratively used for telling a marvellous story, or falsity, and also sometimes to express flattery. *Irish*.

A BLASTED FELLOW or BRIMSTONE. An abandoned rogue or prostitute. *Cant*.

TO BLAST. To curse.

BLATER. A Calf. *Cant*.

BLEACHED MORT. A fair-complexioned wench.

BLEATERS. Those cheated by Jack in a box. *Cant*.—See JACK IN A BOX.

BLEATING CHEAT. A sheep. *Cant*.

BLEATING RIG. Sheep stealing. *Cant*.

BLEEDING CULLY. One who parts easily with his money, or bleeds freely.

BLEEDING NEW. A metaphor borrowed from fish, which will not bleed when stale.

BLESSING. A small quantity over and above the measure, usually given by hucksters dealing in pease, beans, and other vegetables.

BLEW JOHN. Ash or after-wort.

BLIND. A feint, pretence, or shift.

BLIND CHEEKS. The breech. Buss blind cheeks, kiss mine a-se.

BLIND EXCUSE. A poor or insufficient excuse. A blind alehouse, lane, or alley; an obscure, or little-known or frequented alehouse, lane, or alley.

BLIND HARPERS. Beggars counterfeiting blindness, playing on fiddles, &c.

BLINDMAN'S BUFF. A play used by children, where one being blinded by a handkerchief bound over his eyes, attempts to seize any one of the company, who all endeavour to avoid him; the person caught must be blinded in his stead.

BLINDMAN'S HOLIDAY. Night, darkness.

BLOCK HOUSES. Prisons, houses of correction, &c.

BLOOD. A riotous disorderly fellow.

BLOOD FOR BLOOD. A term used by tradesmen for bartering the different commodities in which they deal. Thus a hatter furnishing a hosier with a hat, and taking payment in stockings, is said to deal blood for blood.

BLOODY BACK. A jeering appellation for a soldier, alluding to his scarlet coat.

BLOSS. The pretended wife of a bully, or shop lifter. *Cant*.

TO BLOT THE SKRIP AND JARK IT. To stand engaged or bound for any one. *Cant*.

BLOW. He has bit the blow, i.e. he has stolen the goods. *Cant*.

BLOWER or BLOWEN. A mistress or whore of a gentleman of the scamp.

TO BLOW THE GROUNSILS. To lie with a woman on the floor. *Cant*.

B L U

To Blow the Gab. To confess, or impeach a confederate. *Cant*

Blow-up. A discovery, or the confusion occasioned by one.

A Blowse, or Blowsabella. A woman whose hair is dishevelled, and hanging about her face, a slattern

Blubber. The mouth —I have stopped the cull's blubber; I have stopped the fellow's mouth: meant either by gagging or murdering him.

To Blubber. To cry.

To Sport Blubber. Said of a large coarse woman, who exposes her bosom.

Blubber Cheeks. Large flaccid cheeks, hanging like the fat or blubber of a whale.

Blue To look blue; to be confounded, terrified, or disappointed Blue as a razor, perhaps, blue as azure.

Blue Boar. A venereal bubo

Blue Devils Low spirits

Blue Flag He has hoisted the blue flag, he has commenced publican, or taken a public house, an allusion to the blue aprons worn by publicans See Admiral of the Blue

Blue and Orange This society, styling themselves Loyal and Friendly, met, 1742, at Kouli Kahn's head, Leicester-fields

Blue Pidgeon Fliers. Thieves who steal lead off houses and churches *Cant*

Blue Plumb A bullet.—Surfeited with a blue plumb; wounded with a bullet. A sortment of George R—'s blue plumbs, a volley of ball, shot from soldiers firelocks

Blue Skin A person begotten on a black woman by a white man. One of the blue squadron, any one having a cross of the black breed, or, as it is termed, a lick of the tar brush.

Blue Tape, or Sky Blue. Gin.

Bluff Fierce, surly. He looked as bluff as bull beef

Bluffer. An inn-keeper. *Cant.*

Blunderbuss A short gun, with a wide bore, for carrying slugs, also a stupid, blundering fellow.

Blunt Money *Cant*

To Bluster. To talk big, to hector or bully

Boarding

BOARDING SCHOOL. Bridewell, Newgate, or any other prison, or house of correction.

BOB. A shoplifter's assistant, or one that receives and carries off stolen goods. All is bob, all is safe. *Cant*.

BOBBED. Cheated, tricked, disappointed.

BOBBISH. Smart, clever, spruce.

BOB-STAY. A rope which holds the bowsprit to the stem or cutwater. Figuratively, the frenum of a man's yard.

BOB TAIL. A lewd woman, or one that plays with her tail; also an impotent man, or an eunuch. Tag, rag, and bobtail, a mob of all sorts of low people. To shift one's bob, to move off, or go away. To bear a bob, to join in chorus with any singers.

BODIES. The foot guards, or king's body guards.

BODY SNATCHERS. Bum bailiffs.

BODY OF DIVINITY BOUND IN BLACK CALF. A parson.

BOG LANDER. An Irishman, Ireland being famous for its large bogs, which furnish the chief fuel in many parts of that kingdom.

BOG TROTTER. The same.

BOG HOUSE. The necessary house.

BOG LATIN. Barbarous Latin. *Irish*.—See DOG LATIN and APOTHECARIES LATIN.

BOGY. Ask bogy, i.e. ask mine a-se. *Sea wit*.

BOH. Said to be the name of a Danish general, who so terrified his opponent Foh, that he caused him to bewray himself. Whence, when we smell a stink, it is customary to exclaim, Foh! i.e. I smell general Foh. He cannot say Boh to a goose; i.e. he is a cowardly or sheepish fellow.

BOLD. Bold as a miller's shirt, which every day takes a rogue by the collar.

BOLT. A blunt arrow.

BOLT UPRIGHT. As erect, or straight up, as an arrow set on its end.

TO BOLT. To run suddenly out of one's house, or hiding place, through fear; a term borrowed from a rabbit warren, where the rabbits are made to bolt, by sending ferrets into their burrows: we set the house on fire, and made him bolt. To bolt, also means to swallow meat without chewing.

ing the farmers servants in Kent are famous for bolting large quantities of pickled pork

BOLTER OF WHITE FRIARS, OR THE MINT. One that peeps out, but dares not venture abroad for fear of arrests.

BONE BOX The mouth Shut your bone box, shut your mouth.

BONED. Seized, apprehended, taken up by a constable. *Cant*

BOLUS A nick-name for an apothecary

BONE SETTER A hard-trotting horse

BOOBY, or DOG BOOBY. An aukward lout, clodhopper, or country fellow. See CLODHOPPER and LOUT —A bitch booby, a country wench.

BOOBY HUTCH. A one-horse chaise, noddy, buggy, or leathern bottle.

BOOK KEEPER One who never returns borrowed books. Out of one's books, out of one's favour.

BOOT CATCHER The servant at an inn whose business it is to clean the boots of the guests.

BOOTS. The youngest officer in a regimental mess, whose duty it is to skink, that is, to stir the fire, snuff the candles, and ring the bell. See SKINK —To ride in any one's old boots, to marry or keep his cast off mistress

BOOTY. To play booty, cheating play, where the player purposely avoids winning

BO-PEEP. One who sometimes hides himself, and sometimes appears publicly abroad, is said to play at bo-peep. Also one who lies perdue, or on the watch.

BORACHIO. A skin for holding wine, commonly a goat's; also a nick name for a drunkard.

BORDE. A shilling. A half borde; sixpence.

BORDELLO A bawdy house

BORE A tedious, troublesome man or woman, one who bores the ears of his hearers with an uninteresting tale: a term much in fashion about the years 1780 and 1781.

BORN UNDER A THREEPENNY HALFPENNY PLANET, NEVER TO BE WORTH A GROAT. Said of any person remarkably unsuccessful in their attempts or profession.

BOTCH.

BOTCH. A nick name for a taylor.

BOTHERED, or BOTH-EARED Talked to at both ears by different persons at the same time, confounded, confused. *Irish phrase.*

BOTHERAMS A convivial society.

BOTTLE-HEADED Void of wit

BOTTOM. A polite term for the posteriors Also, in the sporting sense, strength and spirits to support fatigue; as, a bottomed horse. Among bruisers it is used to express a hardy fellow who will bear a good beating. The bottom of a woman's tu quoque; the crown of her head.

BOTTOMLESS PIT The monosyllable

BOUGHS. He is up in the boughs; he is in a passion.

To BOUNCE To brag or hector; also to tell an improbable story.

BOUNCER A large man or woman, also a great lye.

BOUNCING CHEAT. A bottle, from the explosion in drawing the cork *Cant.*

BOUNG. A purse. *Cant.*

BOUNG NIPPER A cut purse. *Cant.*—Formerly purses were worn at the girdle, from whence they were cut.

BOOSE, or BOUSE Drink.

BOOSEY. Drunk.

BOWSING KEN An alehouse or ginshop.

BOWSPRIT The nose, from its being the most projecting part of the human face, as the bowsprit is of a ship

Bow-wow. The childish name for a dog, also a jeering appellation for a man born at Boston in America.

Bow-wow MUTTON Dog's flesh

Bow-wow SHOP. A salesman's shop in Monmouth street, so called because the servant barks, and the master bites. See BARKER

BOWYER. One that draws a long bow, a dealer in the marvellous, a teller of improbable stories, a liar perhaps from the wonderful shots frequently boasted of by archers

To BOX THE COMPASS. To say or repeat the mariner's compass, not only backwards or forwards, but also to be
able

able to answer any and all questions respecting its divisions.
Sea term

TO BOX THE JESUIT, AND GET COCK ROACHES. A sea term for masturbation; a crime, it is said, much practised by the reverend fathers of that society.

BRACE. The brace tavern; a room in the S E corner of the King's Bench, where, for the convenience of prisoners residing thereabouts, beer purchased at the tap house was retailed at a halfpenny per pot advance. It was kept by two brothers of the name of Partridge, and thence called the *Brace*.

BRACKET-FACED Ugly, hard-featured.

BRAGGET. Mead and ale sweetened with honey.

BRAGGADOCIO. A vain-glorious fellow, a boaster

BRAINS. If you had as much brains as guts, what a clever fellow you would be ! a saying to a stupid fat fellow

BRAN-FACED. Freckled. He was christened by a baker, he carries the bran in his face

BRANDY-FACED. Red-faced, as if from drinking brandy.

BRAT A child or infant.

BRAY. A vicar of Bray; one who frequently changes his principles, always siding with the strongest party. an allusion to a vicar of Bray, in Berkshire, commemorated in a well-known ballad for the pliability of his conscience.

BRAZEN-FACED. Bold-faced, shameless, impudent.

BREAD AND BUTTER FASHION. One slice upon the other. John and his maid were caught lying bread and butter fashion.—To quarrel with one's bread and butter; to act contrary to one's interest To know on which side one's bread is buttered, to know one's interest, or what is best for one. It is no bread and butter of mine; I have no business with it

BREAD AND BUTTER WAREHOUSE. Ranelagh.

BREAK-TEETH WORDS. Hard words, difficult to pronounce.

BREAKING SHINS Borrowing money; perhaps from the figurative operation being, like the real one, extremely disagreeable to the patient.

BREAD Employment Out of bread, out of employment In bad bread, in a disagreeable scrape, or situation

BREAD BASKET. The stomach, a term used by boxers. I took him a punch in his bread basket, i. e. I gave him a blow in the stomach.

BREAST FLEET He or she belongs to the breast fleet; i e. is a Roman catholic; an appellation derived from their custom of beating their breasts in the confession of their sins.

BREECHES. To wear the breeches, a woman who governs her husband is said to wear the breeches.

BREECHES BIBLE. An edition of the Bible printed in 1598, wherein it is said that Adam and Eve sewed fig leaves together, and made themselves breeches.

BREEZE. To kick up a breeze; to breed a disturbance.

BRIDGE. To make a bridge of any one's nose, to push the bottle past him, so as to deprive him of his turn of filling his glass; to pass one over.

BRIM. (Abbreviation of Brimstone.) An abandoned woman; perhaps originally only a passionate or irascible woman, compared to brimstone for its inflammability.

BRISKET BEATER A Roman catholic. See BREAST FLEET, and CRAW THUMPER.

BRISTOL MILK. A Spanish wine called sherry, much drank at that place, particularly in the morning.

BROGANEER. One who has a strong Irish pronunciation or accent

BROGUE. A particular kind of shoe without a heel, worn in Ireland, and figuratively used to signify the Irish accent.

BROTHER OF THE
- BLADE. A soldier
- BUSKIN. A player.
- BUNG A brewer
- COIF A serjeant at law.
- GUSSET A pimp.
- QUILL. An author.
- STRING. A fiddler.
- WHIP. A coachman.

BROTHER STARLING. One who lies with the same woman, that is, builds in the same nest

BROUGHTONIAN. A boxer, a disciple of Broughton, who was a beef eater, and once the best boxer of his day.

BROWN BESS A soldier's firelock. To hug Brown Bess, to carry a firelock, or serve as a private soldier.

BROWN GEORGE. An ammunition loaf

BROWN MADAM, or MISS BROWN The monosyllable.

BROWN STUDY. Said of one absent, in a reverie, or thoughtful

BRUISER. A boxer, one skilled in the art of boxing, also an inferior workman among chasers

BRUISING, or rather BREWISING, THE BED Bewraying the bed, from

BREWES, or BROWES Oatmeal boiled in the pot with salt beef.

TO BRUSH To run away. Let us buy a brush and lope; let us go away or off. To have a brush with a woman; to lie with her. To have a brush with a man, to fight with him.

BRUSHER A bumper, a full glass. See BUMPER.

BUB. Strong beer

BUBBER A drinking bowl, also a great drinker; a thief that steals plate from public houses. *Cant.*

THE BUBBLE. The party cheated, perhaps from his being like an air bubble, filled with words, which are only wind, instead of real property.

TO BUBBLE To cheat.

TO BAR THE BUBBLE To except against the general rule, that he who lays the odds must always be adjudged the loser. this is restricted to betts laid for liquor.

BUBBLY JOCK A turkey cock *Scotch*

BUBBLE AND SQUEAK. Beef and cabbage fried together. It is so called from its bubbling up and squeaking whilst over the fire.

BUBE The venereal disease

BUCK. A blind horse, also a gay debauchee.

TO RUN A BUCK To poll a bad vote at an election *Irish term*

BUCK BAIL Bail given by a sharper for one of the gang

A Buck of the first Head. One who in debauchery surpasses the rest of his companions, a blood or choice spirit. There are in London divers lodges or societies of Bucks, formed in imitation of the Free Masons one was held at the Rose, in Monkwell-street, about the year 1750. The president is styled the Grand Buck.—A buck sometimes signifies a cuckold

Buckeen   A bully. *Irish*.

Bucket   To kick the bucket; to die

Buck Fitch   A leacherous old fellow.

Buck's Face   A cuckold.

Buckinger's Boot   The monosyllable. Matthew Buckinger was born without hands and legs; notwithstanding which he drew coats of arms very neatly, and could write the Lord's Prayer within the compass of a shilling he was married to a tall handsome woman, and traversed the country, shewing himself for money.

Budge, or Sneaking Budge. One that slips into houses in the dark, to steal cloaks or other clothes Also lambs fur formerly used for doctors robes, whence they were called budge doctors. Standing budge, a thief's scout or spy.

To Budge   To move, or quit one's station. Don't budge from hence, i. e. don't move from hence, stay here.

Budget   A wallet. To open the budget, a term used to signify the notification of the taxes required by the minister for the expences of the ensuing year, as, Tomorrow the minister will go to the House, and open the budget.

Bufe   A dog. Bufe's nob, a dog's head. *Cant.*

Bufe Nabber   A dog stealer *Cant*.

Buff.   All in buff, stript to the skin, stark naked.

Buff.   To stand buff; to stand the brunt.

Buffer.   One that steals and kills horses and dogs for their skins, also an inn-keeper in Ireland it signifies a boxer.

Buffle-headed   Confused, stupid.

Bug   A nick name given by the Irish to Englishmen, bugs having, as it is said, been introduced into Ireland by the English

To Bug.   A cant word among journeymen hatters, signifying the exchanging some of the dearest materials of which a hat is made for others of less value. Hats are composed of the furs and wools of diverse animals, among which is a small portion of bevers fur. Bugging, is stealing the bever, and substituting in lieu thereof an equal weight of some cheaper ingredient.—Bailiffs who take money to postpone or refrain the serving of a writ, are said to bug the writ.

BUG-HUNTER. An upholsterer.

BUGABOO. A scare-babe, or bully-beggar.

BUGAROCH. Comely, handsome. *Irish*

BUGGY. A one-horse chaise.

BUGHER. A little yelping dog.

BULK AND FILE. Two pickpockets; the bulk jostles the party to be robbed, and the file does the business.

BULKER. One who lodges all night on a bulk or projection before old-fashioned shop windows.

BULL. An Exchange Alley term for one who buys stock on speculation for time, i. e. agrees with the seller, called a Bear, to take a certain sum of stock at a future day, at a stated price. if at that day stock fetches more than the price agreed on, he receives the difference, if it falls or is cheaper, he either pays it, or becomes a lame duck, and waddles out of the Alley. See LAME DUCK and BEAR.

BULL. A blunder, from one Obadiah Bull, a blundering lawyer of London, who lived in the reign of Henry VII.: by a bull, is now always meant a blunder made by an Irishman. A bull was also the name of false hair formerly much worn by women. To look like bull beef, or as bluff as bull beef, to look fierce or surly. Town bull, a great whoremaster.

BULL BEGGAR, or BULLY BEGGAR. An imaginary being with which children are threatened by servants and nurses, like raw head and bloody bones.

BULL CALF. A great hulkey or clumsy fellow. See HULKEY.

BULL CHIN. A fat chubby child.

BULL DOGS. Pistols.

BULL'S EYE. A crown piece.

BULL'S FEATHER. A horn. he wears the bull's feather; he is a cuckold.

TO BULLOCK. To hector, bounce, or bully.

BULLY.

BULLY. A cowardly fellow, who gives himself airs of great bravery. A bully huff cap, a hector. See HECTOR.

BULLY BACK. A bully to a bawdy house, one who is kept in pay, to oblige the frequenters of the house to submit to the impositions of the mother abbess, or bawd, and who also sometimes pretends to be the husband of one of the ladies, and under that pretence extorts money from greenhorns, or ignorant young men, whom he finds with her. See GREENHORN.

BULLY COCK. One who foments quarrels in order to rob the persons quarrelling.

BULLY RUFFIANS. Highwaymen who attack passengers with oaths and imprecations.

BULLY TRAP. A brave man with a mild or effeminate appearance, by whom bullies are frequently taken in.

BUM. The breech, or backside.

BUM BAILIFF. A sheriff's officer, who arrests debtors, so called perhaps from following his prey, and being at their bums, or, as the vulgar phrase is, hard at their a-ses. Blackstone says, it is a corruption of bound bailiff, from their being obliged to give bond for their good behaviour.

BUM BRUSHER. A schoolmaster.

BUM BOAT. A boat attending ships to retail greens, drams, &c. commonly rowed by a woman; a kind of floating chandler's shop.

BUM FODDER. Soft paper for the necessary house or torchecul.

BUMFIDDLE. The backside, the breech. See ARS MUSICA.

BUMBO. Brandy, water, and sugar, also the negro name for the private parts of a woman.

BUMKIN. A raw country fellow.

BUMMED. Arrested.

BUMPER. A full glass, in all likelihood from its convexity or bump at the top; some derive it from a full glass formerly drank to the health of the pope—*au bon pere*.

BUMPING. A ceremony performed on boys perambulating the bounds of the parish on Whitmonday, when they have their posteriors bumped against the stones marking the boundaries, in order to fix them in their memory.

BUN.

BUN. A common name for a rabbit, also for the monosyllable. To touch bun for luck, a practice observed among sailors going on a cruise.

BUNDLING. A man and woman sleeping in the same bed, he with his small clothes, and she with her petticoats on; an expedient practised in America on a scarcity of beds, where, on such an occasion, husbands and parents frequently permitted travellers to bundle with their wives and daughters.

BUNG UPWARDS. Said of a person lying on his face

BUNG YOUR EYE. Drink a dram, strictly speaking, to drink till one's eye is bunged up or closed

BUNT An apron

TO BUNT To run against, or jostle.

BUNTER. A low dirty prostitute, half whore and half beggar

BUNTLINGS. Petticoats. *Cant.*

BURN CRUST. A jocular name for a baker.

BURN THE KEN. Strollers living in an alehouse without paying their quarters, are said to burn the ken *Cant.*

BURNING THE PARADE. Warning more men for a guard than were necessary, and excusing the supernumeraries for money. This was a practice formerly winked at in most garrisons, and was a very considerable perquisite to the adjutants and serjeant majors; the pretence for it was, to purchase coal and candle for the guard, whence it was called burning the parade.

BURNING SHAME. A lighted candle stuck into the parts of a woman, certainly not intended by nature for a candlestick.

BURNER He is no burner of navigable rivers; i. e. he is no conjurer, or man of extraordinary abilities, or rather, he is but a simple fellow See THAMES.

BURNT. Poxed or clapped. He was sent out a sacrifice, and came home a burnt offering, a saying of seamen who have caught the venereal disease abroad. He has burnt his fingers; he has suffered by meddling

BURR. A hanger on, or dependant, an allusion to the field burrs, which are not easily got rid of. Also the Northumbrian pronunciation. the people of that country, but chief-

BUT

ly about Newcastle and Morpeth, are said to have a burr in their throats, particularly called the Newcastle burr.

BUSHEL BUBBY. A full-breasted woman

BUSK. A piece of whalebone or ivory, formerly worn by women, to stiffen the fore part of their stays. hence the toast—Both ends of the busk

BUSS BEGGAR An old superannuated fumbler, whom none but beggars will suffer to kiss them

BUS-NAPPER A constable *Cant.*

BUS-NAPPER'S KENCHIN A watchman *Cant*

BUSY. As busy as the devil in a high wind, as busy as a hen with one chick.

BUTCHER A jocular exclamation used at sea, or by soldiers on a march, when one of their comrades falls down; and means—Butcher! butcher! where are you? here is a calf that has the staggers, and wants bleeding.

BUTCHER'S DOG To be like a butcher's dog, i.e. lie by the beef without touching it, a simile often applicable to married men

BUTCHER'S MEAT Meat taken up on trust, which continues the butcher's till paid for

BUTCHER'S HORSE. That must have been a butcher's horse, by his carrying a calf so well, a vulgar joke on an aukward rider.

BUTT A dependant, poor relation, or simpleton, on whom all kinds of practical jokes are played off, and who serves as a butt for all the shafts of wit and ridicule

BUTTER A butter, in inch of butter, that commodity being sold at Cambridge by the yard, in rolls of about an inch diameter The word is used plurally, as—Send me a roll and two butters

BUTTER BOX. A Dutchman, from the great quantity of butter eaten by the people of that country.

To BUTTER A BET. To double or treble it

BUTTERED BUN. One lying with a woman that has just lain with another man, is said to have a buttered bun.

BUTTER TEETH Large broad fore teeth

BUTTER AND EGGS TROT. A kind of short jogg trot, such as is used by women going to market, with butter

and

and eggs—She looks as if butter would not melt in her mouth, yet I warrant you cheese would not choak her, a saying of a demure-looking woman, of suspected character. Don't make butter dear; a gird at the patient angler

BUTTOCK A whore *Cant.*

BUTTOCK BROKER. A bawd, or match maker. *Cant*

BUTTOCK BALL. The amorous congress *Cant*

BUTTOCK AND FILE A common whore and a pickpocket. *Cant*

BUTTOCK AND TWANG, or A DOWN BUTTOCK AND SHAM FILE A common whore, but no pickpocket.

BUTTON. A bad shilling, among coiners His a-se makes buttons; he is ready to bewray himself through fear. *Cant.*

BUZMAN A pickpocket. *Cant*

BUZZA To buzza one, is to challenge him to pour out all the wine in the bottle into his glass, undertaking to drink it, should it prove more than the glass will hold; it is commonly said to one who hesitates to empty a bottle that is nearly out. Some derive it from *bouze all*, i. e drink it all.

BUZZARD. A simple fellow. A blind buzzard; a purblind man or woman

BYE BLOW. A bastard.

C.

CABALLARIANS. The very honourable order of Caballarians was held at the Magpye Tavern, without Bishopsgate

CABBAGE. Cloth, stuff, or silk purloined by taylors from their

their employers, which they deposit in a place called *hell*, or their *eye* from the first, when taxed with their knavery, they equivocally swear, that if they have taken any, they wish they may find it in *hell*, or, alluding to the second protest, that what they have over and above is not more than they could put in their *eye*.—When the scrotum is relaxed or whiffled, it is said they will not cabbage.

CACAFEUGO A sh-te fire, a furious braggadocio or bully huff.

CACKLE To blab, or discover secrets. The cull is leaky, and cackles; the rogue tells all. *Cant.*—See LEAKY.

CACKLERS KEN. A hen roost. *Cant.*

CACKLING CHEATS Fowls. *Cant.*

CACKLING FARTS. Eggs. *Cant.*

CAFFAN Cheese. *Cant.*

CAGG To cagg, a military term used by the private soldiers, signifying a solemn vow or resolution not to get drunk for a certain time; or, as the term is, till their cagg is out; which vow is commonly observed with the strictest exactness. Ex. I have cagg'd myself for six months. Excuse me this time, and I will cagg myself for a year. This term is also used in the same sense among the common people of Scotland, where it is performed with diverse ceremonies.

CAGG MAGGS. Old Lincolnshire geese, which having been plucked ten or twelve years, are sent up to London to feast the cockneys.

CAKE, or CAKEY. A foolish fellow.

CALF-SKIN FIDDLE. A drum.—To smack calf's skin, to kiss the book in taking an oath. It is held by the St Giles's casuists, that by kissing one's thumb instead of smacking calf's skin, the guilt of taking a false oath is avoided.

CALVES. His calves are gone to grass, a saying of a man with slender legs without calves. Veal will be cheap, calves fall, said of a man whose calves fall away.

CALVES HEAD CLUB A club instituted by the Independents and Presbyterians, to commemorate the decapitation of King Charles I. Their chief fare was calves heads; and they drank their wine and ale out of calves sculls.

CALIBOGUS.

CAN

CALIBOGUS. Rum and spruce beer, an American beverage.

CALLE. A cloak or gown. *Cant.*

CAMBRIDGE FORTUNE. A wind mill and a water mill, used to signify a woman without any but personal endowments.

CAMBRIDGE OAK. A willow.

CAMERADE. A chamber fellow - a Spanish military term. Soldiers were in that country divided into chambers, five men making a chamber, whence it was generally used to signify companion.

CAMESA. A shirt or shift. *Cant, Spanish*

CAMP CANDLESTICK. A bottle, or soldier's bayonet.

CAMPBELL'S ACADEMY. The hulks or lighters, on board of which felons are condemned to hard labour. Mr Campbell was the first director of them. See ACADEMY and FLOATING ACADEMY.

CANARY BIRD. A jail bird, a person used to be kept in a cage; also, in the canting sense, guineas.

CANDLESTICKS. Bad, small, or untunable bells. Hark! how the candlesticks rattle.

CANDY. Drunk. *Irish.*

CANE To lay Cane upon Abel, to beat any one with a cane or stick.

CANK. Dumb.

CANNIKEN. A small can; also, in the canting sense, the plague.

CANT An hypocrite, a double-tongued pallavering fellow. See PALLAVER.

CANT. To cant, to toss or throw. as, Cant a slug into your bread room, drink a dram. *Sea wit.*

CANTICLE. A parish clerk.

CANTING Preaching with a whining, affected tone, perhaps a corruption of chaunting, some derive it from Andrew Cant, a famous Scotch preacher, who used that whining manner of expression. Also a kind of gibberish used by thieves and gypsies, called likewise pedlars French, the slang, &c. &c.

CAP

CANTERS, or THE CANTING CREW. Thieves, beggars, and gypsies, or any others using the canting lingo. See LINGO.

CANTERBURY STORY. A long roundabout tale.

To CAP. To take one's oath. I will cap downright, I will swear home. *Cant.*

To CAP. To take off one's hat or cap. To cap the quadrangle; a lesson of humility, or rather servility, taught undergraduates at the university, where they are obliged to cross the area of the college cap in hand, in reverence to the Fellows who sometimes walk there. The same ceremony is observed on coming on the quarter deck of ships of war, although no officer should be on it.

CAP ACQUAINTANCE. Persons slightly acquainted, or only so far as mutually to salute with the hat on meeting. A woman who endeavours to attract the notice of any particular man, is said to set her cap at him.

CAPER MERCHANT. A dancing master, or hop merchant; marchand des capriolles *French term*—To cut capers; to leap or jump in dancing. See HOP MERCHANT.

CAPPING VERSES. Repeating Latin verses in turn, beginning with the letter with which the last speaker left off.

CAPON. A castrated cock, also an eunuch.

CAPRICORNIFIED. Cuckolded, hornified.

CAPSIZE. To overturn or reverse. He took his broth till he capsized, he drank till he fell out of his chair. *See term.*

CAPTAIN. Led captain, an humble dependant in a great family, who for a precarious subsistence, and distant hopes of preferment, suffers every kind of indignity, and is the butt of every species of joke or ill humour. The small provision made for officers of the army and navy in time of peace, obliges many in both services to occupy this wretched station. The idea of the appellation is taken from a led horse, many of which for magnificence appear in the retinues of great personages on solemn occasions, such as processions, &c.

CAR

THE CAPTAIN IS COME, or AT HOME. The catamenia are come down

CAPTAIN COPPERTHORNE'S CREW. All officers, a saying of a company where every one strives to rule.

CAPTAIN HACKUM A blustering bully

CAPTAIN LIEUTENANT Meat between veal and beef, the flesh of an old calf, a military simile, drawn from the officer of that denomination, who has only the pay of a lieutenant, with the rank of captain, and so is not entirely one or the other, but between both.

CAPTAIN PODD. A celebrated master of a puppet-shew, in Ben Jonson's time, whose name became a common one to signify any of that fraternity.

CAPTAIN QUEERNABS A shabby ill-dressed fellow.

CAPTAIN SHARP A cheating bully, or one in a set of gamblers, whose office it is to bully any pigeon, who, suspecting roguery, refuses to pay what he has lost. *Cant.*

CAPTAIN TOM The leader of a mob, also the mob itself

CARAVAN. A large sum of money, also, a person cheated of such sum *Cant*

CARBUNCLE FACE. A red face, full of pimples.

CARDINAL A cloak in fashion about the year 1760 The cardinal is come, see THE CAPTAIN, &c

To CAROUSE To drink freely or deep from the German word expressing *all out*.

CARRIERS. A set of rogues who are employed to look out and watch upon the roads, at inns, &c, in order to carry information, to their respective gangs, of a booty in prospect

CARRIER PIGEONS. Sharpers who attend the drawing of the lottery in Guildhall, and, as soon as a number or two are drawn, write them on a card, and run with them to a confederate, who is waiting near at hand, ready mounted, with these numbers he rides full speed to some distant insurance office, before fixed on, where there is another of the gang, commonly a decent looking woman, who takes care to be at the office before the hour of drawing to her he secretly gives the number, which she insures for a considerable sum; thus biting the biter.

CARRION

CARRION HUNTER. An undertaker; called also a cold cook, and death hunter. See COLD COOK and DEATH HUNTER

CARROTS. Red hair.

CARROTTY-PATED Ginger-hackled, red-haired See GINGER-HACKLED.

CARRY WITCHET. A fort of conundrum, puzzlewit, or riddle.

CART. To put the cart before the horse, to mention the last part of a story first To be flogged at the cart's a-se or tail; persons guilty of petty larceny are frequently sentenced to be tied to the tail of a cart, and whipped by the common executioner, for a certain distance the degree of severity in the execution is left to the discretion of the executioner, who, it is said, has cats of nine tails of all prices.

CARTING. The punishment formerly inflicted on bawds, who were placed in a tumbrel or cart, and led through a town, that their persons might be known.

CARVEL's RING. The private parts of a woman. Hans Carvel, a jealous old doctor, being in bed with his wife, dreamed that the Devil gave him a ring, which, so long as he had it on his finger, would prevent his being made a cuckold. waking, he found he had got his finger the Lord knows where.

TO CASCADE To vomit

CASE. A house, perhaps from the Italian *casa*. In the canting lingo it meant store or ware house, as well as dwelling house. Tout that case, mark or observe that house. It is all bob, now let's dub the gigg of the case; now the coast is clear, let us break open the door of the house

A CASE VROW. A prostitute attached to a particular bawdy house.

CASH, or CAFFAN. Cheese. *Cant* —See CAFFAN

CASTER A cloak *Cant*.

CASTING UP ONE'S ACCOUNTS Vomiting

CAT A common prostitute. An old cat, a cross old woman

TO CAT, or SHOOT THE CAT. To vomit from drunkenness

CAT

CAT AND BAGPIPEAN SOCIETY. A society which met at their office in the great western road. in their summons, published in the daily papers, it was added, that the kittens might come with the old cats without being scratched

CAT CALL A kind of whistle, chiefly used at theatres, to interrupt the actors, and damn a new piece. It derives its name from one of its sounds, which greatly resembles the modulations of an intriguing boar cat.

CAT-HARPING FASHION Drinking cross ways, and not, as usual, over the left thumb. *Sea term.*

CAT IN PAN. To turn cat in pan, to change sides or parties supposed originally to have been to turn *cate* or *cake* in pan

CAT's FOOT. To live under the cat's foot, to be under the dominion of a wife, hen-pecked. To live like dog and cat; spoken of married persons who live unhappily together As many lives as a cat; cats, according to vulgar naturalists, have nine lives, that is, one less than a woman. No more share than a cat in hell without claws; said of one who enters into a dispute or quarrel with one greatly above his match.

CAT LAP. Tea, called also scandal broth. See SCANDAL BROTH

CAT MATCH. When a rook or cully is engaged amongst bad bowlers.

CAT OF NINE TAILS. A scourge composed of nine strings of whipcord, each string having nine nots.

CAT's PAW To be made a cat's paw of, to be made a tool or instrument to accomplish the purpose of another an allusion to the story of a monkey, who made use of a cat's paw to scratch a roasted chestnut out of the fire.

CAT's SLEEP Counterfeit sleep. cats often counterfeiting sleep, to decoy their prey near them, and then suddenly spring on them

CAT STICKS. Thin legs, compared to sticks with which boys play at cat. See TRAPSTICKS.

CAT WHIPPING, or WHIPPING THE CAT. A trick often practised on ignorant country fellows, vain of their strength,

strength, by laying a wager with them that they may be pulled through a pond by a cat. The bet being made, a rope is fixed round the waist of the party to be catted, and the end thrown across the pond, to which the cat is also fastened by a packthread, and three or four sturdy fellows are appointed to lead and whip the cat: these, on a signal given, seize the end of the cord, and pretending to whip the cat, haul the astonished booby through the water.—To whip the cat, is also a term among taylors for working jobs at private houses, as practised in the country.

CATAMARAN. An old scraggy woman, from a kind of float made of spars and yards lashed together, for saving shipwrecked persons

CATCH CLUB. A member of the catch club; a bum bailiff.

CATCH FART A foot boy; so called from such servants commonly following close behind their master or mistress

CATCH PENNY. Any temporary contrivance to raise a contribution on the public.

CATCH POLE. A bum bailiff, or sheriff's officer.

CATCHING HARVEST. A dangerous time for a robbery, when many persons are on the road, on account of a horse race, fair, or some other public meeting

CATER COUSINS. Good friends. He and I are not cater cousins, i. e. we are not even cousins in the fourth degree, or four times removed; that is, we have not the least friendly connection

CATERPILLAR. A nick name for a soldier In the year 1745, a soldier quartered at a house near Derby, was desired by his landlord to call upon him, whenever he came that way; for, added he, soldiers are the pillars of the nation The rebellion being finished, it happened the same regiment was quartered in Derbyshire, when the soldier resolved to accept of his landlord's invitation, and accordingly obtained leave to go to him: but, on his arrival, he was greatly surprised to find a very cold reception, whereupon expostulating with his landlord, he reminded him of his invitation, and the circumstance of his having said, soldiers

were

were the pillars of the nation. If I did, answered the host, I meant *cater*pillars

CATERWAULING. Going out in the night in search of intrigues, like a cat in the gutters

CATHEDRAL. Old-fashioned. An old cathedral bedstead, chair, &c

CATTLE. Sad cattle; whores or gypsies Black cattle; lice. *Cant.*

CAVAULTING SCHOOL. A bawdy house

CAUDGE-PAWED. Left-handed.

CAULIFLOWER. A large white wig, such as is commonly worn by the dignified clergy, and was formerly by physicians Also the private parts of a woman; the reason for which appellation is given in the following story: A woman, who was giving evidence in a cause wherein it was necessary to express those parts, made use of the term cauliflower, for which the judge on the bench, a peevish old fellow, reproved her, saying she might as well call it artichoke. Not so, my lord, replied she; for an artichoke has a bottom, but a **** and a cauliflower have none.

CAUTIONS. The four cautions — I. Beware of a woman before.—II Beware of a horse behind.—III Beware of a cart side ways.—IV. Beware of a priest every way

CAW-HANDED, or CAW-PAWED. Aukward, not dexterous, ready, or nimble.

CAXON. An old weatherbeaten wig.

CELTIBERIANS A society of the brethren of this most ancient and honourable brotherhood was held at the Swan and Rummer, Fleet-street.

CENT PER CENT. An usurer.

CHAFED Well beaten, from *chauffé*, warmed.

CHALKERS Men of wit, in Ireland, who in the night amuse themselves with cutting inoffensive passengers across the face with a knife. They are somewhat like those facetious gentlemen some time ago known in England by the title of Sweaters and Mohocks

CHALKING. The amusement above described.

CHAP. A fellow. An odd chap, a strange fellow.

CHAPERON. The cicisbeo, or gentleman usher, to a lady; from the French.

CHAPT. Dry or thirsty.

CHARACTERED, or LETTERED. Burnt in the hand. They have palmed the character upon him, they have burned him in the hand. *Cant.*—See LETTERED.

CHARM. A picklock. *Cant.*

CHARREN. The smoke of Charren—his eyes water from the smoke of Charren; a man of that place coming out of his house weeping, because his wife had beat him, told his neighbours the smoke had made his eyes water.

CHATTER BOX. One whose tongue runs twelve score to the dozen, a chattering man or woman.

CHATTER BROTH. Tea. See CAT LAP and SCANDAL BROTH.

CHATTS. Lice: perhaps an abbreviation of chattels, lice being the chief live stock or chattels of beggars, gypsies, and the rest of the canting crew. *Cant.*—Also, according to the canting academy, the gallows.

CHATES. The gallows. *Cant.*

CHAUNTER CULLS. Grub-street writers, who compose songs, carrols, &c. for ballad singers. *Cant.*

CHEAPSIDE. He came at it by way of Cheapside; he gave little or nothing for it, he bought it cheap.

CHEATS. Sham sleeves to put over a dirty shirt or shift. See SHAMS.

CHEEK BY JOWL. Side by side, hand to fist.

CHEEKS. Ask cheeks near cunnyborough; the repartee of a St. Giles's fair one, who bids you ask her backside, *anglicè* her a-se. A like answer is current in France: any one asking the road or distance to Macon, a city near Lyons, would be answered by a French lady of easy virtue, 'Mettez votre nez dans mon cul, & vous serrez dans les Fauxbourgs.'

CHEESE TOASTER. A sword.

CHELSEA. A village near London, famous for the military hospital. To get Chelsea, to obtain the benefit of that hospital. Dead Chelsea, by G-d! an exclamation uttered by a grenadier at Fontenoy, on having his leg carried away by a cannon ball.

CHERRY

CHERRY-COLOURED CAT A black cat, there being black cherries as well as red.

CHERUBIMS Peevish children, because cherubims and seraphims continually do cry

CHESHIRE CAT He grins like a Cheshire cat, said of any one who shews his teeth and gums in laughing

CHICK A-BIDDY, A chicken, so called to and by little children

CHICKEN-BREASTED Said of a woman with scarce any breasts

CHICKEN BUTCHER A poulterer

CHICKEN-HAMMED Persons whose legs and thighs are bent or arched outwards

CHICKEN-HEARTED Fearful, cowardly

CHICKEN NABOB One returned from the East Indies with but a moderate fortune of fifty or sixty thousand pounds, a diminutive nabob a term borrowed from the chicken turtle

CHILD To eat a child, to partake of a treat given to the parish officers, in part of commutation for a bastard child the common price was formerly ten pounds and a greasy chin See GREASY CHIN

CHIMNEY CHOPS An abusive appellation for a negro.

CHINK Money

CHIP A child A chip of the old block, a child who either in person or sentiments resembles its father or mother

CHIPS A nick name for a carpenter

CHIRPING MERRY Exhilarated with liquor Chirping glass, a cheerful glass, that makes the company chirp like birds in spring

CHIT. An infant or baby

CHITTERLINS The bowels There is a rumpus among my chitterlins, i e I have the cholick

CHITTY-FACED. Baby-faced, said of one who has a childish look

CHIVE, or CHIFE A knife, file, or saw To chive the darbies, to file off the irons or fetters To chive the boungs of the frows, to cut off women's pockets

CHIVEY I gave him a good chivey; I gave him a hearty scolding

CHIVING LAY. Cutting the braces of coaches behind, on which the coachman quitting the box, an accomplice robs the boot; also, formerly, cutting the back of the coach to steal the fine large wigs then worn

CHOAK Choak away, the church yard's near, a jocular saying to a person taken with a violent fit of coughing, or who has swallowed any thing, as it is called, the wrong way. Choak, chicken, more are hatching; a like consolation

CHOAK PEAR Figuratively, an unanswerable objection. also a machine formerly used in Holland by robbers; it was of iron, shaped like a pear; this they forced into the mouths of persons from whom they intended to extort money, and, on turning a key, certain interior springs thrust forth a number of points, in all directions, which so enlarged it, that it could not be taken out of the mouth; and the iron, being case-hardened, could not be filed. the only methods of getting rid of it, were either by cutting the mouth, or advertising a reward for the key These pears were also called pears of agony

CHOCOLATE To give chocolate without sugar, to reprove. *Military term*

CHOICE SPIRIT A thoughtless, laughing, singing, drunken fellow

CHOP A blow *Boxing term*

TO CHOP AND CHANGE To exchange backwards and forwards. To chop, in the canting sense, means making dispatch, or hurrying over any business ex The *autem bawler* will soon quit the *hums*, for he *chops up* the *whiners*, the parson will soon quit the pulpit, for he hurries over the prayers See AUTEM BAWLER, HUMS, and WHINERS.

CHOP CHURCHES Simoniacal dealers in livings, or other ecclesiastical preferments.

CHOPPING Lusty A chopping boy or girl, a lusty child.

CHOPS The mouth. I gave him a wherrit or a souse across the chops, I gave him a blow over the mouth See WHERRIT.

CHOSEN

CHOSEN PELLS Highwaymen who rob in pairs, in the streets and squares of London to prevent being followed by the sound of their horses shoes on the stones, they shoe them with leather

CHOUDER. A sea dish, composed of fresh fish, salt pork, herbs, and sea biscuits, laid in different layers, and stewed together.

TO CHOUSE To cheat or trick he choused me out of it Chouse is also the term for a game like chuck farthing

CHRIST-CROSS ROW. The alphabet in a horn book called Christ-cross Row, from having, as an Irishman observed, Christ's cross *prefixed* before and *after* the twenty-four letters.

CHRISTENING Erasing the name of the true maker from a stolen watch, and engraving a fictitious one in its place.

CHRISTIAN PONEY. A chairman.

CHRISTMASS COMPLIMENTS. A cough, kibed heels, and a snotty nose

CHUB. He is a young chub, or a mere chub; i.e. a foolish fellow, easily imposed on an allusion to a fish of that name, easily taken.

CHUBBY. Round-faced, plump

CHUCK. My chuck; a term of endearment.

CHUCK FARTHING A parish clerk.

CHUCKLE-HEADED Stupid, thick-headed.

CHUFFY Round-faced, chubby

CHUM. A chamber fellow, particularly at the universities and in prisons

CHUMMAGE. Money paid by the richer sort of prisoners in the Fleet and King's Bench, to the poorer, for their share of a room. When prisons are very full, which is too often the case, particularly on the eve of an insolvent act, two or three persons are obliged to sleep in a room. A prisoner who can pay for being alone, chuses two poor chums, who for a stipulated price, called chummage, give up their share of the room, and sleep on the stairs, or, as the term is, ruff it.

CHUNK. Among printers, a journeyman who refuses to work for legal wages; the same as a flint among taylors. See FLINT

CHURCH WARDEN. A Sussex name for a shag, or cormorant, probably from its voracity.

CHURCH WORK. Said of any work that advances slowly

CHURCHYARD COUGH. A cough that is likely to terminate in death.

CHURK. The udder.

CHURL. Originally, a labourer or husbandman, figuratively, a rude, surly, boorish fellow To put a churl upon a gentleman; to drink malt liquor immediately after having drank wine.

CINDER GARBLER. A servant maid, from her business of sifting the ashes from the cinders. *Custom-house wt*

CIRCUMBENDIBUS. A round-about way, or story. He took such a circumbendibus, he took such a circuit.

CIT. A citizen of London

CIVILITY MONEY. A reward claimed by bailiffs, for executing their office with civility.

CIVIL RECEPTION. A house of civil reception, a bawdy house, or nanny house See NANNY HOUSE.

CLACK A tongue, chiefly applied to women, a simile drawn from the clack of a water mill.

CLACK-LOFT. A pulpit, so called by orator Henley.

CLAMMED Starved

CLAN A family's tribe or brotherhood, a word much used in Scotland The head of the clan, the chief an allusion to a story of a Scotchman, who, when a very large louse crept down his arm, put him back again, saying he was the head of the clan, and that, if injured, all the rest would resent it.

CLANK. A silver tankard. *Cant*

CLANK NAPPER. A silver tankard stealer. See RUM BUBBER.

CLANKER. A great lye

CLAP. A venereal taint. He went out by Had'em, and came round by Clapham home, i. e. he went out a wenching, and got a clap.

CLAP

CLAP ON THE SHOULDER. An arrest for debt; whence a bum bailiff is called a shoulder clapper.

CLAPPER. The tongue of a bell, and figuratively of a man or woman.

CLAPPER CLAW. To scold, to abuse, or claw off with the tongue.

CLAPPERDOGEON. A beggar born. *Cant.*

CLARET. French red wine, figuratively, blood. I tapped his claret, I broke his head, and made the blood run. Claret-faced, red-faced.

CLAWED OFF. Severely beaten, or whipped, also smartly poxed or clapped

CLEAR Very drunk. The cull is clear, let's bite him; the fellow is very drunk, let's cheat him. *Cant*

CLEAVER One that will cleave, used of a forward or wanton woman

CLERKED. Soothed, funned, imposed on The cull will not be clerked, i. e. the fellow will not be imposed on by fair words.

CLEYMES. Artificial sores, made by beggars to excite charity.

CLICK. A blow A click in the muns, a blow or knock in the face. *Cant.*

To CLICK. To snatch To click a nab, to snatch a hat. *Cant.*

CLICKER A salesman's servant, also, one who proportions out the different shares of the booty among thieves.

CLICKET Copulation of foxes; and thence used, in a canting sense, for that of men and women as, the cull and the mort are at clicket in the dyke; the man and woman are copulating in the ditch

CLICKMAN TOAD. A watch; also an appellation for a West-country man, said to have arisen from the following story: A West-country man, who had never seen a watch, found one on a heath near Pool, which by the motion of the hand, and the noise of the wheels, he concluded to be a living creature of the toad kind; and, from its clicking, he named it a clickman toad.

CLIMB.

CLIMB. To climb the three trees with a ladder; to ascend the gallows.

CLINCH. A pun, or quibble. To clinch, or to clinch the nail; to confirm an improbable story by another as, A man swore he drove a tenpenny nail through the moon, a bystander said it was true, for he was on the other side and clinched it.

CLINK. A place in the Borough of Southwark, formerly privileged from arrests, and inhabited by lawless vagabonds of every denomination, called, from the place of their residence, clinkers. Also a gaol, from the clinking of the prisoners chains or fetters. he is gone to clink.

CLINKERS. A kind of small Dutch bricks; also irons worn by prisoners; a crafty fellow.

To CLIP. To hug or embrace. to clip and cling. To clip the coin; to diminish the current coin. To clip the king's English; to be unable to speak plain through drunkenness.

CLOAK TWITCHERS. Rogues who lurk about the entrances into dark allies, and bye lanes, to snatch cloaks from the shoulders of passengers.

CLOD HOPPER. A country farmer, or ploughman.

CLOD PATE. A dull, heavy booby.

CLOD POLE. The same.

CLOSE. As close as God's curse to a whore's a-se. close as shirt and shitten a-se.

CLOSE-FISTED. Covetous or stingy.

CLOSH. A general name given by the mobility to Dutch seamen, being a corruption of *Claus*, the abbreviation of Nicholas, a name very common among the men of that nation.

CLOTH MARKET. He is just come from the cloth market, i. e. from between the sheets, he is just risen from bed.

CLOUD. Tobacco. Under a cloud, in adversity.

CLOVEN, CLEAVE, or CLEFT. A term used for a woman who passes for a maid, but is not one.

CLOVEN FOOT. To spy the cloven foot in any business; to discover some roguery or something bad in it: a saying

that

that alludes to a piece of vulgar superstition, which is, that let the Devil transform himself into what shape he will, he cannot hide his cloven foot.

To CHUCK. To shew a propensity for a man. The mort chucks; the wench wants to be doing.

CLOUT. A blow. I'll give you a clout on your jolly nob, I'll give you a blow on the head. It also means a handkerchief. *Cant*

CLOUTED SHOON. Shoes tipped with iron.

CLOUTING LAY. Picking pockets of handkerchiefs.

CLOVER. To be, or live, in clover, to live luxuriously. Clover is the most desirable food for cattle.

CLOWES. Rogues.

CLOY. To steal. To cloy the clout; to steal the handkerchief. To cloy the lour; to steal money. *Cant.*

CLOYES. Thieves, robbers, &c.

CLUB. A meeting, or association, where each man is to spend an equal and stated sum, called his club.

CLUB LAW. Argumentum baculinum, in which an oaken stick is a better plea than an act of parliament.

CLUMP. A lump. Clumpish, lumpish, stupid.

CLUNCH. An aukward clownish fellow.

To CLUTCH THE FIST. To clench or shut the hand. Clutch-fisted; covetous, stingy. See CLOSE-FISTED.

CLUTCHES. Hands, gripe, power.

CLUTTER. A stir, noise, or racket. What a confounded clutter here is!

CLY. Money; also a pocket. He has filed the cly, he has picked a pocket. *Cant.*

CLY THE JERK. To be whipped. *Cant.*

CLYSTER PIPE. A nick name for an apothecary.

COACH WHEEL. A half crown piece is a fore coach wheel, and a crown piece a hind coach wheel; the fore wheels of a coach being less than the hind ones.

To COAX. To fondle, or wheedle. To coax a pair of stockings, to pull down the part soiled into the shoes, so as to give a dirty pair of stockings the appearance of clean ones. Coaxing is also used, instead of darning, to hide the holes about the ancles.

C O C

COB   A Spanish dollar.

COB, or COBBING. A punishment used by the seamen for petty offences, or irregularities, among themselves: it consists in bastonadoing the offender on the posteriors with a cobbing stick, or pipe staff, the number usually inflicted is a dozen. At the first stroke the executioner repeats the word *watch*, on which all persons present are to take off their hats, on pain of like punishment. the last stroke is always given as hard as possible, and is called *the purse* Ashore, among soldiers, where this punishment is sometimes adopted, *watch* and *the purse* are not included in the number, but given over and above, or, in the vulgar phrase, free gratis for nothing. This piece of discipline is also inflicted in Ireland, by the school boys, on persons coming into the school without taking off their hats; it is there called school butter

COBBLE   A kind of boat.

TO COBBLE. To mend, or patch; likewise to do a thing in a bungling manner.

COBBLE COLTER   A turkey.

COBLER. A mender of shoes, an improver of the understandings of his customers, a translator.

COBLERS PUNCH   Treacle, vinegar, gin, and water.

COCK, or CHIEF COCK, OF THE WALK. The leading man in any society or body, the best boxer in a village or district

COCK ALE.   A provocative drink

COCK ALLEY, or COCK LANE   The private parts of a woman

COCK AND A BULL STORY. A roundabout story without head or tail, i e beginning or ending.

COCK-A-WHOOP. Elevated, in high spirits, transported with joy

COCK BAWD   A male keeper of a bawdy house.

COCK HOIST   A cross buttock.

COCKISH   Wanton, forward. A cockish wench, a forward coming girl

COCKLES   To cry cockles; to be hanged perhaps from the noise made whilst strangling   *Cant.*—This will rejoice

the

COD

the cockles of one's heart; a saying in praise of wine, ale, or spirituous liquor.

COCK PIMP The supposed husband of a bawd.

COCK ROBIN A soft easy fellow.

COCK-SURE. Certain a metaphor borrowed from the cock of a firelock, as being much more certain to fire than the match

COCK'S TOOTH I live at the sign of the cock's tooth and head-ach; an answer to an impertinent person, who asks where one lives

COCK YOUR EYE Shut one eye thus translated into apothecaries Latin—*Gallus tuus ego.*

COCKER One fond of the diversion of cock-fighting

COCKNEY A nick name given to the citizens of London, or persons born within the sound of Bow bell, derived from the following story A citizen of London being in the country, and hearing a horse neigh, exclaimed, Lord! how that horse laughs! A by-stander telling him that noise was called *neighing*, the next morning, when the cock crowed, the citizen, to shew he had not forgot what was told him, cried out, Do you hear how the *cock neighs?* The king of the Cockneys is mentioned among the regulations for the sports and shows formerly held in the Middle Temple on Childermas Day, where he had his officers, a marshall, constable, butler, &c. See Dugdale's Origines Juridiciales, p 247 — Ray says, the interpretation of the word Cockney, is, a young person coaxed or coquered, made wanton, or a nestle cock, delicately bred and brought up, so as, when arrived at man's estate, to be unable to bear the least hardship Whatever may be the origin of this appellation, we learn from the following verses, attributed to Hugh Bigot, Earl of Norfolk, that it was in use in the time of king Henry II.

>Was I in my castle at Bungay,
>Fast by the river Waveney,
>I would not care for the king of Cockney

i e the king of London

COCKSHUT TIME. The evening, when fowls go to roost

COD A cod of money, a good sum of money.

CODDERS. Persons employed by the gardeners to gather pease.

CODGER. An old codger; an old fellow.

COD PIECE. The fore flap of a man's breeches. Do they bite master? where, in the cod piece or collar?—a jocular attack on a patient angler by watermen, &c.

CODS. The scrotum. Also a nick name for a curate: a rude fellow meeting a curate, mistook him for the rector, and accosted him with the vulgar appellation of Bol—ks the rector. No, Sir, answered he, only Cods the curate, at your service.

COD'S HEAD. A stupid fellow.

CODS HEADS. A society who met in London.

COFFEE HOUSE. A necessary house. To make a coffee-house of a woman's ****, to go in and out and spend nothing.

COG. The money, or whatsoever the sweeteners drop to draw in a bubble.

To COG. To cheat with dice; also to coax or wheedle. To cog a die; to conceal or secure a die. To cog a dinner, to wheedle one out of a dinner.

COGUE. A dram of any spirituous liquor.

COKER. A lye.

COKES. The fool in the play of Bartholomew fair: perhaps a contraction of the word *coxcomb*.

COLCANNON. Potatoes and cabbage pounded together in a mortar, and then stewed with butter: an Irish dish.

COLD. You will catch cold at that, a vulgar threat or advice to desist from an attempt. He caught cold by lying in bed barefoot, a saying of any one extremely tender or careful of himself.

COLD BURNING. A punishment inflicted by private soldiers on their comrades for trifling offences, or breach of their mess laws; it is administered in the following manner. The prisoner is set against the wall, with the arm which is to be burned tied as high above his head as possible. The executioner then ascends a stool, and having a bottle of cold water, pours it slowly down the sleeve of the delinquent, patting him, and leading the water gently down his body, till it runs out at his breeches knees: this is repeated to the other arm, if he is sentenced to be burned in both.

COL

COLD COOK. An undertaker of funerals, or carrion hunter. See CARRION HUNTER.

COLD IRON. A sword, or any other weapon for cutting or stabbing. I gave him two inches of cold iron into his beef.

COLD MEAT. A dead wife is the best cold meat in a man's house.

COLD PIG. To give cold pig, is a punishment inflicted on sluggards who lie too long in bed: it consists in pulling off all the bed clothes from them, and exposing them naked to the cold.

COLD PUDDING. This is said to settle one's love.

COLE. Money. Post the cole, pay down the money.

COLIANDER or CORIANDER SEEDS. Money.

COLLAR DAY. Execution day.

COLLEGE. Newgate, or any other prison. New College; the Royal Exchange.

COLLEGIATES. Prisoners of the one, and shopkeepers of the other of those places.

COLLECTOR. A highwayman.

TO COLLOGUE. To wheedle or coax.

COOK RUFFIAN, who roasted the devil in his feathers. A bad cook.

COOL CRAPE. A shroud.

COOLER. A woman.

COOL LADY. A female follower of the camp who sells brandy.

COOL NANTS. Brandy.

COOL TANKARD. Wine and water, with lemon, sugar, and burrage.

COLQUARRON. A man's neck. His colquarron is just about to be twisted; he is just going to be hanged. *Cant.*

COLT. One who lets horses to highwaymen; also a boy newly initiated into roguery; a grand or petty juryman on his first assize. *Cant.*

COLTAGE. A fine or beverage paid by colts on their first entering into their offices.

COLT BOWL. Laid short of the jack by a colt bowler; i.e. a person raw or unexperienced in the art of bowling.

COLT's TOOTH. An old fellow who marries, or keeps a young girl, is said to have a colt's tooth in his head.

COLT VEAL. Coarse red veal, more like the flesh of a colt than that of a calf.

COLUMBARIANS. The brethren of this honourable society assembled, A. D. 1743, at the Bull-Inn, in Bishopsgate-street.

COMB. To comb one's head, to clapperclaw, or scold any one. a woman who lectures her husband, is said to comb his head. She combed his head with a joint stool, she threw a stool at him.

COME. To come; to lend. Has he come it? has he lent it? To come over any one, to cheat or over-reach him. Coming wench, a forward wench, also a breeding woman.

COMING! SO IS CHRISTMAS. Said of a person who has long been called, and at length answers, Coming!

COMFORTABLE IMPORTANCE. A wife.

COMMISSION. A shirt. *Cant.*

COMMODE. A woman's head dress.

COMMODITY. A woman's commodity; the private parts of a modest woman, and the public parts of a prostitute.

COMMONS. The house of commons; the necessary house.

COMPANY. To see company, to enter into a course of prostitution.

COMPLIMENTS. See CHRISTMAS.

COMUS's COURT. A social meeting formerly held at the Half Moon tavern, Cheapside.

CONFECT. Counterfeited.

CONGER. To conger; the agreement of a set or knot of booksellers of London, that whosoever of them shall buy a good copy, the rest shall take off such a particular number, in quires, at a stated price; also booksellers joining to buy either a considerable or dangerous copy.

CONGO. Will you lap your congo with me? will you drink tea with me?

CONNY WABBLE. Eggs and brandy beat up together. *Irish.*

CONSCIENCE KEEPER. A superior, who by his influence makes his dependents act as he pleases.

CONTENT. The cull's content, the man is past complaining: a saying of a person murdered for resisting the robbers. *Cant*

CONTENT. A thick liquor, in imitation of chocolate, made of milk and gingerbread.

CONTRA DANCE. A dance where the dancers of the different sexes stand opposite each other, instead of side by side as in the minuet, regadoon, louvre, &c. and now corruptly called a country dance.

CONUNDRUMS. Enigmatical conceits.

CONVENIENT. A mistress. *Cant*.

CONY, or TOM CONY. A silly fellow.

COOPED UP. Imprisoned, confined like a fowl in a coop.

COQUET. A jilt.

CORINTH. A bawdy house. *Cant*.

CORINTHIANS. Frequenters of brothels. Also an impudent, brazen-faced fellow, perhaps from the Corinthian brass.

CORK-BRAINED. Light-headed, foolish.

CORNED. Drunk.

CORNELIAN TUB. The sweating tub, formerly used for the cure of the venereal disease.

CORNISH HUG. A particular lock in wrestling, peculiar to the people of that country.

CORNY-FACED. A very red pimpled face.

CORPORAL. To mount a corporal and four; to be guilty of onanism: the thumb is the corporal, the four fingers the privates.

CORPORATION. A large belly. He has a glorious coporation, he has a very prominent belly.

CORPORATION. The magistrates, &c. of a corporate town. *Corpus sine ratione* Freeman of a corporation's work; neither strong nor handsome.

COSSET. A foundling. Cosset colt or lamb; a colt or lamb brought up by hand.

COSTARD. The head. I'll smite your costard; I'll give you a knock on the head.

COSTARD

COSTARD MONGER. A dealer in fruit, particularly apples.

COT, or QUOT. A man who meddles with women's household business, particularly in the kitchen. The punishment commonly inflicted on a quot, is pinning a greasy dishclout to the skirts of his coat.

COTTEREL. Sir James Cotter, or Cotterel's sallad, hemp. Sir James Cotterel was condemned for a rape. *Irish*

COTSWOULD LION. A sheep Cotswould in Gloucestershire is famous for its breed of sheep

COVE. A man, a fellow, a rogue. The cove was bit, the rogue was outwitted The cove has bit the cole, the rogue has got the money. *Cant.*

COVENT, or CONVENT GARDEN, vulgarly called COMMON GARDEN Anciently, the garden belonging to a dissolved monastery, now famous for being the chief market in London for fruit, flowers, and herbs. The two theatres are situated near it. In its environs are many brothels; and, not long ago, the lodgings of the second order of ladies of easy virtue were either there, or in the purlieus of Drury Lane.

COVENT GARDEN ABBESS. A bawd.

COVENT GARDEN AGUE The venereal disease. He broke his shins against Covent Garden rails, he caught the venereal disorder.

COVENT GARDEN NUN. A prostitute.

COVENTRY.— To send one to Coventry; a punishment inflicted by officers of the army on such of their brethren as are testy or have been guilty of improper behaviour, not worthy the cognizance of a court martial. The person sent to Coventry is considered as absent; no one must speak to or answer any question he asks, except relative to duty, under penalty of being also sent to the same place On a proper submission, the penitent is recalled, and welcomed by the mess, as just returned from a journey to Coventry.

COVEY. A collection of whores What a fine covey here is, if the Devil would but throw his net!

To

CRA

TO COUCH A HOGSHEAD. To lie down to sleep. *Cant.*

COUNTERFEIT CRANK A general cheat, assuming all sorts of characters, one counterfeiting the falling sickness

COUNTRY HARRY A waggoner. *Cant.*

COUNTRY PUT. An ignorant country fellow.

COURT CARD. A gay fluttering coxcomb.

COURT HOLY WATER. } Fair speeches and promises, with-
COURT PROMISES. } out performance.

COURT OF ASSISTANTS. A court often applied to by young women who marry old men.

COURT OF NUL TIEL RECORD A society held, A D 1756, at the One Tun, in the Strand

COW. To sleep like a cow, i e with a **** at one's a-se, said of a married man, married men being supposed to sleep with their backs towards their wives, according to the following proclamation

> *All you that in your beds do lie,*
> *Turn to your wives, and occupy,*
> *And when that you have done your best,*
> *Turn a se to a-se, and take your rest.*

COW's BABY A calf

COW's COURANT Gallop and sh——e.

COW-HANDED Aukward.

COW-HEARTED Fearful

COW ITCH The product of a sort of bean, which excites an insufferable itching, used chiefly for playing tricks

COW's SPOUSE A bull.

COW's THUMB. Done to a cow's thumb, done exactly.

COXCOMB. Anciently, a fool. Fools, in great families, wore a cap with bells, on the top of which was a piece of red cloth, in the shape of a cock's comb At present, coxcomb signifies a fop, or vain self conceited fellow

CRAB To catch a crab, to fall backwards by missing one's stroke in rowing.

CRAB LANTHORN. A peevish fellow.

CRAB LOUSE A species of louse peculiar to the human body, the male is denominated a cock, the female a hen

CRAB SHELLS Shoes. *Irish*

CRABS. A losing throw to the main at hazard

CRABBED. Sour, ill-tempered, difficult.

CRACK A whore.

TO CRACK. To boast or brag, also to break. I cracked his napper, I broke his head.

THE CRACK, or ALL THE CRACK The fashionable theme, the go. The Crack Lay, of late is used, in the cant language, to signify the art and mystery of house-breaking.

CRACKER Crust, sea biscuit, or ammunition loaf, also the backside. Farting crackers, breeches.

CRACKISH Whorish.

CRACKMANS Hedges. The cull thought to have loped by breaking through the crackmans, but we fetched him back by a nope on the costard, which stopped his jaw, the man thought to have escaped by breaking through the hedge, but we brought him back by a great blow on the head, which laid him speechless.

CRAG The neck.

CRAMP RINGS Bolts, shackles, or fetters. *Cant.*

CRAMP WORDS Sentence of death passed on a criminal by a judge. He has just undergone the cramp word, sentence has just been passed on him. *Cant.*

CRANK Gin and water, also, brisk, pert.

CRANK. The falling sickness. *Cant.*

CRAP, or CROP Money.

CRAPPED Hanged. *Cant.*

TO CRASH To kill. Crash that cull, kill that fellow. *Cant.*

CRASHING CHEATS. Teeth.

CRAW THUMPERS Roman catholics, so called from their beating their breasts in the confession of their sins. See BRISKET BEATER, and BREAST FLEET.

CREAM-POT LOVE Such as young fellows pretend to dairy maids, to get cream and other good things from them.

TO CREEME To slip or slide any thing into the hands of another. *Cant.*

CREEPERS Gentlemen's companions, lice.

CREW A knot or gang, also, a boat or ship's company. The canting crew are thus divided into twenty-three orders, which see under the different words.

M E N.

1 Rufflers   3 Hookers or Anglers
2 Upright Men   4 Rogues
                                5 Wild

CRI

5 Wild Rogues
6 Priggers of Prancers
7 Palliardes
8 Fraters
9 Jarkmen, or Patricoes
10 Fresh Water Mariners, or Whip Jackets
11 Drummerers
12 Drunken Tinkers
13 Swadders, or Pedlars
14 Abrams

WOMEN

1 Demanders for Glimmer or Fire
2 Bawdy Baskets
3 Morts
4 Autem Morts
5 Walking Morts
6 Doxies
7 Delles
8 Kinching Morts
9 Kinching Coes

TO CRIB To purloin, or appropriate to one's own use, part of any thing intrusted to one's care

TO FIGHT A CRIB. To make a sham fight. *Bear Garden term*

CRIBBAGE-FACED Marked with the small pox, the pits bearing a kind of resemblance to the holes in a cribbage board.

CRIBBEYS, or CRIBBY ISLANDS Blind allies, courts, or bye ways, perhaps from the houses built there being cribbed out of the common way or passage, and islands, from the similarity of sound to the Caribbee Islands

CRIM CON MONEY Damages directed by a jury to be paid by a convicted adulterer to the injured husband, for criminal conversation with his wife

CRIMP A broker or factor, as a coal crimp, who disposes of the cargoes of the Newcastle coal ships, also persons employed to trapan or kidnap recruits for the East Indian and African companies. To crimp, or play crimp, to play foul or booty, also a cruel manner of cutting up fish alive, practised by the London fishmongers, in order to make it eat firm, cod, and other crimped fish, being a favourite dish among voluptuaries and epicures

CRINKUM CRANKUM. A woman's commodity. See SPECTATOR.

CRINKUMS The foul or venereal disease.

CRIPPLE Six pence, that piece being commonly much bent and distorted.

CRISPIN. A shoemaker from a romance, wherein a prince of that name is said to have exercised the art and mystery of a shoemaker, thence called the gentle craft. or rather from the saints Crispinus and Crispianus, who, according to the legend, were brethren born at Rome, from whence they travelled to Soissons in France, about the year 303, to propagate the Christian religion, but, because they would not be chargeable to others for their maintenance, they exercised the trade of shoemakers. the governor of the town discovering them to be Christians, ordered them to be beheaded, about the year 303, from which time they have been the tutelar saints of the shoemakers

CRISPIN'S HOLIDAY Every Monday throughout the year, but most particularly the 25th of October, being the anniversary of Crispinus and Crispianus

CRISPIN'S LANCE An awl

CROAKER One who is always foretelling some accident or misfortune an allusion to the croaking of a raven, supposed ominous

CROAKUMSHIRE Northumberland, from the particular croaking in the pronunciation of the people of that county, especially about Newcastle and Morpeth, where they are said to be born with a burr in their throats, which prevents their pronouncing the letter r

CROCKERS. Forestallers, called also Kidders and Tranters,

CROCODILE'S TEARS The tears of a hypocrite, Crocodiles are fabulously reported to shed tears over their prey before they devour it

CROCUS, or CROCUS METALLORUM. A nick name for a surgeon of the army and navy

CROKER. A groat, or four pence.

CRONE An old ewe whose teeth are worn out · figuratively, a toothless old beldam

CRONY An intimate companion, a camerade; also, a confederate in a robbery

CROOK BACK Six-pence. for the reason of this name, see CRIPPLE

CROOK YOUR ELBOW. To crook one's elbow, and with it

may never come straight, if the fact then affirmed is not true—according to the casuists of Bow Street and St. Giles's, adds great weight and efficacy to an oath.

CROOK SHANKS. A nick name for a man with bandy legs He buys his boots in Crooked Lane, and his stockings in Bandy-legged Walk, his legs grew in the night, therefore could not see to grow straight jeering sayings of men with crooked legs.

CROP A nick name for a presbyterian from their cropping their hair, which they trimmed close to a bowl dish, placed as a guide on their heads, whence they were likewise called roundheads See ROUNDHEADS.

CROP Money See CRAP Cant.

CROP THE CONJUROR Jeering appellation of one with short hair.

CROPPING DRUMS. Drummers of the foot guards, or Chelsea hospital, who find out weddings, and beat a point of war to serenade the new-married couple, and thereby obtain money.

CROPPEN The tail The croppen of the rotan, the tail of the cart. Croppen ken, the necessary house. Cant.

CROPSICK Sickness in the stomach, arising from drunkenness.

CROSS. To come home by weeping cross; to repent at the conclusion

CROSS BITE One who combines with a sharper to draw in a friend, also, to counteract or disappoint. Cant.

CROSS BUTTOCK A particular lock or fall in the Broughtonian art, which, as Mr Fielding observes, conveyed more pleasant sensations to the spectators than the patient.

CROSS PATCH A peevish boy or girl.

To CROW. To brag, boast, or triumph. To crow over any one; to keep him in subjection. an image drawn from a cock, who crows over a vanquished enemy. To pluck a crow, to reprove any one for a fault committed, to settle a dispute To strut like a crow in a gutter; to walk proudly, or with an air of consequence.

CROWD. A fiddle: probably from *crooth*, the Welch name for that instrument.

CROWDERO,

CROWDERO. A fidler

CROWDY. Oatmeal and water, or milk a mefs much eaten in the north

CROW FAIR A vifitation of the clergy. See REVIEW OF THE BLACK CUIRASSERS

CROWN OFFICE. The head.

CRUISERS. Beggars, or highway fpies, who traverfe the road, to give intelligence of a booty, alfo, rogues ready to fnap up any booty that may offer, like privateers or pirates on a cruife.

CRUMMY. Fat, flefhy. A fine crummy dame; a fat woman. He has picked up his crumbs finely of late, he has grown very fat, or rich, of late

CRUMP. One who helps folicitors to affidavit men, or falfe witneffes —'I wifh you had, Mrs Crump,' a Gloucefter-shire faying, in anfwer to a wifh for any thing, implying, you muft not expect any affiftance from the fpeaker. It is faid to have originated from the following incident. One Mrs Crump, the wife of a fubftantial farmer, dining with the old Lady Coventry, who was extremely deaf, faid to one of the footmen, waiting at table, 'I wifh I had 'a draught of fmall beer,' her modefty not permitting her to defire fo fine a gentleman to bring it the fellow, confcious that his miftrefs could not hear either the requeft or anfwer, replied, without moving, ' I wifh you had, Mrs ' Crump.' Thefe wifhes being again repeated by both parties, Mrs Crump got up from the table to fetch it herfelf; and being afked by my Lady where fhe was going, related what had paffed The ftory being told abroad, the expreffion became proverbial.

CRUMP-BACKED Hump-backed.

CRUSTY BEAU One that ufes paint and cofmetics, to obtain a fine complexion.

CRUSTY FELLOW. A furly fellow

CUB. An unlicked cub, an unformed, ill-educated young man, a young nobleman or gentleman on his travels: an allufion to the ftory of the bear, faid to bring its cub into form by licking. Alfo, a new gamefter

CUCKOLD. The hufband of an incontinent wife · cuckolds, however,

however, are Christians, as we learn by the following story: An old woman hearing a man call his dog Cuckold, reproved him sharply, saying, 'Sirrah, are not you ashamed 'to call a dog by a christian's name?' To cuckold the parson, to bed with one's wife before she has been churched.

CUCUMBERS Taylors, who are jocularly said to subsist, during the summer, chiefly on cucumbers

CUFF An old cuff, an old man To cuff Jonas, said of one who is knock-kneed, or who beats his sides to keep himself warm in frosty weather, called also Beating the Booby

CUFFIN. A man

CULL A man, honest or otherwise A bob cull; a good-natured, quiet fellow *Cant*

CULLABILITY A disposition liable to be cheated, an unsuspecting nature, open to imposition

CULLY A fop or fool, also, a dupe to women from the Italian word *coglione*, a blockhead

CULP A kick or blow. from the words *mea culpa*, being that part of the popish liturgy at which the people beat their breasts, or, as the vulgar term is, thump their craws.

CUNDUM The dried gut of a sheep, worn by men in the act of coition, to prevent venereal infection, said to have been invented by one colonel Cundum. These machines were long prepared and sold by a matron of the name of Philips, at the Green Canister, in Half-moon street, in the Strand. That good lady having acquired a fortune, retired from business, but learning that the town was not well served by her successors, she, out of a patriotic zeal for the public welfare, returned to her occupation, of which she gave notice by diverse hand bills, in circulation in the year 1776. Also a false scabbard over a sword, and the oil-skin case for holding the colours of a regiment.

CUNNINGHAM. A punning appellation for a simple fellow.

CUNNING MAN A cheat, who pretends by his skill in astrology to assist persons in recovering stolen goods, and also to tell them their fortunes, and when, how often, and to whom they shall be married, likewise answers all lawful questions,

questions, both by sea and land. This profession is frequently occupied by ladies

CUNNING SHAVER. A sharp fellow, one that trims close, i. e. cheats ingeniously.

CUNNY-THUMBED To double one's fist with the thumb inwards, like a woman.

C**T The κύσος of the Greek, and the *cunnus* of the Latin dictionaries; a nasty name for a nasty thing. *un con.* Miege.

CUP OF THE CREATURE. A cup of good liquor.

CUP-SHOT. Drunk.

CUPBOARD LOVE Pretended love to the cook, or any other person, for the sake of a meal. My guts cry cupboard; i. e. I am hungry.

CUPID, BLIND CUPID. A jeering name for an ugly blind man: Cupid, the god of love, being frequently painted blind.

CUR A cut or curtailed dog According to the forest laws, a man who had no right to the privilege of the chace, was obliged to cut or law his dog among other modes of disabling him from disturbing the game, one was by depriving him of his tail. a dog so cut was called a cut or curtailed dog, and by contraction a cur. A cur is figuratively used to signify a surly fellow.

CURBING LAW. The act of hooking goods out of windows. the curber is the thief, the curb the hook *Cant*

CURE A-SE. A dyachilon plaister, applied to the parts galled by riding.

CURJEW. The vulgar seamen's pronunciation of the Couragieux ship of war.

CURLE. Clippings of money, which curls up in the operation. *Cant.*

CURMUDGEON. A covetous old fellow, derived, according to some, from the French term *cœur mechant*.

CURRY. To curry favour, to obtain the favour of a person by coaxing, or servility. To curry any one's hide; to beat him.

CURSE OF SCOTLAND. The nine of diamonds diamonds, it is said, imply royalty, being ornaments to the imperial crown;

crown, and every ninth king of Scotland has been observed, for many ages, to be a tyrant and a curse to that country. Others say it is from its similarity to the arms of Argyle, the Duke of Argyle having been very instrumental in bringing about the union, which, by some Scotch patriots, has been considered as detrimental to their country.

CURSITORS. Broken pettyfogging attornies, or Newgate solicitors. *Cant*

CURTAILS. Thieves who cut off pieces of stuff hanging out of shop windows, the tails of women's gowns, &c; also thieves wearing short jackets.

CURTAIN LECTURE. A woman who scolds her husband when in bed, is said to read him a curtain lecture.

CURTEZAN. A prostitute.

CUSHION. He has deserved the cushion; a saying of one whose wife is brought to bed of a boy, implying, that having done his business effectually, he may now indulge or repose himself.

CUSHION THUMPER, or DUSTER. A parson; many of whom, in the fury of their eloquence, heartily belabour their cushions.

CUSTARD CAP. The cap worn by the sword-bearer of the City of London, made hollow at the top like a custard.

CUSTOM-HOUSE GOODS. The stock in trade of a prostitute, because fairly entered.

CUT. Drunk. A little cut over the head; slightly intoxicated. To cut, to leave a person or company. To cut up well, to die rich.

TO CUT BENE. To speak gently. To cut bene whiddes; to give good words. To cut queer whiddes, to give foul language. To cut a bosh, or a flash; to make a figure. *Cant*

TO CUTTY-EYE. To look out of the corners of one's eyes, to leer, to look askance. The cull cutty-eyed at us; the fellow looked suspicious at us.

D.

DAM

DAB. An adept, a dab at any feat or exercife. Dab, quoth Dawkins, when he hit his wife on the a-fe with a pound of butter.

DACE. Two pence. Tip me a dace, lend me two pence. *Cant.*

DADDLES. Hands. Tip us your daddle, give me your hand. *Cant.*

DADDY. Father. Old daddy, a familiar addrefs to an old man. To beat daddy mammy; the firft rudiments of drum beating, being the elements of the roll.

DAGGERS. They are at daggers drawing; i. e. at enmity, ready to fight.

DAIRY A woman's breafts, particularly one that gives fuck. She fported her dairy, fhe pulled out her breaft.

DAISY CUTTER. A jockey term for a horfe that does not lift up his legs fufficiently, or goes too near the ground, and is therefore apt to ftumble.

DAISY KICKERS Hoftlers at great inns.

DALMAHOY. A Dalmahoy wig, a particular kind of bufhy bob wig, firft worn by a chymift of that name, and afterwards adopted by tradefmen, apothecaries, &c.

DAM. A fmall Indian coin, mentioned in the Gentoo code of laws. hence etymologifts may, if they pleafe, derive the common expreffion, I do not care a dam, i. e. I do not care half a farthing for it.

DAMBER. A rafcal. See DIMBER.

DAMME BOY. A roaring, mad, bluftering fellow, a fcourer of the ftreets, or kicker up of a breeze.

DAMNED SOUL. A clerk in a counting-houfe, whofe fole bufinefs it is to clear or fwear off merchandize at the cuftom-houfe; and who, it is faid, guards againft the crime of perjury, by taking a previous oath, never to fwear truly on thofe occafions.

DAMPER.

DAMPER. A luncheon, or snap before dinner: so called from its damping, or allaying, the appetite; eating and drinking being, as the proverb wisely observes, apt to take away the appetite.

DANCERS. Stairs.

DANDY. That's the dandy, i. e. the ton, the clever thing: an expression of similar import to "That's the barber." See BARBER.

DANDY GREY RUSSET. A dirty brown. His coat's dandy grey russet, the colour of the Devil's nutting bag.

DANDY PRAT. An insignificant or trifling fellow.

TO DANGLE. To follow a woman without asking the question. Also, to be hanged. I shall see you dangle in the sheriff's picture frame, I shall see you hanging on the gallows.

DANGLER. One who follows women in general, without any particular attachment.

DAPPER FELLOW. A smart, well-made, little man.

DARBIES. Fetters. *Cant.*

DARBY. Ready money. *Cant.*

DARK CULLY. A married man that keeps a mistress, whom he visits only at night, for fear of discovery.

DARKMANS. The night. *Cant.*

DARKMANS BUDGE. One that slides into a house in the dark of the evening, and hides himself, in order to let some of the gang in at night to rob it.

DART. A straight-armed blow in boxing.

DASH. A tavern drawer. To cut a dash, to make a figure.

DAVID JONES. The devil, the spirit of the sea: called Neken in the north countries, such as Norway, Denmark, and Sweden.

DAVID JONES'S LOCKER. The sea.

DAVID'S SOW. As drunk as David's sow, a common saying, which took its rise from the following circumstance: One David Lloyd, a Welchman, who kept an alehouse at Hereford, had a living sow with six legs, which was greatly resorted to by the curious. he had also a wife much addicted to drunkenness, for which he used sometimes to give her due correction. One day David's wife having taken a cup too much, and being fearful of the consequences, turned out the sow, and lay down to sleep herself sober in the stye. A company coming in to see the sow, David ushered them into the stye, exclaiming, There is a sow for you! did any of you ever see such another? all the while supposing the sow had really been there, to which some of the company, seeing the state the woman was in, replied, it was the drunkenest sow they had ever beheld whence the woman was ever after called David's Sow.

DAVY. I'll take my davy of it, vulgar abbreviation of affidavit

TO DAWB To bribe The cull was scragged because he could not dawb; the rogue was hanged because he could not bribe All bedawbed with lace, all over lace.

DAY LIGHTS Eyes To darken his day lights, or sew up his sees; to close up a man's eyes in boxing.

DEAD CARGO. A term used by thieves, when they are disappointed in the value of their booty

DEAD HORSE To work for the dead horse, to work for wages already paid.

DEAD-LOUSE. Vulgar pronunciation of the Dédalus ship of war.

DEAD MEN. A cant word among journeymen bakers, for loaves falsely charged to their master's customers, also empty bottles

DEADLY NEVERGREEN, that bears fruit all the year round The gallows, or three-legged mare. See THREE-LEGGED MARE

DEAR JOYS Irishmen from their frequently making use of that expression.

DEATH HUNTER An undertaker, one who furnishes the necessary articles for funerals. See CARRION HUNTER.

DEATH'S HEAD UPON A MOP-STICK A poor, miserable, emaciated fellow, one quite an otomy. See OTOMY.— He looked as pleasant as the pains of death.

DECUS A crown piece

DEEP-ONE. A thorough-paced rogue, a sly designing fellow in opposition to a shallow or foolish one.

DEFT FELLOW. A neat little man.

DEGEN, or DAGEN. A sword. Nim the degen; steal the sword. Dagen is Dutch for a sword. *Cant*

DELLS. Young buxom wenches, ripe and prone to venery, but who have not lost their virginity, which the *upright man* claims by virtue of his prerogative, after which they become free for any of the fraternity. Also a common strumpet. *Cant*

DEMURE. As demure as an old whore at a christening.

DEMY-REP. Abbreviation of demy-reputation; a woman of doubtful character.

DERICK. The name of the finisher of the law, or hangman, about the year 1608.—' For he rides his circuit with the
' Devil, and Derrick must be his host, and Tiburne the
' inne at which he will lighte.' 'Vide Bellman of London, in art. PRIGGING LAW.—' At the gallows, where I leave
' them, as to the haven at which they must all cast anchor,
' if Derrick's cables do but hold.' *Ibid.*

DEVIL. A printer's errand boy. Also a small thread in the king's ropes and cables, whereby they may be distinguished from all others. The Devil himself; a small streak of blue thread in the king's sails. The Devil may dance in his pocket; i. e. he has no money: the cross on our ancient coins being jocularly supposed to prevent him from visiting that place, for fear, as it is said, of breaking his shins against it. To hold a candle to the Devil, to be civil to any one out of fear: in allusion to the story of the old woman, who set a wax taper before the image of St. Michael, and another before the Devil, whom that saint is commonly represented as trampling under his feet: being reproved for paying such honour to Satan, she answered, as it was uncertain which place she should go to, heaven or hell, she chose to secure a friend in both places. That will be when the Devil is blind, and he has not got sore eyes yet; said of any thing unlikely to happen. It rains whilst the sun shines, the Devil is beating his wife with a shoulder of mutton: this phenomenon is also said to denote that cuckolds are going to heaven; on being informed of this,

a loving

a loving wife cried out with great vehemence, 'Run, huf-
'band, run!'

The Devil was sick, the Devil a monk would be;
The Devil was well, the devil a monk was he.

a proverb signifying that we are apt to forget promises made in times of distress. To pull the Devil by the tail, to be reduced to one's shifts. The Devil go with you and six-pence, and then you will have both money and company

DEVIL. The gizzard of a turkey or fowl, scored, peppered, salted, and broiled it derives its appellation from being hot in the mouth

DEVIL'S BOOKS Cards.

DEVIL CATCHER, or DEVIL DRIVER. A parson. See SNUB DEVIL.

DEVIL'S DAUGHTER. It is said of one who has a termagant for a wife, that he has married the Devil's daughter, and lives with the old folks.

DEVIL'S DAUGHTER'S PORTION.

Deal, Dover, and Harwich,
The Devil gave with his daughter in marriage,
And, by a codicil to his will,
He added Helvoet and the Brill

a saying occasioned by the shameful impositions practised by the inhabitants of those places, on sailors and travellers.

DEVIL DRAWER. A miserable painter

DEVIL'S DUNG Assafœtida.

DEVIL'S GUTS A surveyor's chain. so called by farmers, who do not like their land should be measured by their landlords

DEVILISH. Very: an epithet which in the English vulgar language is made to agree with every quality or thing, as, devilish bad, devilish good; devilish sick, devilish well; devilish sweet, devilish sour; devilish hot, devilish cold, &c. &c.

DEUSEA VILLE The country *Cant.*

DEUSEA VILLE STAMPERS. Country carriers. *Cant.*

DEW BEATERS. Feet. *Cant.*

DEWS WINS, or DEUX WINS. Two-pence. *Cant.*

DEWITTED Torn to pieces by a mob, as that great statesman John de Wit was in Holland, anno 1672

DICE. The names of false dice.
   A bale of bard cinque deuces
   A bale of flat cinque deuces
   A bale of flat fice aces
   A bale of bard cater traes
   A bale of flat cater traes
   A bale of fulhams
   A bale of light graniers
   A bale of langrets contrary to the ventage
   A bale of gordes, with as many highmen as lowmen, for passage
   A bale of demies
   A bale of long dice for even and odd
   A bale of bristles
   A bale of direct contraries.

DICK. That happened in the reign of queen Dick, i. e. never, said of any absurd old story. I am as queer as Dick's hatband, that is, out of spirits, or don't know what ails me.

DICKEY. A woman's under petticoat.

DIDDEYS A woman's breasts or bubbies.

DIDDLE. Gin.

DIGGERS Spurs *Cant.*

DILDO. [From the Italian *diletto*, q. d. a woman's delight, or from our word *dally*, q d. a thing to play withal.] Penis Succedaneus, called in Lombardy Passo Tempo. *Baily.*

DILIGENT. Double diligent, like the Devil's apothecary; said of one affectedly diligent.

DILLY [An abbreviation of the word *diligence*] A public voiture or stage, commonly a post chaise, carrying three persons. the name is taken from the public stage vehicles in France and Flanders. The Dillies first began to run in England about the year 1779.

DIMBER. Pretty A dimber cove, a pretty fellow. Dimber mort, a pretty wench *Cant.*

DIMBER

DIMBER DAMBER. A top man, or prince, among the canting crew; also the chief rogue of the gang, or the completest cheat. *Cant.*

DING To knock down. To ding it in one's ears, to reproach or tell one something one is not desirous of hearing Also to throw away or hide. thus a highwayman who throws away or hides any thing with which he robbed, to prevent being known or detected, is, in the canting lingo, styled a Dinger.

DING BOY. A rogue, a hector, a bully, or sharper *Cant.*

DING DONG. Helter skelter, in a hasty disorderly manner.

DINGEY CHRISTIAN. A mulatto, or any one who has, as the West Indian term is, a lick of the tar brush, that is, some negro blood in him.

DINING ROOM POST A mode of stealing in houses that let lodgings, by rogues pretending to be postmen, who send up sham letters to the lodgers, and, whilst waiting in the entry for the postage, go into the first room they see open, and rob it.

DIP. To dip for a wig. Formerly, in Middle Row, Holborn, wigs of different sorts were, it is said, put into a close-stool box, into which, for three-pence, any one might dip, or thrust in his hand, and take out the first wig he laid hold of, if he was dissatisfied with his prize, he might, on paying three halfpence, return it and dip again.

THE DIP. A cook's shop, under Furnivals Inn, where many attornies clerks, and other inferior limbs of the law, take out the wrinkles from their bellies. *Dip* is also a punning name for a tallow-chandler.

DIPPERS Anabaptists.

DIPT. Pawned or mortgaged.

DIRTY PUZZLE. A nasty slut

DISGUISED. Drunk.

DISGRUNTLED. Offended, disobliged.

DISHED UP He is completely dished up, he is totally ruined. To throw a thing in one's dish, to reproach or twit one with any particular matter.

DISHCLOUT. A dirty, greasy woman. He has made a napkin of his dishclout; a saying of one who has married his

cook

cook maid. To pin a dishclout to a man's tail; a punishment often threatened by the female servants in a kitchen, to a man who pries too minutely into the secrets of that place

DISMAL DITTY. The psalm sung by the felons at the gallows, just before they are turned off.

DISPATCHES A mittimus, or justice of the peace's warrant, for the commitment of a rogue.

DIVE To dive, to pick a pocket. To dive for a dinner, to go down into a cellar to dinner A dive, is a thief who stands ready to receive goods thrown out to him by a little boy put in at a window Cant.

DIVER. A pickpocket, also one who lives in a cellar.

DIVIDE. To divide the house with one's wife; to give her the outside, and to keep all the inside to one's self, i. e. to turn her into the street

Do. To do any one, to rob or cheat him. I have done him; I have robbed him. Also to overcome in a boxing match witness those laconic lines written on the field of battle, by Humphreys to his patron—'Sir, I have done 'the Jew.'

To Do OVER. Carries the same meaning, but is not so briefly expressed, the former having received the polish of the present times.

DOASH A cloak. Cant

DOBIN RIG Stealing ribbands from haberdashers early in the morning, or late at night, generally practised by women in the disguise of maid servants

TO DOCK To lie with a woman. The cull docked the dell all the darkmans, the fellow lay with the wench all night Docked smack smooth, one who has suffered an amputation of his penis, from a venereal complaint. He must go into dock; a sea phrase, signifying that the person spoken of must undergo a salivation. Docking is also a punishment inflicted by sailors on the prostitutes who have infected them with the venereal disease, it consists in cutting off all their clothes, petticoats, shift and all, close to their stays, and then turning them into the street.

DOCTOR.

DOL

DOCTOR Milk and water, with a little rum, and some nutmeg also the name of a composition used by distillers, to make spirits appear stronger than they really are, or, in their phrase, better proof.

DOCTORS. Loaded dice, that will run but two or three chances. They put the doctors upon him; they cheated him with loaded dice.

DODSEY. A woman perhaps a corruption of Doxey. *Cant.*

DOG. An old dog at it, expert or accustomed to any thing. Dog in a manger, one who would prevent another from enjoying what he himself does not want: an allusion to the well-known fable. The dogs have not dined; a common saying to any one whose shirt hangs out behind. To dog, or dodge, to follow at a distance. To blush like a blue dog; i. e. not at all. To walk the black dog on any one, a punishment inflicted in the night on a fresh prisoner, by his comrades, in case of his refusal to pay the usual footing or garnish

DOG BUFFERS. Dog stealers, who kill those dogs not advertised for, sell their skins, and feed the remaining dogs with their flesh

DOG LATIN. Barbarous Latin, such as was formerly used by the lawyers in their pleadings.

DOG'S PORTION. A lick and a smell He comes in for only a dog's portion; a saying of one who is a distant admirer or dangler after women. See DANGLER.

DOG'S RIG. To copulate till you are tired, and then turn tail to it

DOG'S SOUP Rain water

DOG VANE. A cockade. *Sea term.*

DOGGED. Surly.

DOGGESS, DOG'S WIFE or LADY, PUPPY'S MAMMA. Jocular ways of calling a woman a bitch.

DOLL. Bartholomew doll, a tawdry, over-drest woman, like one of the children's dolls sold at Bartholomew Fair. To mill doll; to beat hemp at Bridewell, or any other house of correction.

DOLLY. A Yorkshire dolly; a contrivance for washing, by means of a kind of wheel fixed in a tub, which being

turned

turned about, agitates and cleanses the linen put into it, with soap and water.

DOMINE DO LITTLE, An impotent old fellow.

DOMINEER. To reprove or command in an insolent or haughty manner. Don't think as how you shall domineer here.

DOMMERER. A beggar pretending that his tongue has been cut out by the Algerines, or cruel and blood-thirsty Turks, or else that he was born deaf and dumb. *Cant.*

DONE, or DONE OVER. Robbed; also, convicted or hanged. *Cant.*—See Do.

DONE UP. Ruined by gaming and extravagances. *Modern term.*

DONKEY, DONKEY DICK. A he, or jack ass: called dorkey, perhaps, from the Spanish or don-like gravity of that animal, intitled also the king of Spain's trumpeter.

DOODLE. A silly fellow, or noodle. See NOODLE. Also a child's penis. Doodle doo, or Cock a doodle doo, a childish appellation for a cock, in imitation of its note when crowing.

DOODLE SACK. A bagpipe. *Dutch.*—Also the private parts of a woman.

DOPEY. A beggar's trull.

DOSE. Burglary. He was cast for felon and dose, he was found guilty of felony and burglary. *Cant.*

DOT AND GO ONE. To waddle: generally applied to persons who have one leg shorter than the other, and who, as the sea phrase is, go upon an uneven keel. Also a jeering appellation for an inferior writing master, or teacher of arithmetic.

DOUBLE. To tip any one the double, to run away in his or her debt.

DOUBLE JUGG. A man's backside. *Cotton's Virgil.*

DOVE TAIL. A species of regular answer, which fits in to the subject, like the contrivance whence it takes its name. ex. Who owns this? The dovetail is, Not you by your asking.

DOUGLAS. Roby Douglas, with one eye and a stinking breath, the breech. *Sea wit.*

Dowdy. A coarse, vulgar-looking woman.

Dowdying. A local joke formerly practised at Salisbury, on large companies, or persons boasting of their courage. It was performed by one Pearce, who had the knack of personating madness, and who, by the direction of some of the company, would burst into a room, in a most furious manner, as if just broke loose from his keeper, to the great terror of those not in the secret. Dowdying became so much the fashion of the place, that it was exhibited before his Royal Highness the Prince of Wales, father of our present sovereign. Pearce obtained the name of Dowdy, from a song he used to sing, which had for its burthen the words *dow de dow*.

Down Hills. Dice that run low.

To Dowse. To take down; as, Dowse the pendant. Dowse your dog vane, take the cockade out of your hat. Dowse the glim; put out the candle.

Dowse on the Chops. A blow in the face.

Dowser. Vulgar pronounciation of *douceur*.

Doxies. She beggars, wenches, whores.

Drab. A nasty, sluttish whore.

Drag. To go on the drag, to follow a cart or waggon, in order to rob it. *Cant.*

Draggletail, or Daggletail. One whose garments are bespattered with dag or dew; generally applied to the female sex, to signify a slattern.

Dragooning it. A man who occupies two branches of one profession, is said to dragoon it, because, like the soldier of that denomination, he serves in a double capacity. Such is a physician who furnishes the medicines, and compounds his own prescriptions.

Dram. A glass or small measure of any spirituous liquors, which, being originally sold by apothecaries, were estimated by drams, ounces, &c. Dog's dram, to spit in his mouth, and clap his back.

Dram-a-tick. A dram served upon credit.

Draper. An ale draper, an alehouse keeper.

Draught, or Bill, on the Pump at Aldgate. A bad or false bill of exchange. See Aldgate.

DRAW LATCHES. Robbers of houses whose doors are only fastened with latches. *Cant.*

DRAWERS. Stockings. *Cant.*

DRAWING THE KING'S PICTURE. Coining. *Cant.*

TO DRESS. To beat. I'll dress his hide neatly, I'll beat him soundly.

DRIBBLE. A method of pouring out, as it were, the dice from the box, gently, by which an old practitioner is enabled to cog one of them with his fore finger.

DRIPPER. A gleet.

DROMEDARY. A heavy, bungling thief or rogue. A purple dromedary, a bungler in the art and mystery of thieving. *Cant.*

DROMMERARS. See DOMERARS.

DROP. The new drop, a contrivance for executing felons at Newgate, by means of a platform, which drops from under them: this is also called the last drop. See LEAF.

DROP A COG. To let fall, with design, a piece of gold or silver, in order to draw in and cheat the person who sees it picked up; the piece so dropt is called a dropt cog.

DROP IN THE EYE. Almost drunk.

TO DRUB. To beat any one with a stick, or rope's end: perhaps a contraction of *dry rub*. It is also used to signify a good beating with any instrument.

DRUMBELO. A dull, heavy fellow.

DRUMMER. A jockey term for a horse that throws about his fore legs irregularly: the idea is taken from a kettle drummer, who in beating makes many flourishes with his drumsticks.

DRUNK. Drunk as a wheel-barrow. Drunk as David's sow. See DAVID'S SOW.

DRURY LANE AGUE. The venereal disorder.

DRURY LANE VESTAL. A woman of the town, or prostitute. Drury-lane, and its environs, were formerly the residence of many of those ladies.

DRY BOB. A smart repartee: also copulation without emission, in law Latin, *siccus robertulus*.

DRY BOOTS. A sly humorous fellow.

DUB. A picklock, or master-key. *Cant.*

Dub Lay. Robbing houses by picking the locks.

Dub the Gigger. Open the door. *Cant.*

Dub o' th' Hick. A lick on the head

Dubber. A picker of locks. *Cant.*

Duce. Two-pence.

Duck. A lame duck, an Exchange-alley phrase for a stock jobber, who either cannot or will not pay his losses, or differences, in which case he is said to *waddle out of the alley,* as he cannot appear there again till his debts are settled and paid; should he attempt it, he would be hustled out by the fraternity.

Ducks and Drakes To make ducks and drakes; a school boy's amusement, practised with pieces of tile, oyster-shells, or flattish stones, which being skimmed along the surface of a pond, or still river, rebound many times To make ducks and drakes of one's money, to throw it idly away.

Duck F-ck-r. The man who has the care of the poultry on board a ship of war.

Duck Legs. Short legs

Dudders, or Whispering Dudders. Cheats who travel the country pretending to sell smuggled goods. they accost their intended dupes in a whisper The goods they have for sale are old shop-keepers, or damaged; purchased by them of large manufactories See Duffer

Duddering Rake. A thundering rake, a buck of the first head, one extremely lewd.

Dudgeon. Anger.

Duds. Clothes

Duffers. Cheats who ply in different parts of the town, particularly about Water-lane, opposite St. Clement's Church in the Strand, and pretend to deal in smuggled goods, stopping all country people, or such as they think they can impose on; which they frequently do, by selling them Spital-fields goods at double their current price.

Duke, or Rum Duke A queer unaccountable fellow.

Duke of Limbs A tall, aukward, ill-made fellow.

Duke Humphrey. To dine with Duke Humphrey, to fast Humphrey, Duke of Gloucester, surnamed the Good,

was

DUN

was famous for his voluntary mortifications, particularly frequent fasting

DULL SWIFT. A stupid, sluggish fellow, one long going on an errand

DUMB ARM. A lame arm.

DUMB-FOUNDED. Silenced, also soundly beaten.

DUMB GLUTTON A woman's privities.

DUMB WATCH. A venereal bubo in the groin.

DUMPLIN A short thick man or woman. Norfolk dumplin; a jeering appellation of a Norfolk man, dumplins being a favourite kind of food in that country.

DUMPS Down in the dumps; low-spirited, melancholy: jocularly said to be derived from Dumpos, a king of Egypt, who died of melancholy. Dumps are also small pieces of lead, cast by school boys in the shape of money.

DUN. An importunate creditor. Dunny, in the provincial dialect of several counties, signifies *deaf*, to dun, then, perhaps may mean to deafen with importunate demands: some derive it from the word *donnez*, which signifies *give*. But the true original meaning of the word, owes its birth to one Joe Dun, a famous bailiff of the town of Lincoln, so extremely active, and so dexterous in his business, that it became a proverb, when a man refused to pay, Why do not you *Dun* him? that is, Why do not you set Dun to arrest him? Hence it became a cant word, and is now as old as since the days of Henry VII. Dun was also the general name for the hangman, before that of Jack Ketch

> *And presently a halter got,*
> *Made of the best strong hempen teer,*
> *And ere a cat could lick her ear,*
> *Had tied it up with as much art,*
> *As DUN himself could do for 's heart.*
>
> Cotton's Virgil Trav book iv.

DUNAKER A stealer of cows and calves

DUNGHILL A coward a cockpit phrase, all but game cocks being styled dunghills To die dunghill, to repent, or shew any signs of contrition, at the gallows. Moving dunghill, a dirty, filthy man or woman Dung, an abbreviation of dunghill, also means a journeyman taylor who

submits

submits to the law for regulating journeymen taylors wages, therefore deemed by the flints a coward. See FLINTS.

DUNNOCK. A cow. *Cant*

TO DUP. To open a door. a contraction of *do ope* or *open*. See DUB.

DURGEN. A little trifling fellow.

DURHAM MAN. Knocker-kneed, he grinds mustard with his knees. Durham is famous for its mustard.

DUST. Money. Down with your dust, deposit the money. To raise or kick up a dust; to make a disturbance or riot; see BREEZE. Dust it away, drink about.

DUSTMAN. A dead man; your father is a dustman.

DUTCH COMFORT. Thank God it is no worse.

DUTCH CONCERT. Where every one plays or sings a different tune.

DUTCH FEAST. Where the entertainer gets drunk before his guests.

DUTCH RECKONING, or ALLE-MAL. A verbal or lump account, without particulars, as brought at spunging or bawdy houses.

DUTCHESS. A woman enjoyed with her pattens on, or by a man in boots, is said to be made a dutchess.

DYE HARD, or GAME. To dye hard, is to shew no signs of fear or contrition at the gallows; not to whiddle or squeak. This advice is frequently given to felons going to suffer the law, by their old comrades, anxious for the honour of the gang.

E.

E.

EARNEST. A deposit in part of payment, to bind a bargain.

EASY. Make the cull easy, or quiet, gagg or kill him. As easy as pissing the bed.

EASY VIRTUE. A lady of easy virtue; an impure, or prostitute.

EAT. To eat like a beggar man, and wag his under jaw; a jocular reproach to a proud man. To eat one's words, to retract what one has said.

TO EDGE. To stimulate or provoke, or, as it is vulgarly called, to egg a man on. Fall back, fall edge, i. e. let what will happen. Some derive to egg on, from the Latin word, *age, age*.

EIGHT EYES. I will knock out two of your eight eyes; a common Billingsgate threat from one fish nymph to another. every woman, according to the naturalists of that society, having eight eyes, viz. two seeing eyes, two bub-eyes, a bell-eye, two popes-eyes, and a ***-eye. He has fallen down and trod upon his eye, said of one who has a black eye.

ELBOW GREASE. Labour. Elbow grease will make an oak table shine.

ELBOW ROOM. Sufficient space to act in. Out at elbows; said of an estate that is mortgaged.

ELBOW SHAKER. A gamester, one who rattles Saint Hugh's bones, i. e. the dice.

ELF. A fairy or hobgoblin, a little man or woman.

ELIZABETHS. A society for commemorating the anniversary of queen Elizabeth, who met at the sign of her head, Hicks's Hall, in the room said to be that wherein she received her juvenile education.

ENGLISH BURGUNDY. Porter.

ENSIGN BEARER. A drunken man, who looks red in the face, or hoists his colours in his drink.

EQUIPT. Rich, also, having new clothes. Well equipt, full of money, or well dressed. The cull equipped me with a brace of meggs; the gentleman furnished me with a couple of guineas.

ERIFFS. Rogues just initiated, and beginning to practice.

ESSEX LION. A calf. Essex being famous for calves, and chiefly supplying the London markets.

ESSEX STILE. A ditch. great part of Essex is low marshy ground, in which there are more ditches than stiles.

ETERNITY BOX. A coffin.

EVANS. Mrs Evans, a name frequently given to a she cat owing, as it is said, to a witch of the name of Evans, who frequently assumed the appearance of a cat.

EVES. Hen roosts.

EVE's CUSTOM-HOUSE, where Adam made his first entry. The monosyllable.

EVES DROPPER. One that lurks about to rob hen roosts; also a listener at doors and windows, to hear private conversation.

EVIL. A halter. *Cant.*

EWE. A white ewe, a beautiful woman. An old ewe, drest lamb fashion, an old woman, drest like a young girl.

EXECUTION DAY. Washing day.

EXPENDED. Killed. alluding to the gunner's accounts, wherein the articles consumed are charged under the title of Expended. *Sea phrase.*

EYES AND LIMBS. The foot guards were formerly so called by the marching regiments, from a favourite execration in use among them, which was, damning their eyes, limbs, and blue breeches.

EYE SORE. A disagreeable object. It will be an eye sore as long as she lives; said by a man whose wife was cut for a fistula in ano.

F.

F.

FAM

FACE MAKING Begetting children. To face it out; to persist in a falsity. No face but his own, a saying of one who has no money in his pocket, or no court cards in his hand.

FACER A bumper, a glass filled so full as to leave no room for the lip.

FADGE It won't fadge, it won't do.

To FAG To beat. Fag the bloss, beat the wench. *Cant.* A fag also means a boy of an inferior form or class, who acts as a servant to one of a superior, who is said to fag him—he is my fag, whence, perhaps, fagged out, for jaded or tired.

FAGGER A little boy put in at a window to rob the house.

FAGGOT A man hired at a muster to appear as a soldier. To faggot, in the canting sense, means to bind; an allusion to the faggots made up by the woodmen, which are all bound. Faggot the culls, bind the men.

FAITHFUL One of the faithful, a taylor who gives long credit. His faith has made him unwhole, i. e. trusting too much, broke him.

FALLALIS Ornaments, chiefly women's, such as ribbands, necklaces, &c.

FALLEN AWAY FROM A HORSE LOAD TO A CART LOAD. A saying on one grown fat.

FAM LAY Going into a goldsmith's shop, under pretence of buying a wedding ring, and palming one or two, by daubing the hand with some viscous matter.

FAMS, or FAMBLES Hands. Famble cheats, rings or gloves. *Cant.*

To FAMGRASP To shake hands; figuratively, to agree or make up a difference. Famgrasp the cove, shake hands with the fellow. *Cant.*

FAMILY OF LOVE. Lewd women, also, a religious sect.

F E A

To Fan. To beat any one. I fanned him sweetly; I beat him heartily

Fart He has let a brewer's fart, grains and all, said of one who has bewrayed his breeches.

> Piss and fart,
> Sound at heart.
> *Mingere cum bumbis,*
> *Res saluberrima est lumbis.*

I dare not trust my a-se with a fart, said by a person troubled with a looseness

Fart Catcher A valet or footman, from his walking behind his master or mistress

Farting Crackers Breeches

Fartleberries Excrement hanging about the tail of a sheep

Fastner A warrant.

Fastnesses Bogs.

Fat. The last landed, inned, or stowed, of any sort of merchandise so called by the water-side porters, carmen, &c All the fat is in the fire, that is, it is all over with us: a saying used in case of any miscarriage or disappointment in an undertaking; an allusion to overturning the frying-pan into the fire. Fat, among printers, means void spaces.

As Fat as a Hen in the Forehead A saying of a meagre person

Fat Cull A rich fellow.

Fat-headed. Stupid.

Faulkner. A tumbler, juggler, or shewer of tricks · perhaps because they lure the people, as a faulconer does his hawks. *Cant.*

Faytors, or Fators. Fortune tellers.

Fawney Rig. A common fraud, thus practised · A fellow drops a brass ring, double gilt, which he picks up before the party meant to be cheated, and to whom he disposes of it for less than its supposed, and ten times more than its real, value. See Money Dropper

Feague To feague a horse; to put ginger up a horse's fundament, and formerly, as it is said, a live eel, to make him

him lively and carry his tail well. it is said, a forfeit is incurred by any horse dealer's servant, who shall shew a horse without first feaguing him. Feague is used, figuratively, for encouraging or spiriting one up.

To FEATHER ONE'S NEST. To enrich one's self.

FEATHER-BED LANE. A rough or stony lane.

FEE, FAW, FUM. Nonsensical words, supposed in childish story books to be spoken by giants. I am not to be frighted by fee, faw, fum; I am not to be scared by nonsense.

FEEDER. A spoon. To nab the feeder, to steal a spoon.

FEET. To make feet for children's stockings, to beget children. An officer of feet, a jocular title for an officer of infantry.

FEINT. A sham attack on one part, when a real one is meant at another.

FELLOW COMMONER. An empty bottle; so called at the University of Cambridge, where fellow commoners are not in general considered as over full of learning. At Oxford an empty bottle is called a gentleman commoner for the same reason.

FEN. A bawd, or common prostitute. *Cant.*

FENCE, or FENCING CULLY. A receiver of stolen goods. To fence, to spend or lay out. He fenced his hog, he spent his shilling. *Cant.*

FENCING KEN. The magazine, or warehouse, where stolen goods are secreted.

FERME. A hole. *Cant.*

FERMERDY BEGGARS. All those who have not the sham sores or clymes.

FERRARA. Andrea Ferrara; the name of a famous sword cutler. most of the Highland broad swords are marked with his name; whence an Andrea Ferrara has become the common name for the glaymore or Highland broad sword. See GLAYMORE.

FERRET. A tradesman who sells goods to young unthrifty heirs, at excessive rates, and then continually duns them for the debt. To ferret, to search out or expel any one from his hiding place, as a ferret drives out rabbits, also to cheat. Ferret-eyed, red-eyed. ferrets have red eyes.

FETCH.

FIL

FETCH. A trick, wheedle, or invention to deceive.

FEUTERER. A dog keeper; from the French *vautrier*, or *vaultrier*, one that leads a lime hound for the chace.

TO FIB. To beat. Fib the cove's quarron in the rumpad for the lour in his bung; beat the fellow in the highway for the money in his purse. *Cant.*—A fib is also a tiny lye.

FICE, or FOYSE. A small windy escape backwards, more obvious to the nose than ears; frequently by old ladies charged on their lap dogs. See FIZZLE.

FID OF TOBACCO. A quid, from the small pieces of towe with which the vent or touch-hole of a cannon is stopped. *Sea term.*

FIDDLE. A writ to arrest.

FIDDLE FADDLE. Trifling discourse, nonsense. A mere fiddle faddle fellow; a trifler.

FIDDLESTICK'S END. Nothing; the ends of the ancient fiddlesticks ending in a point; hence metaphorically used to express a thing terminating in nothing.

FIDGETS. He has got the fidgets; said of one that cannot sit long in a place.

FIDLAM BEN. General thieves; called also St. Peter's sons, having every finger a fish hook. *Cant.*

FIDLER'S MONEY. All sixpences: sixpence being the usual sum paid by each couple, for music at country wakes and hops. Fidler's fare, meat, drink and money. Fidler's pay; thanks and wine.

FIELD LANE DUCK. A baked sheep's head.

FIERI FACIAS. A red-faced man is said to have been served with a writ of fieri facias.

FIGGER. A little boy put in at a window to hand out goods to the diver. See DIVER.

FIGGING LAW. The art of picking pockets. *Cant.*

FIGURE DANCER. One who alters figures on bank notes, converting tens to hundreds.

FILCH, or FILEL. A beggar's staff, with an iron hook at the end, to pluck clothes from an hedge, or any thing out of a casement. Filcher; the same as angler. Filching cove; a man thief. Filching mort, a woman thief.

FILE, FILE CLOY, or BUNGNIPPER. A pickpocket. To file, to rob or cheat. The file, or bungnipper, goes generally in company with two affiftants, the adam tiler, and another called the bulk or bulker, whofe bufinefs it is to joftle the perfon they intend to rob, and pufh him againft the wall, while the file picks his pocket, and gives the booty to the adam tiler, who fcours off with it. *Cant.*

FIN. An arm. A one-finned fellow, a man who has loft an arm. *Sea phrafe.*

FINE Fine as fivepence. Fine as a cow-turd ftuck with primrofes.

FINGER IN EYE. To put finger in eye, to weep: commonly applied to women. The more you cry the lefs you'll p-fs, a confolatory fpeech ufed by failors to their doxies. It is as great a pity to fee a woman cry, as to fee a goofe walk barefoot, another of the fame kind.

FINGER POST A parfon, fo called, becaufe, like the finger poft, he points out a way he has never been, and probably will never go, i. e. the way to heaven.

FIRING A GUN. Introducing a ftory by head and fhoulders. A man, wanting to tell a particular ftory, faid to the company, Hark! did you not hear a gun?—but now we are talking of a gun, I will tell you a ftory of one.

TO FIRE A SLUG To drink a dram.

FIRE PRIGGERS Villains who rob at fires, under pretence of affifting in removing the goods.

FIRE SHIP. A wench who has the venereal difeafe.

FIRE SHOVEL. He or fhe, when young, was fed with a fire fhovel, a faying of perfons with wide mouths

FISH. A feaman. A fcaly fifh, a rough, blunt tar.

FIVE SHILLINGS. The fign of five fhillings, i. e the crown. Fifteen fhillings, the fign of the three crowns.

FIZZLE. An efcape backward

FLABAGASTED. Confounded.

FLABBY. Relaxed, flaccid, not firm or folid.

FLAG. A groat. *Cant.*—The flag of defiance, or bloody flag, is out; fignifying, the man is drunk, and alluding to the rednefs of his face. *Sea phrafe.*

FLAM. A lye, or fham ftory; alfo a fingle ftroke on a drum.

FLAP DRAGON. A clap, or pox.

To FLARE. To blaze, shine, or glare

FLASH. A periwig. Rum flash, a fine long wig. Queer flash; a miserable weather-beaten caxon.

To FLASH. To shew ostentatiously To flash one's ivory; to laugh and shew one's teeth Don't flash your ivory, but shut your potatoe trap, and keep your guts warm, the Devil loves hot tripes

To FLASH THE HASH. To vomit *Cant*.

FLASH KEN. A house that harbours thieves.

FLASH LINGO. The canting or slang language.

FLASH MAN. A bully to a bawdy house

FLAT. A bubble, gull, or silly fellow.

FLAT COCK. A female.

FLAWD. Drunk.

FLAYBOTTOMIST. A bum brusher, or schoolmaster.

To FLAY, or FLEA, THE FOX. To vomit.

FLEA BITE. A trifling injury. To send any one away with a flea in his ear; to give any one a hearty scolding.

To FLEECE To rob, cheat, or plunder

FLEMISH ACCOUNT. A losing, or bad account.

FLESH BROKER A match maker, a bawd

FLIBUSTIERS West India pirates, buccanneers, or free booters.

FLICKER. A drinking glass *Cant*.

FLICKERING. Grinning or laughing in a man's face

FLICKING Cutting Flick 'me some panam and caftan; cut me some bread and cheese. Flick the peter, cut off the cloak bag or portmanteau.

To FLING To trick or cheat. He flung me fairly out of it, he cheated me out of it.

FLINTS. Journeymen taylors, who on a late occasion refused to work for the wages settled by law. Those who submitted, were, by the mutineers, styled dungs, i e. dunghills.

FLIP. Small beer, brandy, and sugar this mixture, with the addition of a lemon, was, by sailors, formerly called Sir Cloudsly, in memory of Sir Cloudsly Shovel, who used frequently to regale himself with it.

FLOATING ACADEMY. See CAMPBELL'S ACADEMY.

To

FLY

To FLOG. To whip

FLOGGER. A horsewhip *Cant*

FLOGGING CULLY. A debilitated letcher (commonly an old one), whose torpid powers require stimulating by flagellation

FLOGGING COVE. The beadle, or whipper, in Bridewell

FLOGGING STAKE. The whipping post.

FLORENCE. A wench that has been towzed and ruffled.

FLOURISH. To take a flourish; to enjoy a woman in a hasty manner, to take a flyer. See FLYER

To FLOUT. To jeer, to ridicule.

FLUMMERY. Oatmeal and water boiled to a jelly, also compliments, neither of which are over nourishing.

FLUSH IN THE POCKET. Full of money. The cull is flush in the fob; the fellow is full of money.

FLUSTERED. Drunk.

FLUTE. The recorder of a corporation. a recorder was an ancient musical instrument.

To FLUX. To cheat, cozen, or over-reach; also to salivate. To flux a wig, to put it up in curl, and bake it.

FLY. A waggon *Cant*.

FLY-BY-NIGHT. You old fly-by-night, an ancient term of reproach to an old woman, signifying that she was a witch, and alluding to the nocturnal excursions attributed to witches, who were supposed to fly abroad to their meetings, mounted on brooms.

FLY SLICERS. Life-guard men, from their sitting on horseback, under an arch, where they are frequently observed to drive away flies with their swords.

FLYER. To take a flyer, to enjoy a woman with her clothes on, or without going to bed.

FLYERS. Shoes.

FLY-FLAPPED. Whipt in the stocks, or at the cart's tail.

FLYING CAMPS. Beggars plying in a body at funerals.

FLYING GIGGERS. Turn-pike gates.

FLYING HORSE. A lock in wrestling, by which he who uses it throws his adversary over his head.

FLYING PORTERS. Cheats who obtain money by pretending to persons, who have been lately robbed, that they come from a place or party where, and from whom, they may receive information respecting the goods stolen from them, and demand payment as porters.

FOB   A cheat, trick, or contrivance. I will not be fobbed off so, I will not be thus deceived with false pretences. The fob is also a small breeches pocket for holding a watch.

FOG. Smoke. *Cant.*

FOGEY. Old fogey; a nick-name for an invalid soldier: derived from the French word *fougeux*, fierce or fiery.

FOGRAM. An old fogram; a fusty old fellow.

FOGUS. Tobacco. Tip me a gage of fogus; give me a pipe of tobacco. *Cant.*

FOOL. A fool at the end of a stick; a fool at one end, and a maggot at the other; gibes on an angler.

FOOLISH. An expression among impures, signifying the cully who pays, in opposition to a flash man. Is he foolish or flash?

FOOT PADS, or LOW PADS. Rogues who rob on foot.

FOOT WABBLER. A contemptuous appellation for a foot soldier, commonly used by the cavalry.

FOOTMAN'S MAWND. An artificial sore, made with unflacked lime, soap, and the rust of old iron, on the back of a beggar's hand, as if hurt by the bite or kick of a horse.

FOOTY DESPICABLE. A footy fellow, a despicable fellow: from the French *foutue*.

FORE FOOT, or PAW. Give us your fore foot; give us your hand.

FOREMAN OF THE JURY. One who engrosses all the talk to himself, or speaks for the rest of the company.

FORK. A pickpocket. Let us fork him; let us pick his pocket.—' The newest and most dextrous way, which is, to ' thrust the fingers strait, stiff, open, and very quick, into ' the pocket, and so closing them, hook what can be held ' between them.' N. B. This was taken from a book written many years ago: doubtless the art of picking pockets, like all others, must have been much improved since that time.

FORLORN HOPE. A gamester's last stake.

FORTUNE HUNTERS. Indigent men, seeking to enrich themselves by marrying a woman of fortune.

FORTUNE TELLER, or CUNNING MAN. A judge, who tells every prisoner his fortune, lot, or doom. To go before the fortune teller, lambskin men, or conjurer; to be tried at an assize. See LAMBSKIN MEN.

FOUL-MOUTHED. Abusive.

FOUNDLING. A child dropped in the streets, and found, and educated at the parish expence.

FOX. A sharp, cunning fellow. Also an old term for a sword, probably a rusty one, or else from its being dyed red with blood. some say this name alluded to certain swords, of remarkable good temper, or metal, marked with the figure of a fox, probably the sign, or rebus, of the maker.

FOX's PAW. The vulgar pronunciation of the French words *faux-pas*. He made a confounded fox's paw.

FOXED. Intoxicated.

FOYST. A pickpocket, cheat, or rogue. See WOTTON's GANG.

TO FOYST. To pick a pocket.

FOYSTED IN. Words or passages surreptitiously interpolated or inserted into a book or writing.

FRATERS. Vagabonds who beg with sham patents, or briefs, for hospitals, fires, inundations, &c.

FREE. Free of fumblers hall; a saying of one who cannot get his wife with child.

FREE BOOTERS. Lawless robbers and plunderers: originally soldiers who served without pay, for the privilege of plundering the enemy.

FREEHOLDER. He whose wife accompanies him to the alehouse.

FREEZE. A thin, small, hard cyder, much used by vintners and coopers in parting their wines, to lower the price of them, and to advance their gain. A freezing vintner; a vintner who balderdashes his wine.

FRENCH CREAM. Brandy: so called by the old tabbys and dowagers when drank in their tea.

FRENCH DISEASE. The venereal disease, said to have been imported

imported from France. French gout, the same. He suffered by a blow over the snout with a French faggot stick; i. e. he lost his nose by the pox.

FRENCH LEAVE. To take French leave; to go off without taking leave of the company: a saying frequently applied to persons who have run away from their creditors.

FRENCHIFIED. Infected with the venereal disease. The mort is Frenchified; the wench is infected.

FRESHMAN. One just entered a member of the university.

FRIBBLE. An effeminate fop: a name borrowed from a celebrated character of that kind, in the farce of Miss in her Teens, written by Mr. Garrick.

FRIDAY FACE. A dismal countenance. Before, and even long after the Reformation, Friday was a day of abstinence, or *jour maigre*. Immediately after the restoration of king Charles II. a proclamation was issued, prohibiting all publicans from dressing any suppers on a Friday.

To FRIG. To be guilty of the crime of self pollution. Frigging is also figuratively used for trifling.

FRIG PIG. A trifling, fiddle-faddle fellow.

FRIGATE. A well-rigged frigate; a well-dressed wench.

FRISK. To dance the Paddington frisk, to be hanged.

To FRIZ, or FRISK. Used by thieves to signify searching a person whom they have robbed. Blast his eyes! friz, or frisk h·m.

FROE, or VROE. A woman, wife, or mistress. Brush to your froe, or blofs, and wheedle for crop, run to your mistress, and soothe and coax her out of some money, *Dutch*.

FROGLANDER. A Dutchman.

FROSTY FACE. One pitted with the small pox.

FRUMMAGEMMED. Choaked, strangled, or hanged. *Cant.*

FUBSEY. Plump. A fubsey wench; a plump, healthy wench.

To F—K. To copulate.

F—K BEGGAR. See BUSS BEGGAR.

FUDDLE. Drink. This is rum fuddle; this is excellent tipple, or drink. Fuddled, drunk. Fuddle cap, a drunkard.

FULHAMS.

FULHAMS. Loaded dice are called high and lowmen, or high and low fulhams, by Ben Jonson and other writers of his time; either because they were made at Fulham, or from that place being the resort of sharpers.

To FULK. To use an unfair motion of the hand in plumping at taw. *School boys term.*

FULL OF EMPTINESS. Jocular term for empty.

FUMBLER An old or impotent man. To fumble, also means to go aukwardly about any work, or manual operation

FUN. A cheat, or trick. Do you think to fun me out of it? do you think to cheat me?—Also the breech, perhaps from being the abbreviation of fundament. I'll kick your fun. *Cant*

FUNK. To smoke figuratively, to smoke or stink through fear. I was in a cursed funk. To funk the cobler, a school boy's trick, performed with assafœtida and cotton, which are stuffed into a pipe the cotton being lighted, and the bowl of the pipe covered with a coarse handkerchief, the smoke is blown out at the small end, through the crannies of a cobler's stall.

FURMEN. Aldermen.

FURMITY, or FROMENTY. Wheat boiled up to a jelly. To simper like a furmity kettle, to smile, or look merry about the gills.

FUSS. A confusion, a hurry, an unnecessary to do about trifles.]

FUSSOCK. A lazy fat woman. An old fussock; a frowzy old woman.

FUSTIAN. Bombast language. Red fustian; port wine.

FUSTY LUGGS. A beastly, sluttish woman.

To FUZZ To shuffle cards minutely, also, to change the pack

G.

G.

GAB, or GOB. The mouth. Gift of the gab; a facility of speech, nimble-tongued eloquence. To blow the gab, to confess, or peach.

GAB, or GOB, STRING. A bridle.

GAD-SO. An exclamation said to be derived from the Italian word *cazzo*.

GAG. An instrument used chiefly by house-breakers and thieves, for propping open the mouth of a person robbed, thereby to prevent his calling out for assistance.

GAGE. A quart pot, or a pint, also a pipe. *Cant.*

GAGE OF FOGUS. A pipe of tobacco.

GAGGERS, High and Low. Cheats, who by sham pretences, and wonderful stories of their sufferings, impose on the credulity of well-meaning people. See RUM GAGGER.

GALIMAUFREY. A hodge-podge made up of the remnants and scraps of the larder.

GALL. His gall is not yet broken; a saying used in prisons of a man just brought in, who appears dejected.

GALLEY. Building the galley; a game formerly used at sea, in order to put a trick upon a landsman, or fresh water sailor. It being agreed to play at that game, one sailor personates the builder, and another the merchant or contractor. the builder first begins by laying the keel, which consists of a number of men laid all along on their backs, one after another, that is, head to foot; he next puts in the ribs or knees, by making a number of men sit feet to feet, at right angles to, and on each side of, the keel. he now fixing on the person intended to be the object of the joke, observes he is a fierce-looking fellow, and fit for the lion; he accordingly places him at the head, his arms being held or locked in by the two persons next to him, representing the ribs. After several other dispositions, the builder delivers over the galley to the contractor as complete: but he, among other faults and objections, observes the lion is not gilt; on which the builder, or one of his assistants, runs to the head, and dipping a mop in the excrement, thrusts it into the face of the lion.

GAR

GALLEY FOIST. A city barge, used formerly on the lord mayor's day, when he was sworn in at Westminster.

GALLIED. Hurried, vexed, over-fatigued, perhaps like a galley slave.

GALLIGASKINS. Breeches.

GALLIPOT. A nick name for an apothecary.

GALLORE, or GOLORE. Plenty.

GALLOWS BIRD. A thief, or pickpocket, also one that associates with them.

GAMBS. Thin, ill-shaped legs: a corruption of the French word *jambes*.

GAMBADOES. Leathern cases of stiff leather, used in Devonshire instead of boots; they are fastened to the saddle, and admit the leg, shoe and all: the name was at first jocularly given.

GAMBLER. A sharper, a tricking gamester.

GAME. Bubbles or pigeons drawn in to be cheated. Also, at bawdy houses, lewd women. Mother, have you any game? mother, have you any girls? To die game, to suffer at the gallows without shewing any signs of fear or repentance. Game pullet, a young whore, or forward girl in the way of becoming one.

GAMON AND PATTER. Common-place talk of any profession, as the gamon and patter of a horse dealer, sailor, &c.

GAN. The mouth or lips. *Cant.*

GANDER MONTH. That month in which a man's wife lies in, wherefore, during that time, husbands plead a sort of indulgence in matters of gallantry.

GANG. A company of men, a body of sailors, a knot of thieves, pickpockets, &c. A gang of sheep trotters, the four feet of a sheep.

GAP STOPPER. A whoremaster.

GAPESEED. Sights, any thing to feed the eye. I am come abroad for a little gape-seed.

GARNISH. An entrance fee demanded by the old prisoners of one just committed to gaol.

GARRET, or UPPER STORY. The head. His garret, or upper story, is empty, or unfurnished, i. e. has no brains, he is a fool.

GARRET ELECTION. A ludicrous ceremony, practised every

every new parliament: it confists of a mock election of two members to reprefent the borough of Garret (a few ftraggling cottages near Wandfworth in Surry); the qualification of a voter is, having enjoyed a woman in the open air within that diftrict: the candidates are commonly fellows of low humour, who drefs themfelves up in a ridiculous manner. As this brings a prodigious concourfe of people to Wandfworth, the publicans of that place jointly contribute to the expence, which is fometimes confiderable.

GAWKEY. A tall, thin, aukward young man or woman.

GAZEBO. An elevated obfervatory or fummer houfe.

GEE. It won't gee, it won't hit or do, it does not fuit or fit.

GELDING. An eunuch.

GELT. Money, *German*.—Alfo, caftrated.

GENTLE CRAFT. The art of fhoemaking. One of the gentle craft; a fhoemaker, fo called becaufe once practifed by St. Crifpin.

GENTLEMAN COMMONER. An empty bottle; an univerfity joke, gentlemen commoners not being deemed overfull of learning.

GENTLEMAN'S COMPANION. A loufe.

GENTLEMAN'S MASTER. A highway robber, becaufe he makes a gentleman obey his commands, i. e. ftand and deliver.

GENTLEMAN OF THREE INNS. In debt, in gaol, and in danger of remaining there for life, or, in gaol, indicted, and in danger of being hanged in chains.

GENTLEMAN OF THREE OUTS. That is, without money, without wit, and without manners. fome add another out, i e without credit.

GENTRY COVE. A gentleman. *Cant.*

GENTRY COVE KEN. A gentleman's houfe. *Cant.*

GENTRY MORT. A gentlewoman.

GEORGE. A half-crown piece. Yellow George; a guinea; Brown George; an ammunition loaf.

GEORGES. The brethren of the honourable fociety of Royal Georges; a fociety which met at the St. Luke's Head and Eight Bells, Smithfield.

GERMAN DUCK. Half a fheep's head boiled with onions.

GET. One of his get; one of his offspring, or begetting.

GIB CAT A northern name for a he cat, there commonly called Gilbert. As melancholy as a gib cat, as melancholy as a he cat who has been catterwauling, whence they always return scratched, hungry, and out of spirits. Aristotle says, *Omne animal post coitum est triste*; to which an anonymous author has given the following exception. *preter gallum, gallinaceum, et sacerdotem gratis fornicantem*

GIBBERISH. The cant language of thieves and gypsies, called Pedlars French, and St. Giles's Greek see ST. GILES'S GREEK. Also the mystic language of Geber, used by chymists. Gibberish likewise means a sort of disguised language, formed by inserting any consonant between each syllable of an English word, in which case it is called the gibberish of the letter inserted if F, it is the F gibberish, if G, the G gibberish; as in the sentence, How do you do? Howg dog youg dog.

GIBLETS. To join giblets; said of a man and woman who cohabit as husband and wife, without being married, also to copulate

GIBSON, or SIR JOHN GIBSON. A two-legged stool, used to support the body of a coach whilst finishing

GIFTS Small white specks under the finger nails, said to portend gifts or presents. A stingy man is said to be as full of his gifts as a brazen horse of his farts.

GIFT OF THE GAB. A facility of speech.

GIGG. A nose. Snitchel his gigg, fillip his nose. Grunter's gigg; a hog's snout. Gigg is also a high one-horse chaise, and a woman's privities To gigg a Smithfield hank, to hamstring an over-drove ox, vulgarly called a mad bullock.

GIGGER. A latch, or door. Dub the gigger, open the door. Gigger dubber; the turnkey of a gaol.

TO GIGGLE To suppress a laugh. Gigglers, wanton women

GILES'S, or ST GILES'S, BREED Fat, ragged, and saucy Newton and Dyot streets, the grand head-quarters of most of the thieves and pickpockets about London, are in St Giles's parish St Giles's Greek, the cant language, called also Slang, Pedlars French and Flash.

GILFLURT.

GIN

GILFLURT A proud minks, a vain capricious woman.

GILL. The abbrevation of Gillian, figuratively used for woman. Every jack has his gill, i e. every jack has his gillian, or female mate.

GILLS The cheeks. To look rosy about the gills; to have a fresh complexion. To look merry about the gills, to appear cheerful.

GILLY GAUPUS A Scotch term for a tall, aukward fellow.

GILT, or RUM DUBBER. A thief who picks locks, so called from the gilt or pick-lock key. many of them are so expert, that, from the lock of a church door to that of the smallest cabinet, they will find means to open it these go into reputable public houses, where, pretending business, they contrive to get into private rooms, up stairs, where they open any bureaus or trunks they happen to find there.

GIMBLET-EYED. Squinting, either in man or woman.

GIMCRACK, or JIMCRACK. A spruce wench; a gimcrack also means a person who has a turn for mechanical contrivances

GIN SPINNER. A distiller.

GINGAMBOBS Toys, bawbles; also a man's testicles. See THINGAMBOBS

GINGER-PATED, or GINGER-HACKLED. Red-haired: a term borrowed from the cockpit, where red cocks are called gingers

GINGERBREAD. A cake made of treacle, flour, and grated ginger, also money. He has the gingerbread, he is rich.

GINGERBREAD WORK Gilding and carving. these terms are particularly applied by seamen on board Newcastle colliers, to the decorations of the sterns and quarters of West-India-men, which they have the greatest joy in defacing.

GINGERLY. Softly, gently, tenderly. To go gingerly to work, to attempt a thing gently, or cautiously.

GINNY. An instrument to lift up a grate, in order to steal what is in the window. *Cant.*

GIRDS.

GIRDS. Quips, taunts, severe or biting reflections.

GIZZARD. To grumble in the gizzard, to be secretly displeased.

GLASS EYES A nick name for one wearing spectacles.

GLAYMORE. A Highland broad sword: from the Erse *glay*, or *glaive*, a sword, and *more*, great.

GLAZE. A window. *Cant.*

GLAZIER. One who breaks windows and shew glasses, to steal goods exposed for sale Glaziers, eyes. *Cant.*—Is your father a glazier? a question asked to a lad or young man, who stands between the speaker and the candle, or fire. If it is answered in the negative, the rejoinder is—I wish he was, that he might make a window through your body, to enable us to see the fire or light.

GLIB. Smooth, slippery Glib-tongued, talkative.

GLIM A candle, or dark lanthorn, used in housebreaking; also fire. To glim; to burn in the hand. *Cant.*

GLIMFENDERS. Andirons. *Cant.*

GLIMFLASHY. Angry, or in a passion *Cant.*

GLIMJACK. A link boy. *Cant*

GLIMMER. Fire. *Cant.*

GLIMMERERS. Persons begging with sham licences, pretending losses by fire.

GLIMSTICK. A candlestick. *Cant.*

GLOBE. Pewter. *Cant.*

GLOVES. To give any one a pair of gloves; to make them a present or bribe. To win a pair of gloves, to kiss a man whilst he sleeps. for this a pair of gloves is due to any lady who will thus earn them

GLUEPOT. A parson. from joining men and women together in matrimony.

GLUM. Sullen.

GLYBE A writing. *Cant.*

GO BETWEEN A pimp or bawd.

GO BY THE GROUND. A little short person, man or woman.

GO SHOP. The Queen's Head in Duke's court, Bow street, Covent garden; frequented by the under players: where gin and water is sold in three-halfpenny bowls, called

GOL

Goes; the gin is called Arrack. The go, the fashion: as, large hats are all the go.

GOADS Those who wheedle in chapmen for horse dealers.

GOALER's COACH. A hurdle. traitors being usually conveyed from the goal, to the place of execution, on a hurdle or sledge.

GOAT. A lascivious person. Goats gigg; making the beast with two backs, copulation.

GOB The mouth, also a bit or morsel: whence gobbets. Gift of the gob, wide-mouthed, or one who speaks fluently, or sings well.

GOB STRING. A bridle.

GOBBLE P—K. A rampant, lustful woman.

GOBBLER. A turkey cock

GOD PERMIT. A stage coach from that affectation of piety, frequently to be met with in advertisements of stage coaches or waggons, where most of their undertakings are premised with, "if God permit," or, "God willing."

GODFATHER He who pays the reckoning, or answers for the rest of the company. as, Will you stand godfather, and we will take care of the brat; i. e. repay you another time. Jurymen are also called godfathers, because they name the crime the prisoner before them has been guilty of, whether felony, petit larceny, &c.

GOG All-a-gog, impatient, anxious or desirous of a thing

GOG AND MAGOG. Two giants, whose effigies stand on each side of the clock in Guildhall, London, of whom there is a tradition, that, when they hear the clock strike one, on the first of April, they will walk down from their places

GOGGLES. Eyes see OGLES. Goggle eyes; large prominent eyes. To goggle, to stare.

GOING UPON THE DUB. Going out to break open, or pick the locks of, houses.

GOLD DROPPERS Sharpers who drop a piece of gold, which they pick up in the presence of some unexperienced person, for whom the trap is laid, this they pretend to have found, and, as he saw them pick it up, they invite him

him to a public house to partake of it: when there, two or three of their comrogues drop in, as if by accident, and propose cards, or some other game, when they seldom fail of stripping their prey.

GOLD FINDER. One whose employment is to empty necessary houses, called also a tom turd man, and night man: the latter, from that business being always performed in the night.

GOLDEN FLEECE. The knights of this ancient and honourable order, were a society about the year 1749.

GOLDFINCH. One who has commonly a purse full of gold. Goldfinches; guineas

GOLGOTHA, OR THE PLACE OF SCULLS. Part of the Theatre at Oxford, where the heads of houses sit; those gentlemen being, by the wits of the university, called Sculls.

GOLLUMPUS. A large, clumsy fellow.

GOLOSHES, i.e. Goliah's shoes. Large leathern clogs, worn by invalids over their ordinary shoes.

GOOD MAN. A word of various imports, according to the place where it is spoken in the city it means a rich man; at Hockley in the Hole, or St. Giles's, an expert boxer; at a bagnio in Covent Garden, a vigorous fornicator, at an alehouse or tavern, one who loves his pot or bottle; and sometimes, though but rarely, a virtuous man.

GOOD WOMAN. A nondescript, represented on a famous sign in St. Giles's, in the form of a common woman, but without a head.

GOODYER'S PIG. Like Goodyer's pig; never well but when in mischief.

GOOSE. A taylor's goose; a smoothing iron used to press down the seams, for which purpose it must be heated: hence it is a jocular saying, that a taylor, be he ever so poor, is always sure to have a goose at his fire. He cannot say boh! to a goose; a saying of a bashful or sheepish fellow.

GOOSE RIDING. A goose, whose neck is greased, being suspended by the legs to a cord tied to two trees or high posts, a number of men on horseback, riding full speed, attempt to pull off the head, which if they effect, the goose is their prize.

GRA

prize. This has been practised in Derbyshire within the memory of persons now living.

GOOSEBERRY. He played up old gooseberry among them; said of a person who, by force or threats, suddenly puts an end to a riot or disturbance

GOOSEBERRY-EYED. One with dull grey eyes, like boiled gooseberries

GOOSEBERRY WIG. A large frizzled wig: perhaps, from a supposed likeness to a gooseberry bush.

GOOSECAP. A silly fellow, or woman.

GOREE. Money, chiefly gold: perhaps from the traffick carried on at that place, which is chiefly for gold dust. *Cant.*

GORMAGON. A monster with six eyes, three mouths, four arms, eight legs, five on one side and three on the other, three arses, two tarses, and a **** upon its back; a man on horseback, with a woman behind him.

GOTCH-GUTTED. Pot-bellied: a gotch in Norfolk signifying a pitcher, or large round jug

To GOUGE. To squeeze out a man's eye with the thumb: a cruel practice used by the Bostonians in America.

To GRABBLE. To seize. To grabble the bit; to seize any one's money. *Cant.*

GRAFTED. Cuckolded, i. e. having horns grafted on his head.

GRANNAM. Corn.

GRANNUM's GOLD. Hoarded money: supposed to have belonged to the grandmother of the possessor.

GRANNY. An abbrevation of grandmother; also the name of an ideot, famous for licking her eye, who died Nov. 14, 1719. Go teach your granny to suck eggs; said to such as would instruct any one in a matter he knows better than themselves.

GRAPPLE THE RAILS A cant name used in Ireland for whiskey.

GRAVE DIGGER. Like a grave digger, up to the a-se in business, and don't know which way to turn.

GRAVY-EYED Blear-eyed, one whose eyes have a running humour.

To

To GREASE. To bribe. To greafe a man in the fift; to bribe him. To greafe a fat fow in the a-fe; to give to a rich man. Greafy chin, a treat given to parifh officers in part of commutation for a baftard, called alfo, Eating a child.

GREAT JOSEPH. A furtout. *Cant.*

GREEDY GUTS. A covetous or voracious perfon.

GREEK. St Giles's Greek; the flang lingo, cant, or gibberifh.

GREEN Doctor Green; i. e. grafs a phyfician, or rather medicine, found very fuccefsful in curing moft diforders to which horfes are liable. My horfe is not well, I fhall fend him to Doctor Green.

GREEN BAG. An attorney. thofe gentlemen carry their clients deeds in a green bag, and, it is faid, when they have no deeds to carry, frequently fill them with an old pair of breeches, or any other trumpery, to give themfelves the appearance of bufinefs.

GREEN GOWN. To give a girl a green gown, to tumble her on the grafs.

GREEN SICKNESS. The difeafe of maids occafioned by celibacy.

GREENHEAD. An inexperienced young man.

GREENHORN. A novice on the town, an undebauched young fellow, juft initiated into the fociety of bucks and bloods.

GREENWICH BARBERS. Retailers of fand from the pits at and about Greenwich in Kent. perhaps they are ftyled Barbers, from their conftant fhaving the fand banks.

GREENWICH GOOSE. A penfioner of Greenwich Hofpital.

GREGORIAN TREE. The gallows. fo named from Gregory Brandon, a famous finifher of the law; to whom Sir William Segar, garter king of arms (being impofed on by Brooke, a herald), granted a coat of arms.

GREY BEARD. Earthen juggs formerly ufed in public houfes for drawing ale. they had the figure of a man with a large beard ftamped on them; whence probably they took their name. fee *Ben Jonfon's Plays, Bartholomew Fair, &c &c.* Dutch earthen juggs, ufed for fmuggling

gin

gin on the coasts of Essex and Suffolk, are at this time called grey beards.

GREY MARE The grey mare is the better horse; said of a woman who governs her husband

GREY PARSON A farmer who rents the tythes of the rector or vicar.

GRIG. A farthing. A merry grig; a fellow as merry as a grig; an allusion to the apparent liveliness of a grig, or young eel.

GRIM. Old Mr Grim; death.

GRIMALKIN. A cat. mawkin signifies a hare in Scotland.

GRIN. To grin in a glass case; to be anatomized for murder. the skeletons of many criminals are preserved in glass cases, at surgeons hall.

GRINAGOG, THE CAT'S UNCLE A foolish grinning fellow, one who grins without reason.

GRINDERS Teeth. Gooseberry grinder, the breech. Ask bogey, the gooseberry grinder; ask mine a-se.

GROATS. To save his groats; to come off handsomely: at the universities, nine groats are deposited in the hands of an academic officer, by every person standing for a degree, which if the depositor obtains with honour, the groats are returned to him.

GROG. Rum and water. Grog was first introduced into the navy, about the year 1740, by Admiral Vernon, to prevent the sailors intoxicating themselves with their allowance of rum or spirits Groggy, or grogified, drunk.

GROGGED. A grogged horse, a foundered horse.

GROGHAM. A horse. *Cant*.

GROPERS. Blind men; also midwives

GROUND SWEAT A grave.

GRUB. Victuals. To grub, to dine To ride grub; to be sullen, or out of temper.

GRUB STREET. A street near Moorfields, formerly the supposed habitation of many persons who wrote for the booksellers: hence a Grub-street writer, means a hackney author, who manufactures books for the booksellers.

GRUB STREET NEWS. Lying intelligence

To

GUT

To Grubshite. To make foul or dirty.

Grumble. To grumble in the gizzard, to murmur or repine. He grumbled like a bear with a sore ear.

Grumbletonian. A discontented person; one who is always railing at the times, or ministry.

Grunter. A hog, also a shilling. To grunt, to groan, or complain of sickness.

Grunter's Gig. A smoaked hog's face.

Grunting Peck. Pork, bacon, or any kind of hog's flesh.

Gudgeon. One easily imposed on. To gudgeon, to swallow the bait, or fall into a trap. from the fish of that name, which is easily taken.

Gull. A simple credulous fellow, easily cheated.

Gulled. Deceived, cheated, imposed on.

Gullgropers. Usurers who lend money to the gamesters.

Gum. Abusive language. Come, let us have no more of your gum.

Gummy. Clumsy particularly applied to the ancles of men or women, and the legs of horses.

Gumption, or Rum Gumption. Docility, comprehension, capacity.

Gun. He is in the gun; he is drunk. perhaps from an allusion to a vessel called a gun, used for ale in the universities.

Gundiguts. A fat, pursy fellow.

Gunner's Daughter. To kiss the gunner's daughter; to be tied to a gun and flogged on the posteriors. a mode of punishing boys on board a ship of war.

Gunpowder. An old woman. *Cant.*

Guts. My great guts are ready to eat my little ones; my guts begin to think my throat's cut, my guts curse my teeth: all expressions signifying the party is extremely hungry.

Guts and Garbage. A very fat man or woman. More guts than brains, a silly fellow.

Gutfoundered. Exceeding hungry.

Gut Scraper, or Tormentor of Catgut. A fidler.

Gutter Lane. The throat, the swallow, the red lane. See Red Lane.

Gutting a Quart Pot. Taking out the lining of it;

GYP

i. e. drinking it off. Gutting an oyster, eating it. Gutting a house, clearing it of its furniture.

GUZZLE. Liquor. To guzzle, to drink greedily.

GUZZLE GUTS. One greedy of liquor.

GYBE, or JYBE. Any writing or pass with a seal.

GIBING. Jeering or ridiculing.

GYLES, or GILES. Hopping Giles; a nick name for a lame person. St. Giles was the tutelar saint of cripples.

GYPSIES. A set of vagrants, who, to the great disgrace of our police, are suffered to wander about the country. They pretend that they derive their origin from the ancient Egyptians, who were famous for their knowledge in astronomy, and other sciences, and, under the pretence of fortune telling, find means to rob or defraud the ignorant and superstitious. To colour their impostures, they artificially discolour their faces, and speak a kind of gibberish peculiar to themselves. They rove up and down the country in great companies, to the great terrour of the farmers, from whose geese, turkeys, and fowls, they take very considerable contributions.

When a fresh recruit is admitted into the fraternity, he is to take the following oath, administered by the principal maunder, after going through the annexed forms.

First a new name is given him, by which he is ever after to be called, then standing up in the middle of the assembly, and directing his face to the dimber damber, or principal man of the gang, he repeats the following oath; which is dictated to him by some experienced member of the fraternity:

I, Crank Cuffin, do swear to be a true brother, and that I will in all things obey the commands of the great tawney prince, and keep his counsel, and not divulge the secrets of my brethren.

I will never leave nor forsake the company, but observe and keep all the times of appointment, either by day or by night, in every place whatever.

I will not teach any one to cant, nor will I disclose any of our mysteries to them.

I will take my prince's part against all that shall oppose him, or any of us, according to the utmost of my ability, nor will I suffer him, or any one belonging to us, to be abused by any strange abrams, rufflers, hookers, pailliards, swaddlers, Irish toyles, swigmen, whip jacks, jarkmen, bawdy baskets, dommerars, clapper dogeons, patricoes, or curtals, but will defend him, or them, as much as I can, against all other outliers whatever. I will not conceal aught I win out of libkins or from the ruffmans, but will preserve it for the use of the company. Lastly, I will cleave to my doxy wap stiffly, and will bring her duds, margery praters, goblers, grunting cheats, or tibs of the buttery, or any thing else I can come at, as winnings for her wappings.

The canters have, it seems, a tradition, that from the three first articles of this oath, the first founders of a certain boastful, worshipful fraternity (who pretend to derive their origin from the earliest times) borrowed both the hint and form of their establishment; and that their pretended derivation from the first *Adam* is a forgery, it being only from the first *Adam Tiler*: see ADAM TILER. At the admission of a new brother, a general stock is raised for booze, or drink, to make themselves merry on the occasion. As for peckage, or eatables, they can procure it without money, for while some are sent to break the ruffmans, or woods and bushes, for firing, others are detached to filch geese, chickens, hens, ducks (or mallards), and pigs. Their morts are their butchers, who presently make bloody work with what living things are brought them; and having made holes in the ground, under some remote hedge in an obscure place, they make a fire, and boil or broil their food, and, when it is enough, fall to work tooth and nail: and having eaten more like beasts than men, they drink more like swine than human creatures, entertaining one another all the time with songs in the canting dialect.

As they live, so they lie, together promiscuously, and know not how to claim a property either in their goods or children, and this general interest ties them more firmly together, than if all their rags were twisted into ropes, to bind them indissolubly from a separation; which detestable union is farther consolidated by the above oath.

They stroll up and down all summer time in droves, and dextrously pick pockets, while they are telling of fortunes; and the money, rings, silver thimbles, &c which they get, are instantly conveyed from one hand to another, till the remotest person of the gang (who is not suspected because they come not near the person robbed) gets possession of it, so that, in the strictest search, it is almost impossible to recover it. while the wretches with imprecations, oaths, and protestations, disclaim the thievery

That by which they are said to get the most money, is, when young gentlewomen of good families and reputation have happened to be with child before marriage, a round sum is often bestowed among the gypsies, for some one mort to take the child; and as that is never heard of more by the true mother and family, so the disgrace is kept concealed from the world, and, if the child lives, it never knows its parents

Gyp. A college runner or errand boy at Cambridge, called at Oxford a scout. See Scout.

H.

HAD

HABERDASHER OF PRONOUNS. A schoolmaster, or usher.

HACKNEY WRITER. One who writes for attornies or booksellers.

HACKUM Captain Hackum; a bravo, a slasher.

HAD 'EM. He has been at Had 'em, and come home by Clapham, said of one who has caught the venereal disease.

HALBERT,

HALBERT. A weapon carried by a serjeant of foot. To get a halbert; to be appointed a serjeant. To be brought to the halberts, to be flogged *a la militaire*. soldiers of the infantry, when flogged, being commonly tied to three halberts, set up in a triangle, with a fourth fastened across them. He carries the halbert in his face, a saying of one promoted from a serjeant to a commission officer.

HALF A HOG. Sixpence.

HALF AN OUNCE Half a crown: silver being formerly estimated at a crown, or five shillings, an ounce

HALF BORD. Sixpence *Cant*

HALF SEAS OVER. Almost drunk

HALLOW It was quite a hallow thing, i. e. a certainty, or decided business

HAMLET A high constable. *Cant*.

HAMS, or HAMCASES. Breeches.

HAND. A sailor. We lost a hand, we lost a sailor Bear a hand; make haste. Hand to fist; opposite the same as tête a tête, or cheek by jowl.

HAND AND POCKET SHOP. An eating house where ready money is paid for what is called for.

HAND BASKET PORTION. A woman whose husband receives frequent presents from her father, or family, is said to have a hand basket portion

HANDLE. To know how to handle one's fists, to be skilful in the art of boxing.

HANDSOME He is a handsome-bodied man in the face, a jeering commendation of an ugly fellow. Handsome is that handsome does, a proverb frequently cited by ugly women.

HANDSOME REWARD. This, in advertisements, means a horse-whipping

To HANG AN ARSE. To hang back, to hesitate

HANG GALLOWS LOOK. A thievish or villainous appearance.

HANG IN CHAINS. A vile, desperate fellow. Persons guilty of murder, or other atrocious crimes, are frequently, after execution, hanged on a gibbet, to which they are fastened by iron bandages the gibbet is commonly

placed

HAR

placed on or near the place where the crime was committed.

HANG IT UP. Score it up. fpeaking of a reckoning

HANGER ON A dependant

HANGMAN'S WAGES Thirteen pence halfpenny, which, according to the vulgar tradition, was thus allotted one fhilling for the execution, and three halfpence for the rope. N.B This refers to former times, the hangmen of the prefent day having, like other artificers, raifed their prices. The true ftate of this matter is, that a Scottifh mark was the fee allowed for an execution, and the value of that piece was fettled by a proclamation of James I at thirteen pence halfpenny

HANK. He has a hank on him; i e an afcendancy over him, or a hold upon him A Smithfield hank, an ox rendered furious by over-driving and barbarous treatment

HANKER To hanker after any thing, to have a longing after or for it.

HANKTELO A filly fellow.

HANS IN KELDER Jack in the cellar, i e the child in the womb a health frequently drank to breeding women, or their hufbands.

HAP WORTH A COPERAS. A vulgar pronunciation of habeas corpus

HARD Stale beer, nearly four, is faid to be hard. Hard alfo means fevere; as, hard fate, a hard mafter.

HARD AT HIS A-SE Clofe after him.

HARE. He has fwallowed a hare, he is drunk more probably a *hair*, which requires wafhing down.

HARK-YE-ING. Whifpering on one fide to borrow money.

HARMAN A conftable *Cant*

HARMAN BECK. A beadle. *Cant*.

HARMANS The ftocks *Cant*.

HARP. To harp upon, to dwell upon a fubject. Have among you, my blind harpers; an expreffion ufed in throwing or fhooting at random among a crowd. Harp is alfo the Irifh expreffion for woman, or tail, ufed in toffing up in Ireland: from Hibernia being reprefented with a harp on the reverfe of the copper coins of that country;

for

for which reason it is, in hoisting the copper, i. e tossing up, sometimes likewise called music.

HARRIDAN. A hagged old woman; a miserable, scraggy, worn-out harlot, fit to take her bawd's degree. derived from the French word *haridelle*, a worn-out jade of a horse or mare.

HARRY. A country fellow *Cant*.—Old Harry; the Devil

HARUM SCARUM He was running harum scarum; said of any one running or walking carelessly, and in a hurry, after they know not what

HASH To flash the hash, to vomit. *Cant*.

HASTY. Precipitate, passionate He is none of the Hastings sort; a saying of a slow, loitering fellow an allusion to the Hastings pea, which is the first in season

HASTY PUDDING Flour and milk boiled to a moderate thickness, and eaten with sugar and butter Figuratively, a wet, muddy road as, The way through Wandsworth is quite a hasty pudding To eat hot hasty pudding for a laced hat, or some other prize, is a common feat at wakes and fairs

HAT Old hat, a woman's privities. because frequently felt.

HATCHES. Under the hatches, in trouble, distress, or debt

HATCHET FACE. A long thin face.

HAVIL A sheep. *Cant*

HAVY CAVY Wavering, doubtful, shilly shally.

HAWK. Ware hawk, the word to look sharp, a bye word when a bailiff passes Hawk also signifies a sharper, in opposition to pigeon. See PIGEON.

HAWKERS Licensed itinerant retailers of different commodities, called also pedlars; likewise the sellers of news papers Hawking, an effort to spit up the thick phlegm, called *oysters*. whence it is wit upon record, to ask the person so doing whether he has a licence, a punning allusion to the Act of hawkers and pedlars.

To HAZLE GILD To beat any one with a hazle stick

HEAD CULLY OF THE PASS OR PASSAGE BANK The top tilter of that gang throughout the whole army, who demands

mands and receives contribution from all the pass banks in the camp.

HEAD RAILS. Teeth. *Sea phrase.*

HEARING CHEATS Ears *Cant*

HEART'S EASE A twenty shilling piece, also one of the names for gin.

HEARTY CHOAK. He will have a hearty choak and caper sauce for breakfast; i. e he will be hanged

HEATHEN PHILOSOPHER One whose breech may be seen through his pocket hole. this saying arose from the old philosophers, many of whom despised the vanity of dress to such a point, as often to fall into the excess complained of.

TO HEAVE. To rob. To heave a case; to rob a house. To heave a bough, to rob a booth. *Cant.*

HEAVER The breast. *Cant.*

HEAVERS. Thieves who make it their business to steal tradesmen's shop books. *Cant*

HECTOR. A bully, a swaggering coward. To hector, to bully: probably from such persons affecting the valour of Hector, the Trojan hero.

HEDGE. To make a hedge; to secure a bet, or wager, laid on one side, by taking the odds on the other, so that, let what will happen, a certain gain is secured, or hedged in, by the person who takes this precaution, who is then said to be on velvet.

HEDGE ALEHOUSE. A small obscure alehouse.

HEDGE CREEPER. A robber of hedges.

HEDGE PRIEST. An illiterate unbeneficed curate, a patrico

HEDGE WHORE An itinerant harlot, who bilks the bagnios and bawdy houses, by disposing of her favours on the way side, under a hedge, a low beggarly prostitute.

HEELS. To be laid by the heels, to be confined, or put in prison. Out at heels; worn, or diminished his estate or affairs are out at heels

HEEL TAP. A peg in the heel of a shoe, taken out when it is finished. A person leaving any liquor in his glass, is frequently called upon by the toast master to take off his heel tap.

HELL

HELL. A taylor's repository for his stolen goods, called cabbage: see CABBAGE. Little hell; a small dark covered passage, leading from London Wall to Bell Alley.

HELL-BORN BABE. A lewd graceless youth, one naturally of a wicked disposition.

HELL CAT. A termagant, a vixen, a furious scolding woman. See TERMAGANT and VIXEN.

HELL HOUND. A wicked abandoned fellow.

HELTER SKELTER. In defiance of order, composed of the Cumberland words, *helter*, to halter or hang, and *skelter*, or *kelter*, order or condition, i. e. hang order, as we say, hang sorrow, &c.

HEMP. Young hemp, an appellation for a graceless boy.

HEMPEN FEVER. A man who was hanged is said to have died of a hempen fever, and, in Dorsetshire, to have been stabbed with a Bridport dagger; Bridport being a place famous for manufacturing hemp into cords.

HEMPEN WIDOW. One whose husband was hanged.

HEN-HEARTED. Cowardly.

HEN HOUSE. A house where the woman rules; called also a *she house*, and *hen frigate*: the latter a sea phrase, originally applied to a ship, the captain of which had his wife on board, supposed to command him.

HENPECKED. A husband governed by his wife, is said to be henpecked.

HERE AND THEREIAN. One who has no settled place of residence.

HERRING. The devil a barrel the better herring; all equally bad.

HERRING-GUTTED. Thin, as a shotten herring.

HERRING POND. The sea. To cross the herring pond at the king's expence; to be transported.

HERTFORDSHIRE KINDNESS. Drinking twice to the same person.

HICCOBITES. The brethren of this most ancient and joyous order, held their general court, Dec. 5, 1750, at the Sun tavern, Fish-street hill.

HICK. A country hick; an ignorant clown. *Cant.*

HICKEY. Tipsey quasi, hickuping.

P   HICKSIUS

HIS

HICKSIUS DOXIUS. Drunk.

HIDE AND SEEK   A childish game. He plays at hide and seek; a saying of one who is in fear of being arrested for debt, or apprehended for some crime, and therefore does not chuse to appear in public, but secretly skulks up and down. See SKULK

HIDEBOUND   Stingy, hard of delivery: a poet poor in invention, is said to have a hidebound muse.

HIGGLEDY PIGGLEDY   Confusedly mixed.

HIGH EATING   To eat skylarks in a garret

HIGH FLYERS. Tories, Jacobites.

HIGH JINKS   A gambler at dice, who, having a strong head, drinks to intoxicate his adversary, or pigeon.

HIGH LIVING   To lodge in a garret, or cockloft.

HIGH PAD.   A highwayman *Cant*

HIGH ROPES   To be on the high ropes, to be in a passion.

HIGH SHOON, or CLOUTED SHOON   A country clown

HIGH WATER   It is high water with him, he is full of money

HIGHGATE   Sworn at Highgate—a ridiculous custom formerly prevailed at the public houses in Highgate, to administer a ludicrous oath to all travellers of the middling rank who stopped there. The party was sworn on a pair of horns, fastened on a stick the substance of the oath was, never to kiss the maid when he could kiss the mistress, never to drink small beer when he could get strong, with many other injunctions of the like kind, to all which was added the saving clause of, " unless you like it " best." The person administering the oath was always to be called Father by the juror, and he, in return, was to style him Son, under the penalty of a bottle.

HIKE.   To hike off, to run away. *Cant*.

HIND LEG.   To kick out a hind leg; to make a rustic bow.

HINNEY, MY HONEY. A north country hinney, particularly a Northumbrian in that county, hinney is the general term of endearment.

HISTORY OF THE FOUR KINGS, OR CHILD'S BEST GUIDE TO THE GALLOWS.   A pack of cards. He studies the
history

H O B

history of the four kings assiduously, he plays much at cards.

HOAXING. Bantering, ridiculing. Hoaxing a quiz; joking an odd fellow. *University wit.*

HOB, or HOBBINOL A clown.

HOB OR NOB. Will you hob or nob with me? a question formerly in fashion at polite tables, signifying a request or challenge to drink a glass of wine with the proposer; if the party challenged answered Nob, they were to chuse whether white or red. This foolish custom is said to have originated in the days of good Queen Bess, thus When great chimnies were in fashion, there was at each corner of the hearth, or grate, a small elevated projection, called the hob, and behind it a seat In winter time the beer was placed on the hob to warm, and the cold beer was set on a small table, said to have been called the nob. so that the question, Will you have hob or nob? seems only to have meant, Will you have warm or cold beer? i. e. beer from the hob, or beer from the nob.

HOBBERDEHOY. Half a man and half a boy, a lad between both.

HOBBLED. Impeded, interrupted, puzzled To hobble, to walk lamely

HOBBLEDYGEE A pace between a walk and a run, a dog-trot.

HOBBY Sir Posthumous's hobby, one nice or whimsical in his clothes

HOBBY HORSE A man's favourite amusement, or study, is called his hobby horse. It also means a particular kind of small Irish horse; and also a wooden one, such as is given to children

HOBBY-HORSICAL. A man who is a great keeper or rider of hobby horses, one that is apt to be strongly attached to his systems of amusement

HOBNAIL. A country clodhopper from the shoes of country farmers and ploughmen being commonly stuck full of hob nails, and even often clouted, or tipped with iron. The Devil ran over his face with hob nails in his shoes; said of one pitted with the small pox.

HOG

HOBSON's CHOICE. That or none from old Hobson, a famous carrier of Cambridge, who used to let horses to the students, but never permitted them to chuse, always allotting each man the horse he thought properest for his manner of riding and treatment

HOCKS. A vulgar appellation for the feet. You have left the marks of your dirty hocks on my clean stairs; a frequent complaint from a mop-squeezer to a footman.

HOCKEY. Drunk with strong stale beer, called old hock. See HICKSIUS DOXIUS, and HICKEY.

HOCKING, or HOUGHING. A piece of cruelty practised by the butchers of Dublin, on soldiers, by cutting the tendon of Achilles: this has been by law made felony.

HOCUS POCUS. Nonsensical words used by jugglers, previous to their deceptions, as a kind of charm, or incantation. A celebrated writer supposes it to be a ludicrous corruption of the words, *hoc est corpus*, used by the popish priests in consecrating the host. Hocus is also used to express drunkenness: as, he is quite hocus, he is quite drunk.

HOD. Brother Hod; a familiar name for a bricklayer's labourer, from the hod which is used for carrying bricks and mortar.

HODDY DODDY, ALL A-SE AND NO BODY. A short clumsy person, either male or female.

HODGE. An abbreviation of Roger, a general name for a country booby.

HODGE PODGE, or HOTCH POT. A mixture.

HODMANDODS. Snails in their shells.

HOG. A shilling. To drive one's hogs, to snore; the noise made by some persons in snoring, being not much unlike the notes of that animal. He has brought his hogs to a fine market; a saying of any one who has been remarkably successful in his affairs, and is spoken ironically to signify the contrary. A hog in armour, an aukward or mean looking man or woman, finely dressed, is said to look like a hog in armour. To hog a horse's mane, to cut it short, so that the ends of the hair stand up like hogs bristles. Jonian hogs; an appellation given to the members of St John's College, Cambridge.

HOL

HOG GRUBBER. A mean stingy fellow.

HOGGISH. Rude, unmannerly, filthy.

HOGO. Corruption of *haut goust*, high taste, or flavour; commonly said of flesh somewhat tainted. It has a confounded hogo, it stinks confoundedly.

HOIST. To go upon the hoist, to get into windows accidentally left open; this is done by the assistance of a confederate, called the hoist, who leans his head against the wall, making his back a kind of step or ascent.

HOISTING. A ludicrous ceremony formerly performed on every soldier, the first time he appeared in the field after being married, it was thus managed: As soon as the regiment, or company, had grounded their arms to rest a while, three or four men of the same company to which the bridegroom belonged, seized upon him, and putting a couple of bayonets out of the two corners of his hat, to represent horns, it was placed on his head, the back part foremost. He was then hoisted on the shoulders of two strong fellows, and carried round the arms, a drum and fife beating and playing the pioneers call, named Round Heads and Cuckolds, but on this occasion styled the Cuckold's March, in passing the colours, he was to take off his hat; this, in some regiments, was practised by the officers on their brethren. Hoisting, among pickpockets, is, setting a man on his head, that his money, watch, &c. may fall out of his pockets; these they pick up, and hold to be no robbery. See REVERSED.

HOITY-TOITY. *A hoity-toity wench*, a giddy, thoughtless, romping girl.

HOLBORN HILL. To ride backwards up Holborn hill, to go the gallows; the way to Tyburn, the place of execution for criminals condemned in London, was up that hill. Criminals going to suffer, always ride backwards; as some conceive, to increase the ignominy, but more probably to prevent their being shocked with a distant view of the gallows; as, in amputations, surgeons conceal the instruments with which they are going to operate. The last execution at Tyburn, and consequently of this procession,

was

was in the year 1784, since which the criminals have been executed near Newgate.

HOLIDAY. A holiday bowler, a bad bowler. Blind man's holiday; darkness, night. A holiday is any part of a ship's bottom, left uncovered in paying it. *Sea term.* It is all holiday see ALL HOLIDAY.

HOLY FATHER. A butcher's boy of St Patrick's Market, Dublin, or other Irish blackguard; among whom the exclamation, or oath, By the Holy Father (meaning the Pope), is common.

HOLY LAMB. A thorough-paced villain. *Irish.*

HOLY WATER. He loves him as the Devil loves holy water; i. e. hates him mortally. Holy water, according to the Roman Catholics, having the virtue to chase away the Devil and his imps.

HONEST MAN. A term frequently used by superiors to inferiors. As honest a man as any in the cards when all the kings are out, i. e. a knave. I dare not call thee rogue for fear of the law, said a Quaker to an attorney, but I will give thee five pounds, if thou canst find any creditable person who will say thou art an honest man.

HONEST WOMAN. To marry a woman with whom one has cohabited as a mistress, is termed, making an honest woman of her.

HONEY MOON. The first month after marriage. A poor honey; a harmless, foolish, good-natured fellow. It is all honey or all t—d with them, said of persons who are either in the extremity of friendship or enmity, either kissing or fighting.

HOOD-WINKED. Blindfolded by a handkerchief, or other ligature, bound over the eyes.

HOOF. To beat the hoof, to travel on foot. He hoofed it, or beat the hoof, every step of the way from Chester to London.

HOOK AND SNIVEY, WITH NIX THE BUFFER. This rig consists in feeding a man and a dog for nothing, and is carried on thus. Three men, one of whom pretends to be sick and unable to eat, go to a public house, the two well men

men make a bargain with the landlord for their dinner, and, when he is out of sight, feed their pretended sick companion and dog gratis.

HOOKED. Over-reached, tricked, caught. a simile taken from fishing. **** hooks; fingers.

HOOKERS See ANGLERS.

HOOP To run the hoop, an ancient marine custom. Four or more boys having their left hands tied fast to an iron hoop, and each of them a rope, called a nettle, in their right, being naked to the waist, wait the signal to begin; this being made by a stroke with a cat of nine tails, given by the boatswain to one of the boys, he strikes the boy before him, and every one does the same at first the blows are but gently administered, but each irritated by the strokes from the boy behind him, at length lays it on in earnest. This was anciently practised when a ship was wind-bound.

To HOOP. To beat. I'll well hoop his or her barrel; I'll beat him or her soundly

To HOP THE TWIG. To run away *Cant*

HOP MERCHANT. A dancing master See CAPER MERCHANT

HOP-O-MY-THUMB A diminutive person, man or woman. She was such a hop-o-my-thumb, that a pigeon, sitting on her shoulder, might pick a pea out of her a-se.

HOPKINS. Mr. Hopkins, a ludicrous address to a lame or limping man, being a pun on the word *hop*

HOPPING GILES A jeering appellation given to any person who limps, or is lame St Giles was the patron of cripples, lepers, &c. Churches dedicated to that saint commonly stand out of town, many of them having been chapels to hospitals See GYLES.

HOPPER-ARSED Having large projecting buttocks: from their resemblance to a small basket, called a hopper, or hoppet, worn by husbandmen for containing seed corn, when they sow the land.

HORNS To draw in one's horns; to retract an assertion through fear. metaphor borrowed from a snail, who, on the apprehension of danger, draws in his horns, and retires to his shell.

HORN CHOLICK. A temporary priapism.

HORN FAIR. An annual fair held at Charlton, in Kent, on St. Luke's day, the 18th of October. It consists of a riotous mob, who, after a printed summons dispersed through the adjacent towns, meet at Cuckolds Point, near Deptford, and march from thence in procession, through that town and Greenwich, to Charlton, with horns of different kinds upon their heads; and at the fair there are sold rams horns, and every sort of toy made of horn, even the gingerbread figures have horns. The vulgar tradition gives the following history of the origin of this fair: King John, or some other of our ancient kings, being at the palace of Eltham, in this neighbourhood, and having been out a hunting one day, rambled from his company to this place, then a mean hamlet, when entering a cottage to enquire his way, he was struck with the beauty of the mistress, whom he found alone, and having prevailed over her modesty, the husband returning suddenly, surprised them together; and threatening to kill them both, the king was obliged to discover himself, and to compound for his safety by a purse of gold, and a grant of the land from this place to Cuckolds Point, besides making the husband master of the hamlet. It is added that, in memory of this grant, and the occasion of it, this fair was established, for the sale of horns, and all sorts of goods made with that material. A sermon is preached at Charlton church on the fair day.

HORN MAD. A person extremely jealous of his wife, is said to be horn mad. Also a cuckold, who does not cut or breed his horns easily.

HORN WORK. Cuckold making.

HORNIFIED. Cuckolded.

HORSE BUSS. A kiss with a loud smack; also a bite.

HORSE COSER. A dealer in horses vulgarly and corruptly pronounced *horse courser*. The verb *to cose* was used by the Scots, in the sense of bartering or exchanging.

HUG

HORSE GODMOTHER. A large masculine woman, a gentlemanlike kind of a lady.

HORSE LADDER. A piece of Wiltshire wit, which consists in sending some raw lad, or simpleton, to a neighbouring farm house, to borrow a horse ladder, in order to get up the horses, to finish a hay mow.

HORSE'S MEAL. A meal without drinking.

HOSTELER, i. e. oat stealer. Hosteler was originally the name for an inn-keeper; inns being in old English styled hostels, from the French signifying the same.

HOT POT. Ale and brandy made hot.

HOT STOMACH. He has so hot a stomach, that he burns all the clothes off his back; said of one who pawns his clothes to purchase liquor.

HOUSE, or TENEMENT, TO LET. A widow's weeds, also an atchievement marking the death of a husband, set up on the outside of the mansion both supposed to indicate that the dolorous widow wants a male comforter.

HOYDON. A romping girl.

HUBBLE-BUBBLE. Confusion. A hubble-bubble fellow; a man of confused ideas, or one thick of speech, whose words sound like water bubbling out of a bottle. Also an instrument used for smoaking through water in the East Indies, called likewise a caloon, and hooker.

HUBBLE DE SHUFF. Confusedly. To fire hubble de shuff; to fire quick and irregularly. *Old military term.*

HUBBUB. A noise, riot, or disturbance.

HUCKLE MY BUFF. Beer, egg, and brandy, made hot.

HUCKSTERS. Itinerant retailers of provisions. He is in hucksters hands, he is in a bad way.

TO HUE. To lash. The cove was hued in the nask, in the rogue was soundly lashed in bridewell. *Cant.*

TO HUFF. To reprove, or scold at any one, also to bluster, bounce, ding, or swagger. A captain huff; a noted bully. To stand the huff, to be answerable for the reckoning in a public house.

HUG. To hug brown bess, to carry a firelock, or serve as a private soldier. He hugs it as the Devil hugs a witch; said of one who holds any thing as if he was afraid of losing it.

H U M

HUGGER MUGGER. By stealth, privately, without making an appearance. They spent their money in a hugger mugger way.

HUGOTONTHEONBIQUIFFINARIANS A society existing in 1748.

HULKY, or HULKING. A great hulky fellow, an overgrown clumsy lout, or fellow.

HULVER-HEADED. Having a hard impenetrable head. hulver, in the Norfolk dialect, signifying holly, a hard and solid wood

TO HUM, or HUMBUG. To deceive, or impose on one by some story or device. A humbug; a jocular imposition, or deception. To hum and haw, to hesitate in speech, also to delay, or be with difficulty brought to consent to any matter or business

HUMS. Persons at church. There is a great number of hums in the autem, there is a great congregation in the church.

HUM BOX. A pulpit.

HUM CAP. Very old and strong beer, called also stingo. See STINGO.

HUM DRUM. A hum drum fellow, a dull tedious narrator, a bore; also a set of gentlemen, who (Bailey says) used to meet near the Charter House, or at the King's Head in St. John's Street, who had more of pleasantry, and less of mystery, than the Free Masons.

HUM DURGEON. An imaginary illness. He has got the hum durgeon, the thickest part of his thigh is nearest his a-se, i e nothing ails him except low spirits.

HUMBUGS. The brethren of the venerable society of humbugs was held at brother Hallam's, in Goodman's Fields

HUMMER. A great lye, a rapper. See RAPPER

HUMMING LIQUOR. Double ale, stout pharaoh. See PHARAOH

HUMMUMS A bagnio, or bathing house.

HUMSTRUM. A musical instrument made of a mopstick, a bladder, and some packthread, thence also called bladder and string, and hurdy gurdy, it is played on like a violin,

which

which is sometimes ludicrously called a humstrum: sometimes, instead of a bladder, a tin canister is used.

Hump. To hump; once a fashionable word for copulation.

Humpty Dumpty. A little humpty dumpty man or woman; a short clumsy person of either sex. also ale boiled with brandy.

To Hunch. To jostle, or thrust.

Hunch-backed. Hump-backed.

Hunks. A covetous miserable fellow, a miser; also the name of a famous bear, mentioned by Ben Jonson.

Hunt's Dog. He is like Hunt's dog, will neither go to church nor stay at home. One Hunt, a labouring man at a small town in Shropshire, kept a mastiff, who on being shut up on Sundays, whilst his master went to church, howled so terribly as to disturb the whole village; wherefore his master resolved to take him to church with him. but when he came to the church door, the dog having perhaps formerly been whipped out by the sexton, refused to enter, whereupon Hunt exclaimed loudly against his dog's obstinacy, who would neither go to church nor stay at home. This shortly became a bye word for discontented and whimsical persons.

Hunting. Drawing in unwary persons to play or game. *Cant.*

Hunting the Squirrel. An amusement practised by post boys, and stage coachmen, which consists in following a one-horse chaise, and driving it before them, passing close to it, so as to brush the wheel, and by other means terrifying any woman or person that may be in it. A man whose turn comes for him to drink, before he has emptied his former glass, is said to be hunted.

Huntsup. The reveillier of huntsmen, sounded on the French horn, or other instrument.

Hurdy Gurdy. A kind of fiddle, made perhaps out of a gourd. at present it is confounded with the humstrum. See Humstrum.

Hurly Burly. A rout, riot, bustle, or confusion.

Hush. Hush the cull; murder the fellow.

Hush Money. Money given to hush up or conceal a robbery

bery, theft, or any other offence, or to take off the evidence from appearing against a criminal.

HUSKYLOUR. A guinea, or job. *Cant.*

HUSSAR-LEG ROLL UP. A meeting of a club so called, was advertised A. D. 1747.

HUSSY. An abbreviation of housewife, but now always used as a term of reproach; as, How now, hussy? or, She is a light hussy.

HUZZA Said to have originally been the cry of the huzzars, or Hungarian light horse, but now the national shout of the English, both civil and military, in the sea phrase termed a cheer; to give three cheers being to huzza thrice.

HYP, or HIP A mode of calling to one passing by. Hip, Michael, your head's on fire, a piece of vulgar wit to a red-haired man.

J.

JABBER. To talk thick and fast, as great praters usually do, to chatter like a magpye; also to speak a foreign language. He jabbered to me in his damned outlandish parlez vous, but I could not understand him, he chattered to me in French, or some other foreign language, but I could not understand him

JACK. A farthing, a small bowl serving as the mark for bowlers, an instrument for pulling off boots.

JACK ADAMS. A fool. Jack Adams's parish; Clerkenwell.

JACK AT A PINCH. A poor hackney parson.

JACK IN A BOX. A sharper, or cheat.

JACK IN AN OFFICE. An insolent fellow in authority.

JACK KETCH. The hangman. vide DERRICK and KETCH.

JACK NASTY FACE. A sea term, signifying a common sailor.

JACK OF LEGS. A tall long-legged man; also a giant, said to be buried in Weston church, near Baldock, in Hertfordshire, where there are two stones fourteen feet distant, said to be the head and feet stones of his grave. This giant, says Salmon, as fame goes, lived in a wood here, and was a great robber, but a generous one; for he plundered the rich to feed the poor he frequently took bread for this purpose from the Baldock bakers, who catching him at an advantage, put out his eyes, and afterwards hanged him upon a knoll in Baldock field. At his death he made one request, which was, that he might have his bow and arrow put into his hand, and on shooting it off, where the arrow fell, they would bury him; which being granted, the arrow fell in Weston churchyard. About seventy years ago, a very large thigh bone was taken out of the church chest, where it had lain many years for a show, and was sold by the clerk to Sir John Tredeskin, who, it is said, put it up among the rarities of Oxford.

JACK PUDDEN. The merry andrew, zany, or jester to a mountebank.

JACK ROBINSON. Before one could say Jack Robinson, a saying to express a very short time, originating from a very volatile gentleman of that appellation, who would call on his neighbours, and be gone before his name could be announced.

JACK SPRAT. A dwarf, or diminutive fellow.

JACK TAR A sailor.

JACK WEIGHT. A fat man.

JACK WHORE A large masculine overgrown wench.

JACKANAPES. An ape, a pert, ugly, little fellow.

JACKED. Spavined. A jacked horse.

JACKMEN. See JARKMEN.

JACOB. A ladder. perhaps from Jacob's dream. *Cant.* Also the common name for a jay, jays being usually taught to say, Poor Jacob! a cup of sack for Jacob.

JACOBITES.

JACOBITES. Sham or collar shirts. Also partizans for the Stuart family. from the name of the abdicated king, i e. James or Jacobus. It is said by the whigs, that God changed Jacob's name to Israel, least the descendants of that patriarch should be called Jacobites.

JADE. A term of reproach to women

JAGUE. A ditch perhaps from jakes

JAIL BIRDS Prisoners.

JAKES. A house of office, a cacatorium.

JAMMED. Hanged. *Cant.*

JANIZARIES. The mob, sometimes so called, also bailiffs, their setters, and followers.

JAPANNED. Ordained To be japanned; to enter into holy orders, to become a clergyman, to put on the black cloth: from the colour of the japan ware, which is black.

JARK. A seal.

JARKMEN Those who fabricate counterfeit passes, licences, and certificates for beggars.

JASON'S FLEECE. A citizen cheated of his gold.

JAW Speech, discourse. Give us none of your jaw; let us have none of your discourse. A jaw-me-dead, a talkative fellow. Jaw work; a cry used in fairs by the sellers of nuts.

JAZEY. A bob wig.

IDEA POT. The knowledge box, the head. See KNOWLEDGE BOX.

JEHU. To drive jehu-like; to drive furiously from a king of Israel of that name, who was a famous charioteer, and mentioned as such in the Bible.

JEM. A gold ring. *Cant*

JEMMY FELLOW. A smart spruce fellow.

JENNY. An instrument for lifting up the grate or top of a show glass, in order to rob it. *Cant*

JERRYCUMMUMBLE To shake, towzle, or tumble about.

JERRY SNEAK. A henpecked husband from a celebrated character in one of Mr. Foote's plays, representing a man governed by his wife.

JESSAMY. A smart jemmy fellow, a fopling,

JESUIT.

JESUIT. See TO BOX THE JESUIT.

JESUITICAL. Sly, evasive, equivocal. A jesuitical answer; an equivocal answer.

JET. A lawyer. Autem jet; a parson.

JEW An over-reaching dealer, or hard, sharp fellow; an extortioner. the brokers behind St Clement's church in the Strand, were formerly called Jews by their brethren the taylors.

JEW BAIL Insufficient bail, commonly Jews, who for a sum of money will bail any action whatsoever, and justify, that is, swear to their sufficiency, but, when called on, are not to be found.

JEW'S EYE That's worth a Jew's eye; a pleasant or agreeable sight: a saying taken from Shakespeare.

JIBBER THE KIBBER. A method of deceiving seamen, by fixing a candle and lanthorn round the neck of a horse, one of whose fore feet is tied up; this at night has the appearance of a ship's light Ships bearing towards it, run on shore, and being wrecked, are plundered by the inhabitants. This diabolical device is, it is said, practised by the inhabitants of our western coasts

JIG. A trick. A pleasant jig; a witty arch trick. Also a lock or door.

JIGGER. A whipping post. *Cant.*

JILT. A tricking woman, who encourages the addresses of a man whom she means to deceive and abandon.

JILTED. Rejected by a woman who has encouraged one's advances.

JINGLE BOXES Leathern jacks tipped with silver, and hung with bells, formerly in use among fuddle caps. *Cant.*

JINGLE BRAINS. A wild, thoughtless, rattling fellow.

JINGLERS Horse cosers, frequenting country fairs. *Cant.*

ILL-FORTUNE, or THE PICTURE OF ILL-LUCK. A ninepenny piece

IMPOST TAKERS. Usurers who attend the gaming tables, and lend money at great premiums.

IMPUDENT STEALING. Cutting out the backs of coaches, and robbing the seats.

IMPURE. A modern term for a lady of easy virtue.

INCHING.

INCHING. Encroaching.

INDIES. Black Indies; Newcastle.

INDORSER. A sodomite. To indorse with a cudgel; to drub or beat a man over the back with a stick, to lay *cane* upon Abel.

INKLE WEAVERS. Supposed to be a very brotherly set of people; 'as great as two inkle weavers' being a proverbial saying.

INLAID. Well inlaid, in easy circumstances, rich, or well to pass.

INNOCENTS. One of the innocents; a weak or simple person, man or woman.

JOB A guinea.

JOB's COMFORT. Reproof instead of consolation.

JOB's COMFORTER. One who brings news of some additional misfortune.

JOB's DOCK. He is laid up in Job's dock; i. e in a salivation. The apartments for the foul or venereal patients in St. Bartholomew's hospital, are called Job's ward.

JOBATION. A reproof.

JOBBERNOLE. The head.

To JOBE. To reprove or reprehend. *Cambridge term.*

JOCK, or CROWDY-HEADED JOCK. A jeering appellation for a north-country seaman, particularly a collier; Jock being a common name, and crowdy the chief food, of the lower order of the people in Northumberland.

To JOCK, or JOCKUM CLOY. To enjoy a woman.

JOCKUM GAGE. A chamber pot, jordan, looking-glass, or member-mug *Cant.*

JOGG-TROT To keep on a jogg-trot; to get on with a slow but regular pace.

JOHNNY BUM. A he or jack ass. so called by a lady that affected to be extremely polite and modest, who would not say Jack because it was vulgar, nor ass because it was indecent.

JOINT. To hit a joint in carving, the operator must think of a cuckold. To put one's nose out of joint; to rival one in the favour of a patron or mistress.

JOLLY.

JOLLY, or JOLLY NOB. The head. I'll lump your jolly nob for you; I'll give you a knock on the head.

JOLLY DOG. A merry facetious fellow; a *bon vivant*, who never flinches from his glass, nor cries to go home to bed.

JOLTER HEAD. A large head, metaphorically, a stupid fellow

JORDAIN. A great blow, or staff. I'll tip him a jordain if I transnear, i e I'll give him a blow with my staff, if I come near him. *Cant*

JORDAN. A chamber pot.

JORUM. A jug, or large pitcher

JOSEPH. A woman's great coat. Also, a sheepish bashful young fellow. an allusion to Joseph who fled from Potiphar's wife. You are Josephus rex; you are joking, i e. joking.

JOWL. The cheek. Cheek by jowl; close together, or cheek to cheek

IRISH APRICOTS. Potatoes. It is a common joke against the Irish vessels, to say they are loaded with fruit and timber, that is, potatoes and broomsticks. Irish assurance, a bold forward behaviour· as being dipt in the river Styx was formerly supposed to render persons invulnerable, so it is said that a dipping in the river Shannon totally annihilates bashfulness, whence arises the saying of an impudent Irishman, that he has been dipped in the Shannon.

IRISH EVIDENCE. A false witness

IRISH LEGS. Thick legs, jocularly styled the Irish arms. It is said of the Irish women, that they have a dispensation from the Pope to wear the thick end of their legs downwards

IRISH TOYLES. Thieves who carry about pins, laces, and other pedlars wares and under the pretence of offering their goods to sale, rob houses, or pilfer any thing they can lay hold of.

IRON. Money in general. To polish the king's iron with one's eye brows, to look out of grated or prison windows, or, as the Irishman expressed them, the iron glass windows. Iron doublet; a prison. See STONE DOUBLET.

IRONMONGER'S SHOP. To keep an ironmonger's shop by

the fide of a common, where the fheriff fets one up; to be hanged in chains. Iron-bound, laced. An iron-bound hat; a filver-laced hat.

ISLAND. He drank out of the bottle till he faw the ifland the ifland is the rifing bottom of a wine bottle, which appears like an ifland in the center, before the bottle is quite empty.

ITCHLAND, or SCRATCHLAND. Scotland.

JUGG. See DOUBLE JUGG.

JUGLER'S BOX. The engine for burning culprits in the hand. *Cant.*

JUKRUM. A licence

JUMBLEGUT LANE. A rough road or lane.

JUMP. The jump, or dining room jump; a fpecies of robbery effected by afcending a ladder placed by a fham lamp-lighter, againft the houfe intended to be robbed. It is fo called, becaufe, fhould the lamp-lighter be put to flight, the thief who afcended the ladder has no means of efcape but that of jumping down.

JUMPERS. Perfons who rob houfes by getting in at the windows. Alfo a fect of Methodifts eftablifhed in South Wales.

JUNIPER LECTURE. A round fcolding bout

JURY LEG. A wooden leg. allufion to a jury maft, which is a temporary fubftitute for a maft carried away by a ftorm, or any other accident *Sea phrafe.*

JURY MAST. A *journiere* maft; i. e. a maft for the day or occafion.

JUST-ASS. A punning appellation for a juftice.

IVY BUSH. Like an owl in an ivy bufh, a fimile for a meagre or weazle faced man, with a large wig, or very bufhy hair.

K.

K.

KATE A picklock. 'Tis a rum kate; it is a clever picklock. *Cant.*

KEEL BULLIES. Men employed to load and unload the coal vessels

KEELHAULING. A punishment in use among the Dutch seamen, in which, for certain offences, the delinquent is drawn once, or oftener, under the ship's keel, ludicrously defined, undergoing a great hard-ship

TO KEEP To inhabit. Lord, where do you keep? i. e. where are your rooms? *Academical phrase.*

TO KEEP IT UP To prolong a debauch. We kept it up finely last night, metaphor drawn from the game at shuttlecock.

KEEPING CULLY. One who keeps a mistress, as he supposes, for his own use, but really for that of the public.

KEFFEL. A horse. *Welsh.*

KELTER. Condition, order. Out of kelter; out of order.

KEMP'S MORRIS. William Kemp, said to have been the original Dogberry in Much ado about Nothing, danced a morris from London to Norwich in nine days; of which he printed the account, A. D. 1600, intitled, Kemp's Nine Days Wonder, &c.

KEMP'S SHOES. Would I had Kemp's shoes to throw after you *Ben Jonson* Perhaps Kemp was a man remarkable for his good luck or fortune, throwing an old shoe, or shoes, after any one going on an important business, being by the vulgar deemed lucky.

KEN. A house A bob ken, or a bowman ken; a well-furnished house, also a house that harbours thieves. Biting the ken; robbing the house *Cant*

KEN MILLER, or **KEN CRACKER** A housebreaker. *Cant.*

KENT-STREET EJECTMENT. To take away the street door; a method practised by the landlords in Kent-street, Southwark, when their tenants are above a fortnight's rent in arrear.

KERRY SECURITY. Bond, pledge, oath, and keep the money

KETCH Jack Ketch; a general name for the finishers of the law, or hangmen, ever since the year 1682, when the office was filled by a famous practitioner of that name, of whom his wife said, that any bungler might put a man to death, but only her husband knew how to make a gentleman die sweetly This officer is mentioned in Butler's Ghost, page 54, published about the year 1682, in the following lines

Till Ketch observing he was chous'd,
And in his profits much abus'd,
In open hall the tribute dunn'd,
To do his office, or refund.

Mr. Ketch had not long been elevated to his office, for the name of his predecessor Dun occurs in the former part of this poem, page 29.

For you yourself to act squire Dun,
Such ignominy ne'er saw the sun.

The addition of 'squire,' with which Mr. Dun is here dignified, is a mark that he had beheaded some state criminal for high treason; an operation which, according to custom for time out of mind, has always entitled the operator to that distinction. The predecessor of Dun was Gregory Brandon, from whom the gallows was called the Gregorian tree, by which name it is mentioned in the prologue to Mercurius Pragmaticus, a tragi-comedy acted at Paris, &c. 1641

This trembles under the black rod, and he
Doth fear his fate from the Gregorian tree.

Gregory Brandon succeeded Derrick. See DERRICK.

KETTLE DRUMS. Cupid's kettle drums; a woman's breasts, called by sailors chest and bedding.

KETTLE OF FISH. When a person has perplexed his affairs in general, or any particular business, he is said to have made a fine kettle of fish of it.

KHAJBAR. The worthy brethren of this order met, A. D. 1749, at the Nag's Head, Tothill-street, Westminster.

KICKS. Breeches. A high kick, the top of the fashion.

It is all the kick, it is the present mode. Tip us your kicks, we'll have them as well as your lour, pull off your breeches, for we must have them as well as your money. A kick, sixpence. Two and a kick; half-a-crown. A kick in the guts; a dram of gin, or any other spirituous liquor. A kick up, a disturbance, also a hop or dance. An odd kick in one's gallop; a strange whim or peculiarity

To KICK THE BUCKET. To die. He kicked the bucket one day, he died one day.

KICKERAPOO. Dead. *Negro word.*

KICKSHAWS. French dishes. corruption of *quelque chose.*

KID. A child.

KID LAY Rogues who make it their business to defraud young apprentices, or errand boys, of goods committed to their charge, by prevailing on them to execute some trifling message, pretending to take care of their parcels till they come back, these are, in cant terms, said to be on the kid lay.

KIDDER. A forestaller see CROCKER. Kidders are also persons employed by the gardeners to gather pease.

KIDDY NIPPERS Taylors out of work, who cut off the waistcoat pockets of their brethren, when cross-legged on the board, thereby grabbling their bit. *Cant.*

KIDNAPPER. Originally one who stole or decoyed children or apprentices from their parents or masters, to send them to the colonies, called also spiriting but now used for all recruiting crimps for the king's troops, or those of the East India company, and agents for indenting servants for the plantations, &c.

KIDNEY. Disposition, principles, humour. Of a strange kidney; of an odd or unaccountable humour. A man of a different kidney; a man of different principles.

KILKENNY. An old frize coat.

KILL CARE CLUB The members of this club, styled also the Sons of Sound Sense and Satisfaction, met at their fortress, the Castle tavern, in Pater-noster-row.

KILL DEVIL New still-burnt rum.

KILL PRIEST. Port wine.

KIT

To KIMBAW To trick, cheat, or cozen; also to beat or to bully. Let's kimbaw the cull, let's bully the fellow. To set one's arms a-kimbaw, vulgarly pronounced a-kimbo, is to rest one's hands on the hips, keeping the elbows square, and sticking out from the body, an insolent bullying attitude. *Cant.*

KINCHIN. A little child. Kinchin coes; orphan beggar boys, educated in thieving. Kinchin morts, young girls under the like circumstances and training. Kinchin morts, or coes in slates, beggars children carried at their mothers backs in sheets Kinchin cove; a little man. *Cant.*

KING'S BAD BARGAIN. One of the king's bad bargains; a malingeror, or soldier who shirks his duty.

KING'S HEAD INN, or CHEQUER INN, IN NEWGATE-STREET. The prison of Newgate

KING JOHN'S MEN. He is one of king John's men, eight score to the hundred, a saying of a little undersized man.

KING OF THE GYPSIES The captain, chief, or ringleader of the gang of misrule, in the cant language called also the upright man.

KING'S PICTURES. Coin, money.

KINGDOM COME. He is gone to kingdom come; he is dead.

KIP. The skin of a large calf, in the language of the Excise Office.

KISS MINE A-SE. An offer, as Fielding observes, very frequently made, but never, as he could learn, literally accepted. A kiss mine a-se fellow; a sycophant.

KISSING CRUST. That part where the loaves have touched in the oven.

KIT. A dancing master. so called from his kit or cittern, a small fiddle, which dancing masters always carry about with them, to play to their scholars. The kit is likewise the whole of a soldier's necessaries, the contents of his knapsack: and is used also to express the whole of different commodities, as, Here, take the whole kit, i. e. take all.

KIT-CAT CLUB. A society of gentlemen, eminent for wit and learning, who in the reign of Queen Anne and George I. met at a house kept by one Christopher Cat.

The

The portraits of most of the members of this society were painted by Sir Godfrey Kneller, of one size; thence still called the kit-cat size.

KITCHEN PHYSICK. Food, good meat roast or boiled. A little kitchen physic will set him up, he has more need of a cook than a doctor.

KITTLE PITCHERING. A jocular method of hobbling or bothering a troublesome teller of long stories: this is done by contradicting some very immaterial circumstance at the beginning of the narration, the objections to which being settled, others are immediately started to some new particular of like consequence, thus impeding, or rather not suffering him to enter into, the main story. Kittle pitchering is often practised in confederacy, one relieving the other, by which the design is rendered less obvious.

KNACK SHOP. A toy shop, a nick-nack-atory.

KNAPPER'S POLL. A sheep's head. *Cant.*

KNAVE IN GRAIN. A knave of the first rate; a phrase borrowed from the dyehouse, where certain colours are said to be in grain, to denote their superiority, as being dyed with cochineal, called grain. Knave in grain is likewise a pun applied to a cornfactor or miller.

KNIGHT OF THE BLADE. A bully.

KNIGHT OF THE POST. A false evidence, one that is ready to swear any thing for hire.

KNIGHT OF THE RAINBOW. A footman, from the variety of colours in the liveries and trimmings of gentlemen of that cloth.

KNIGHT OF THE ROAD. A highwayman.

KNIGHT of the SHEERS. A taylor.

KNIGHT OF THE THIMBLE, or NEEDLE. A taylor or stay maker.

KNIGHT OF THE TRENCHER. A great eater.

KNIGHT AND BARROW PIG, more hog than gentleman. A saying of any low pretender to precedency.

KNOB. The head. See NOB.

KNOCK. To knock a woman, to have carnal knowledge of her. To knock off, to conclude; phrase borrowed from the blacksmith. To knock under, to submit.

KNOCK ME DOWN. Strong ale or beer, stingo.

KNOT. A crew, gang, or fraternity. He has tied a knot with his tongue, that he cannot untie with his teeth; i. e. he is married.

KNOWING ONES. Sportsmen on the turf, who, from experience and an acquaintance with the jockies, are supposed to be in the secret, that is, to know the true merits or powers of each horse; notwithstanding which it often happens that the knowing ones are taken in.

KNOWLEDGE BOX. The head.

KNUCKLES. Pickpockets who attend the avenues to public places, to steal pocket books, watches, &c a superior kind of pickpockets. To knuckle to; to submit.

KNUCKLEDABS, or KNUCKLE CONFOUNDERS. Ruffles.

L.

LACED MUTTON. A woman.

LACING. Beating. I'll lace your jacket handsomely.

LADDER. To go up the ladder to rest; to be hanged.

LADY. A crooked or hump-backed woman.

LADY OF EASY VIRTUE A woman of the town, an impure, a prostitute.

LADYBIRDS. Light or lewd women.

To LAG. To drop behind, to keep back. Lag last, the last of a company

LAGE. Water. *Cant*

LAGE OF DUDS. A buck of linen.

LAID ON THE SHELF, or LAID UP IN LAVENDER. Pawned.

To LAMB, or LAMBASTE. To beat Lamb pye, a beating from *lambo*.

L A T

LAMB's WOOL. Apples roasted and put into strong ale.

LAMBSKIN MEN. The judges, from their robes lined and bordered with ermine.

LAND. How lies the land? how stands the reckoning? Who has any land in Appleby? a question asked the man at whose door the glass stands long, or who does not circulate it in due time

LAND LOPERS, or LAND LUBBERS. Vagabonds lurking about the country, who subsist by pilfering.

LAND PIRATES. Highwaymen.

LANK SLEEVE. The empty sleeve of a one-armed man. A fellow with a lank sleeve, a man who has lost an arm.

LANSPRISADO. One who has only two-pence in his pocket. Also a lance, or deputy corporal, that is, one doing the duty without the pay of a corporal. Formerly a lancier, or horseman, who being dismounted by the death of his horse, served in the foot, by the title of lansprisado, or *lancepessato*, a broken lance

LANTHORN-JAWED. Thin-visaged ; from their cheeks being almost transparent. Or else, lenten jawed, i e. having the jaws of one emaciated by a too rigid observation of Lent. Dark lanthorn ; a servant or agent at court, who receives a bribe for his principal or master

LAP. Butter milk or whey. *Cant.*

LARBOVERS FOR MEDLERS. An answer frequently given to children, or young people, as a rebuke for their impertinent curiosity, in enquiring what is contained in a box, bundle, or any other closed conveyance perhaps from a layover, or turnover, a kind of tart not baked in a pan, but made to contain the fruit by turning one end of the crust over the other. Medlar tarts were probably so made in former times.

LARK. A boat.

LARRY DUGAN'S EYE WATER. Blacking Larry Dugan was a famous shoeblack at Dublin.

LATCH. Let in.

LATHY. Thin, slender A lathy wench, a girl almost as slender as a lath.

LEA

LATITAT. A nick-name for an attorney, from the name of a writ.

LAVENDER. Laid up in lavender, pawned.

LAUGH. To laugh on the wrong side of the mouth; to cry. I'll make him laugh on the wrong (or t'other) side of his mouth.

LAUNCH. The delivery, or labour, of a pregnant woman; a crying out or groaning.

LAW. To give law to a hare; a sporting term, signifying to give the animal a chance of escaping, by not setting on the dogs till the hare is at some distance. It is also more figuratively used for giving any one a chance of succeeding in a scheme or project.

LAY. Enterprise, pursuit, or attempt: to be sick of the lay. It also means a hazard, or chance. He stands a queer lay, i. e. he is in danger. *Cant.*

LAYSTALL. A dunghill about London, on which the soil brought from necessary houses is emptied; or, in more technical terms, where the old gold collected at weddings by the Tom t—d man, is stored.

LAZY. As lazy as Ludlam's dog, who leaned against the wall to bark. As lazy as the tinker who laid down his budget to f—t.

LAZY MAN'S LOAD. Lazy people frequently take up more than they can safely carry, to save the trouble of coming a second time.

LAZYBONES. An instrument like a pair of tongs, for old or very fat people to take any thing from the ground without stooping.

LEAF. To go off with the fall of the leaf, to be hanged: criminals in Dublin being turned off from the outside of the prison by the falling of a board, propped up, and moving on a hinge, like the leaf of a table. *Irish term.*

To LEAK. To make water.

LEAKY. Apt to blab: one who cannot keep a secret is said to be leaky.

LEAPING OVER THE SWORD. An ancient ceremonial said to constitute a military marriage. A sword being laid down on the ground, the parties to be married joined hands,

hands, when the corporal or ferjeant of the company repeated thefe words

Leap rogue, and jump whore,
And then you are married for evermore.

Whereupon the happy couple jumped hand in hand over the fword, the drum beating a ruffle; and the parties were ever after confidered as man and wife.

LEAST IN SIGHT. To play leaft in fight; to hide, keep out of the way, or make one's felf fcarce.

LEATHER. To lofe leather; to be galled with riding on horfeback, or, as the Scotch exprefs it, to be faddle fick. To leather alfo means to beat, perhaps originally with a ftrap. I'll leather you to your heart's content. Leather-headed, ftupid. Leathern conveniency, term ufed by quakers for a ftage-coach.

LEFT-HANDED WIFE. A concubine: an allufion to an ancient German cuftom, according to which, when a man married his concubine, or a woman greatly his inferior, he gave her his left hand.

LEG. To make a leg, to bow. To give leg bail and land fecurity; to run away. To fight at the leg, to take unfair advantages; it being held unfair by back-fword players to ftrike at the leg. To break a leg, a woman who has had a baftard, is faid to have broken a leg.

LEGGERS. Sham leggers; cheats who pretend to fell fmuggled goods, but in reality only deal in old fhop-keepers or damaged goods.

LENTEN FARE. Spare diet.

LEVITE. A prieft or parfon.

TO LIB. To lie together. *Cant.*

LIBBEGE. A bed. *Cant.*

LIBBEN. A private dwelling houfe. *Cant.*

LIBKEN. A houfe to lie in. *Cant.*

TO LICK. To beat, alfo to wafh, or to paint flightly over. I'll give you a good lick o' the chops; I'll give you a good ftroke or blow on the face. Jack tumbled into a cow-t—d, and naftied his beft clothes, for which his father ftept up, and licked him neatly. — I'll lick you! the dovetail to which is, If you lick me all over, you won't mifs ——

LICKSPITTLE. A parasite, or talebearer.
LIFT. To give one a lift; to assist. A good hand at a dead lift; a good hand upon an emergency. To lift one's hand to one's head; to drink to excess, or to drink drams. To lift or raise one's elbow; the same.
LIFT. See SHOPLIFTER, &c.
LIFTER. A crutch.
LIG. A bed. See LIB.
LIGHT BOB. A soldier of the light infantry company.
LIGHT-FINGERED. Thievish, apt to pilfer.
LIGHT-HEELED. Swift in running. A light-heeled wench; one who is apt, by the flying up of her heels, to fall flat on her back, a willing wench.
LIGHTMANS. The day. *Cant.*
LILIPUTIAN. A diminutive man or woman, from Gulliver's Travels, written by Dean Swift, where an imaginary kingdom of dwarfs of that name is described.
LILY WHITE. A chimney sweeper.
LIMBS. Duke of limbs, a tall aukward fellow.
LIMB OF THE LAW. An inferior or pettyfogging attorney.
LIMBO. A prison, confinement.
To LINE. A term for the act of coition between dog and bitch
LINE OF THE OLD AUTHOR. A dram of brandy.
LINGO. Language. An outlandish lingo, a foreign tongue. The parlezious lingo; the French language.
LINEN ARMOURERS Taylors
LION. To tip the lion; to squeeze the nose of the party tipped, flat to his face with the thumb. To shew the lions and tombs; to point out the particular curiosities of any place, to act the ciceroni. an allusion to Westminster Abbey, and the Tower, where the tombs and lions are shewn. A lion is also a name given by the gownsmen of Oxford to an inhabitant or visitor. It is a standing joke among the city wits to send boys and country folks, on the first of April, to the Tower Ditch, to see the lions washed.
LIQUOR. To liquor one's boots, to drink before a journey: among Roman Catholics, to administer the extreme unction.

L O B

LITTLE BARBARY. Wapping.

LITTLE BREECHES. A familiar appellation used to a little boy.

LITTLE CLERGYMAN. A young chimney-sweeper.

LITTLE EASE. A small dark cell in Guildhall, London, where disorderly apprentices are confined by the City Chamberlain: it is called Little Ease, from its being so low that a lad cannot stand upright in it.

LITTLE SNAKESMAN. A little boy who gets into a house through the sink hole, and then opens the door for his accomplices: he is so called, from writhing and twisting like a snake, in order to work himself through the narrow passage.

LIVE LUMBER. A term used by sailors, to signify all landsmen on board their ships.

LIVE STOCK. Lice or fleas.

LOAF. To be in bad loaf; to be in a disagreeable situation, or in trouble.

TO LOAP. To run away. He loaped down the dancers; he ran down stairs.

LOB. Going on the lob; going into a shop to get change for gold, and secreting some of the change.

LOB'S POUND. A prison. Dr Grey, in his notes on Hudibras, explains it to allude to one Doctor Lob, a dissenting preacher, who used to hold forth when conventicles were prohibited, and had made himself a retreat by means of a trap door at the bottom of his pulpit. Once being pursued by the officers of justice, they followed him through divers subterraneous passages, till they got into a dark cell, from whence they could not find their way out, but calling to some of their companions, swore they had got into Lob's Pound.

LOBCOCK. A large relaxed penis; also a dull inanimate fellow.

LOBKIN. A house to lie in; also a lodging.

LOBLOLLEY BOY. A nick name for the surgeon's servant on board a man of war, sometimes for the surgeon himself: from the water gruel prescribed to the sick, which is called loblolley.

LOBONIAN

L O L

LOBONIAN SOCIETY A society which met at Lob Hall, at the King and Queen, Norton Falgate, by order of Lob the Great.

LOBSCOUSE. A dish much eaten at sea, composed of salt beef, biscuit, and onions, well peppered and stewed together.

LOBSTER A nick-name for a soldier, from the colour of his clothes To boil one's lobster, for a churchman to become a soldier lobsters, which are of a bluish black, being made red by boiling I will not make a lobster kettle of my ****; a reply frequently made by the nymphs of the Point of Portsmouth, when requested by a soldier to grant him a favour.

LOCK Character. He stood a queer lock, he bore but an indifferent character A lock is also a buyer of stolen goods, as well as the receptacle for them

LOCK HOSPITAL An hospital for venereal patients.

LOCK UP HOUSE. A spunging house, a public house kept by sheriffs officers, to which they convey the persons they have arrested, where they practise every species of imposition and extortion with impunity. Also houses kept by agents or crimps, who enlist, or rather trepan, men to serve the East India or African Company as soldiers

LOCKERAM-JAWED. Thin-faced, or lanthorn-jawed See LANTHORN-JAWED

LOCKSMITH'S DAUGHTER A key.

LOGE. A watch He filed a cloy of a loge, or scout; he picked a pocket of a watch. See SCOUT.

LOGGERHEAD. A blockhead, or stupid fellow. We three loggerheads be; a sentence frequently written under two heads, and the reader by repeating it makes himself the third A loggerhead is also a double-headed or bar shot of iron. To go to loggerheads, to fall to fighting

LOLL. Mother's loll, a favourite child, the mother's darling

LOLL TONGUE He has been playing a game at loll tongue, he has been salivated.

LOLLIPOPS Sweet lozenges purchased by children.

To LOLLOP To lean with one's elbows on a table.

LOLLPOOP.

LOLLPOOP. A lazy, idle drone.

LOMBARD FEVER. Sick of a lombard fever; i. e. of the idles.

LONG. Great. A long price; a great price.

LONG GALLERY. Throwing, or rather trundling, the dice the whole length of the board.

LONG MEG A jeering name for a very tall woman from one famous in story, called Long Meg of Westminster.

LONG SHANKS A long-legged person.

LONG SHILLING. This among hackney coachmen, before the alteration in the fares, was from the Royal Exchange to the east corner of Catherine-street in the Strand

LONG STOMACH. A voracious appetite

LONG-TONGUED. Loquacious, not able to keep a secret. He is as long-tongued as Granny Granny was an ideot who could lick her own eye. See GRANNY.

LONG-WINDED. A long-winded parson, one who preaches long, tedious sermons. A long-winded paymaster; one who takes long credit

LOO. For the good of the loo, for the benefit of the company or community.

LOOBY. An aukward, ignorant fellow

LOOKING AS IF ONE COULD NOT HELP IT. Looking like a simpleton, or as if one could not say boh! to a goose.

LOOKING GLASS A chamber pot, jordan, or member mug.

LOON, or LOUT. A country bumpkin, or clown.

LOONSLATE Thirteen pence halfpenny.

LOOPHOLE. An opening, or means of escape To find a loophole in an act of parliament, i. e. a method of evading it.

LOP-SIDED. Uneven, having one side larger or heavier than the other boys paper kites are often said to be lop-sided

LORD A crooked or hump-backed man. These unhappy people afford great scope for vulgar raillery, such as, 'Did you come straight from home? if so, you have got 'confoundedly bent by the way.' 'Don't abuse the 'gemman,'

'gemman,' adds a by-stander, 'he has been grossly insulted already; don't you see his back's up?' Or some one asks him if the show is behind, 'because I see,' adds he, 'you have the drum at your back.' Another piece of vulgar wit is let loose on a deformed person: If met by a party of soldiers on the march, one of them observes that that gentleman is on his march too, for he has got his knapsack at his back. It is said, in the British Apollo, that the title of Lord was first given to deformed persons in the reign of Richard III. from several persons labouring under that misfortune being created peers by him; but it is more probably derived from the Greek word λοϱδος, *crooked*.

LORD MANSFIELD'S TEETH. The chevaux de frize round the top of the wall of the King's Bench prison.

LOVE-BEGOTTEN CHILD. A bastard.

LOUNGE. A loitering place, or gossiping shop.

LOUSE. A gentleman's companion. He will never louse a grey head of his own; he will never live to be old.

LOUSE BAG. A black bag worn to the hair or wig.

LOUSE HOUSE. The round house, cage, or any other place of confinement.

LOUSE LADDER. A stitch fallen in a stocking.

LOUSE LAND. Scotland.

LOUSE TRAP. A small-toothed comb.

LOUT. A clumsy stupid fellow.

LOW PAD. A footpad.

LOW TIDE, or LOW WATER. When there is no money in a man's pocket.

LOWRE. Money. *Cant.*

LUBBER. An aukward fellow: a name given by sailors to landsmen.

LUCK, or GOOD LUCK. To tread in a sirreverence, to be bewrayed: an allusion to the proverb, Sh-tt'n luck is good luck.

LUD'S BULWARK. Ludgate prison.

LUGS. Ears or wattles. See WATTLES.

LULLABY CHEAT. An infant. *Cant.*

LULLIES. Wet linen. *Cant.*

LULLY PRIGGERS. Thieves who steal wet linen. *Cant*

LUMB. Too much.

LUMBER. Live lumber; soldiers or passengers on board a ship are so called by the sailors.

LUMBER TROOP. A club or society of citizens of London

TO LUMP. To beat; also to include a number of articles under one head

TO LUMP THE LIGHTER To be transported

LUMPERS Persons who contract to unload ships; also thieves who lurk about wharfs to pilfer goods from ships, lighters, &c

LUMPING. Great A lumping pennyworth, a great quantity for the money, a bargain. He has got a lumping pennyworth; frequently said of a man who marries a fat woman

LUN Harlequin

LURCH To be left in the lurch, to be abandoned by one's confederates or party, to be left in a scrape

LURCHED. Those who lose a game of whist, without scoring five, are said to be lurched.

LURCHER A lurcher of the law, a bum bailiff, or his setter.

LURRIES. Money, watches, rings, or other moveables

LYE. Chamber lye, urine.

M.

MAC

MACCARONI An Italian paste made of flour and eggs Also a fop which name arose from a club, called the Maccaroni Club, instituted by some of the most dressy

T travelled

travelled gentlemen about town, who led the fashions; whence a man foppishly dressed, was supposed a member of that club, and by contraction styled a Maccaroni.

MACE. The mace is a rogue assuming the character of a gentleman, or opulent tradesman, who under that appearance defrauds workmen, by borrowing a watch, or other piece of goods, till one that he bespeaks is done. *Cant.*

MACHINES. Mrs. Philips's ware. See CUNDUM.

MACKEREL. A bawd. from the French *maquerel*. Mackerel-backed, long-backed.

MAD TOM, or TOM OF BEDLAM, otherwise an Abram Man. A rogue that counterfeits madness. *Cant.*

MADAM. A kept madam, a kept mistress.

MADAM RAN. A whore. *Cant.*

MADE. Stolen *Cant.*

MADGE. The private parts of a woman.

MADGE CULLS. Sodomites. *Cant.*

MAGGOT BOILER. A tallow-chandler.

MAGGOTTY. Whimsical, capricious.

MAHOMETAN GRUEL. Coffee. because formerly used chiefly by the Turks.

MAIDEN SESSIONS. A sessions where none of the prisoners are capitally convicted.

MAKE. A halfpenny. *Cart.*

MAKE WEIGHT. A small candle: a term applied to a little slender man.

MALINGEROR. A military term for one who, under pretence of sickness, evades his duty.

MALKIN, or MAULKIN. A general name for a cat; also a parcel of rags fastened to the end of a stick, to clean an oven; also a figure set up in a garden to scare the birds, likewise an aukward woman.

MALKINTRASH. One in a dismal garb.

MALMSEY NOSE. A red pimpled snout, rich in carbuncles and rubies.

MALTOUT. A nick-name for a marine, used by sailors and soldiers of other corps: probably a corruption of *matelot*, the French word for a sailor.

MAN OF THE TOWN. A rake, a debauchee.

MAT

MAN OF THE TURF. A horse racer, or jockey.

MANOEUVERING THE APOSTLES. Robbing Peter to pay Paul, i. e. borrowing of one man to pay another.

MAN TRAP. A woman's commodity.

MANUFACTURE. Liquors prepared from materials of English growth.

MARE'S NEST. He has found a mare's nest, and is laughing at the eggs; said of one who laughs without any apparent cause.

MARGERY PRATER. A hen. *Cant.*

MARINATED. Transported to some foreign plantation.

MARINE OFFICER. An empty bottle: marine officers being held useless by the seamen. *Sea wit.*

MARRIAGE MUSIC. The squalling and crying of children.

MARRIED. Persons chained or handcuffed together, in order to be conveyed to gaol, or on board the lighters for transportation, are in the cant language said to be married together.

MARROW BONES. The knees. To bring any one down on his marrow bones: to make him beg pardon on his knees. Some derive this from Mary's bones, i. e. the bones bent in honour of the Virgin Mary, but this seems rather far-fetched. Marrow bones and cleavers, principal instruments in the band of rough music: these are generally performed on by butchers, on marriages, elections, riding skimmington, and other public or joyous occasions.

MARTINET. A military term for a strict disciplinarian: from the name of a French general, famous for restoring military discipline to the French army. He first disciplined the French infantry, and regulated their method of encampment: he was killed at the siege of Doesbourg in the year 1672.

MASON'S MAUND. A sham sore above the elbow, to counterfeit a broken arm by a fall from a scaffold.

MASTER OF THE MINT. A gardener.

MASTER OF THE ROLLS. A baker.

MASTER OF THE WARDROBE. One who pawns his clothes to purchase liquor.

MATRIMONIAL PEACE-MAKER. The sugar stick, or arbor vitæ.

MAULED. Extremely drunk, or foundly beaten.

MAUDLIN DRUNK. Crying drunk. perhaps from Mary Magdalene, called Maudlin, who is always painted in tears.

MAUNDERING BROTH Scolding

MAUNDING. Afking or begging *Cant.*

MAWKES A vulgar flattern

MAW-WALLOP. A filthy compofition, fufficient to provoke vomiting

MAY BEES May bees don't fly all the year long; an anfwer to any one who prefaces a propofition with, It may be

MEALY-MOUTHED Over modeft or backward in fpeech

MEDLAR. A fruit, vulgarly called an open a-fe, of which it is more truly than delicately faid, that unlefs it is as rotten as a t—d, it is not worth a f—t.

MEGGS Guineas We forked the rum cull's meggs to the tune of fifty, we picked the gentleman's pockets of full fifty guineas. *Cant.*

MELLOW Almoft drunk.

To MELT. To fpend. Will you melt a borde? will you fpend a fhilling? The cull melted a couple of decuffes upon us, the gentleman fpent a couple of crowns upon us *Cant.*

MEMBER MUG. A chamber pot

MEN OF KENT Men born eaft of the river Medway, who are faid to have met the Conqueror in a body, each carrying a green bough in his hand, the whole appearing like a moving wood; and thereby obtaining a confirmation of their ancient privileges. The inhabitants of Kent are divided into Kentifh Men and Men of Kent Alfo a fociety held at the Fountain Tavern, Bartholomew Lane, A. D. 1743

MERCURIANS. A convivial fociety held in London.

MERKIN. Counterfeit hair for women's privy parts. See *Bailey's Dict.*

MERRY ANDREW, or MR MERRYMAN The jack pudding, jefter, or zany of a mountebank, ufually dreffed in a partycoloured coat.

MERRY-BEGOTTEN. A baftard.

MESS JOHN.

MESSJOHN A Scotch presbyterian teacher or parson.

MESSMATE. One who eats at the same mess, companion, or camerade.

METTLE The semen To fetch mettle, the act of self pollution. Mettle is also figuratively used for courage.

METTLESOME Bold, courageous.

MICHAEL Hip, Michael, your head's on fire. See HYP.

MIDSHIPMAN'S WATCH AND CHAIN A sheep's heart and pluck

MILCH COW One who is easily tricked out of his property a term used by gaolers, for prisoners who have money and bleed freely

To MILK THE PIDGEON. To endeavour at impossibilities.

MILL A chisel.

To MILL. To rob, also to break, beat out, or kill. I'll mill your glaze, I'll beat out your eye To mill a bleating cheat, to kill a sheep To mill a ken, to rob a house To mill doll, to beat hemp in Bridewell *Cant*

MILL LAY. To force open the doors of houses in order to rob them *Cant*.

MILLER. A murderer

MINE A-SE ON A BANDBOX. An answer to the offer of any thing inadequate to the purpose for which it is wanted, just as a bandbox would be if used for a seat.

MINE UNCLE'S. A pawnbroker's shop; also a necessary house. Carried to mine uncle's, pawned New-married men are also said to go to their uncle, when they leave their wives soon after the honey moon.

MINIKIN A little man or woman, also the smallest sort of pin

MINOR CLERGY Young chimney sweepers.

MINT. Gold A mint of money, common phrase for a large sum.

MISCHIEF. A man loaded with mischief, i. e. a woman on one shoulder, and a monkey on t'other.

MISH. A shirt, smock, or sheet. *Cant*.

MISH TOPPER. A coat, or petticoat.

MISS. A miss or kept mistress; a harlot.

MON

MISS LAYCOCK. The monosyllable.

MITE. A nick-name for a cheesemonger, from the small insect of that name found in cheese.

MIX METTLE. A silversmith.

MOABITES. Bailiffs, or Philistines.

MOB, or MAB. A wench, or harlot.

MOBILITY. The mob; a sort of opposite to nobility.

MOHAIR. A man in the civil line, a townsman, or tradesman: a military term, from the mohair buttons worn by persons of those descriptions, or any others not in the army, the buttons of military men being always of metal; this is generally used as a term of contempt, meaning a bourgeois, tradesman, or mechanic.

MOIETY. Half, but vulgarly used to signify a share or portion: as, He will come in for a small moiety.

MOLL. A whore.

MOLL PEATLY'S JIGG. A rogering bout.

MOLL THOMPSON'S MARK. M.T. i.e. empty: as, Take away this bottle, it has Moll Thompson's mark upon it.

MOLLY. A Miss Molly; an effeminate fellow, a sodomite.

MONDAY. Saint Monday. See SAINT.

MONEY. A girl's private parts, commonly applied to little children: as, Take care, Miss, or you will shew your money.

MONEY DROPPERS. Cheats who drop money, which they pretend to find just before some country lad; and by way of giving him a share of their good luck, entice him into a public house, where they and their confederates cheat or rob him of what money he has about him.

MONGREL. A hanger on among cheats, a spunger; also a child whose father and mother are of different countries.

MONKS AND FRIARS. Terms used by printers: monks are sheets where the letters are blotted, or printed too black; friars, those letters where the ink has failed touching the type, which are therefore white or faint.

MONKEY. To suck the monkey, to suck or draw wine, or any other liquor, privately out of a cask, by means of a straw, or small tube. Monkey's allowance, more kicks than halfpence. Who put that monkey on horseback without tying his legs? vulgar wit on a bad horseman.

MONOSYLLABLE. A woman's commodity.

MOON CURSER. A link boy: link boys are said to curse the moon; because it renders their assistance unnecessary; these gentry frequently, under colour of lighting passengers over kennels, or through dark passages, assist in robbing them. *Cant.*

MOON-EYED HEN. A squinting wench.

MOON MEN. Gypsies.

MOON RAKERS. Wiltshire men: because it is said that some men of that country, seeing the reflection of the moon in a pond, endeavoured to pull it out with a rake.

MOONSHINE. A matter or mouthful of moonshine; a trifle, nothing. The white brandy smuggled on the coasts of Kent and Sussex, is also called moonshine.

MOP. A kind of annual fair in the west of England, where farmers usually hire their servants.

MOPED. Stupid, melancholy for want of society.

MOPSEY. A dowdy, or homely woman.

MOPSQUEEZER. A maid servant, particularly a house maid.

MOPUSSES. Money.

MORE-ISH. This wine has but one fault, and that is, it is more-ish; i. e. more of it is wanted, or there is too little of it.

MORGLAG. A brown bill, or kind of halbert, formerly carried by watchmen, corruption of *more*, great or broad, and *glave*, blade.

MORRIS. Come, morris off; dance off, or get you gone: allusion to morris, i. e. *morisco*, or moorish dancing.

MORT. A woman or wench; also a yeoman's daughter. To be taken all-a-mort, to be confounded, surprised, or motionless through fear.

MOSS. A cant term for lead, because both are found on the tops of buildings.

MOSSY FACE. The mother of all saints.

MOT. A girl, or wench. See MORT.

MOTHER, or THE MOTHER. A bawd. Mother abbess, the same. Mother midnight; a midwife. Mother in law's bit, a small piece, mothers in law being supposed not apt to overload the stomachs of their husbands children.

MOTHER

MOTHER OF ALL SAINTS. The monosyllable.

MOTHER OF THE MAIDS. A bawd.

MOUCHETS. Small patches worn by ladies. from the French word *mouches*.

MOVEABLES. Rings, watches, or any toys of value.

MOUSE To speak like a mouse in a cheese; i. e. faintly or indistinctly.

MOUSETRAP. The parson's mousetrap; the state of matrimony.

MOUTH A noisy fellow Mouth half cock'd; one gaping and staring at every thing he sees To make any one laugh on the wrong or t'other side of his mouth, to make him cry or grieve

To MOW A Scotch word for the act of copulation.

MOW HEATER. A drover from their frequent sleeping on hay mows. *Cant.*

MOWER A cow.

MUCK. Money; also dung.

MUCKWORM A miser

MUCKINDER. A child's handkerchief tied to the side.

MUD. A fool, or thick-sculled fellow, also, among printers, the same as dung among journeymen taylors See DUNG.

MUD LARK A hog.

MUFF. The private parts of a woman. To the well wearing of your muff, mort, to the happy consummation of your marriage, girl a health

MUFFLING CHEAT. A napkin.

MUGGLETONIANS. The sect or disciples of Lodowick Muggleton

MULLIGRUBS Sick of the mulligrubs with eating chopped hay, low-spirited, having an imaginary sickness.

MUM. An interjection directing silence Mum for that; I shall be silent as to that. You sit like Mumchance, who was hanged for saying nothing, a friendly reproach to any one who seems low-spirited and silent

MUMCHANCE An ancient game like hazard, played with dice probably so named from the silence observed in playing at it

MUM GLASS. The monument erected on Fish-street hill, London, in memory of the great fire in 1666.

MUMBLE A SPARROW. A cruel sport practised at wakes and fairs, in the following manner. A cock sparrow whose wings are clipped, is put into the crown of a hat; a man having his arms tied behind him, attempts to bite off the sparrow's head, but is generally obliged to desist, by the many pecks and pinches he receives from the enraged bird.

MUMMER. The mouth.

MUMPERS. Originally beggars of the genteel kind, but since used for beggars in general.

MUMPERS HALL. An alehouse where beggars are harboured.

MUNDUNGUS. Bad or rank tobacco: from *mondongo*, a Spanish word signifying tripes, or the uncleaned entrails of a beast, full of filth.

MUNS. The face, or rather the mouth: from the German word *mund*, the mouth. Toute his muns, look at his face.

MUNSTER PLUMBS. Potatoes. *Irish.*

MURDER. He looked like God's revenge against murder; he looked angrily.

MUSHROOM. A person or family suddenly raised to riches and eminence: an allusion to that fungus, which starts up in a night.

MUSIC. The watch word among highwaymen, signifying the person is a friend, and must pass unmolested. Music is also an Irish term, in tossing up, to express the harp side, or reverse, of a farthing or halfpenny, opposed to the head.

MUTE. An undertaker's servant, who stands at the door of a person lying in state: so named from being supposed mute with grief.

MUTTON-HEADED. Stupid.

MUTTON MONGER. A man addicted to wenching.

MUZZLE. A beard.

MYNT. See MINT.

MYRMIDONS. The constable's assistants, watchmen, &c.

N.

NAZ

NAB, or NAB CHEAT. A hat. Penthouse nab, a large hat.

TO NAB To seize, or catch unawares. To nab the teize; to be privately whipped. To nab the stoop, to stand in the pillory. To nab the rust; a jockey term for a horse that becomes restive. To nab the snow, to steal linen left out to bleach or dry. *Cant.*

NAB GIRDER, or NOB GIRDER. A bridle.

NACK. To nave a nack, to be ready at any thing, to have a turn for it.

NACKY Ingenious.

NAILED. Secured, fixed. He offered me a deeus, and I nailed him; he offered me a crown, and I struck or fixed him.

NANNY HOUSE. A brothel.

TO NAP To cheat at dice by securing one chance. Also to catch the venereal disease. You've napt it, you are infected.

NAPPING To take any one napping, i. e. to come upon him unexpectedly, to find him asleep. as, He caught him napping, as Morse caught his mare.

NAPPER The head; also a cheat or thief.

NAPPER OF NAPS A sheep stealer. *Cant.*

NAPPY ALE Strong ale.

NASK, or NASKIN. A prison or bridewell. The new nask; Clerkenwell bridewell. Tothill-fields nask, the bridewell at Tothill-fields. *Cant.*

NATION An abbreviation of damnation a vulgar term used in Kent, Sussex, and the adjacent counties, for very Nation good, very good. A nation long way; a very long way.

NATTY LADS. Young thieves or pickpockets. *Cant*

NATURAL. A mistress, a child; also an ideot. A natural son or daughter, a love or merry begotten child, a bastard.

NAY WORD. A bye word, a proverb.

NAZARENE FORETOP The foretop of a wig made in imitation of Christ's head of hair, as represented by the painters and sculptors

NAZY

N I C

Nazy Drunken. Nazy cove or mort, a drunken rogue or harlot. Nazy nabs, drunken coxcombs.

Neb, or **Nib**. The bill of a bird, and the flit of a pen. Figuratively, the face and mouth of a woman, as, She holds up her neb, she holds up her mouth to be kissed.

Neck Stamper. The boy who collects the pots belonging to an alehouse, sent out with beer to private houses.

Neck Verse. Formerly the persons claiming the benefit of clergy were obliged to read a verse in a Latin manuscript psalter, this saving them from the gallows, was termed their neck verse; it was the first verse of the fifty-first psalm, *Miserere mei*, &c.

Neck Weed. Hemp.

Needle Point. A sharper.

Negligee. A woman's undressed gown, vulgarly termed a niggledigee.

Negroe. A black-a-moor; figuratively used for a slave. I'll be no man's negroe, I will be no man's slave.

Negroes Heads. Brown loaves delivered to the ships in ordinary.

Nettled. Teized, provoked, out of temper. He or she has pissed on a nettle, said of one who is peevish or out of temper.

New College Students. Golden scholars, silver batchelors, and leaden masters.

New Drop. The scaffold used at Newgate for hanging criminals, which dropping down, leaves them suspended. By this improvement, the use of that vulgar vehicle, a cart, is entirely left off.

New Light. One of the new light, a methodist.

Newgate Bird. A thief or sharper, frequently caged in Newgate.

Newgate Solicitor. A pettyfogging and roguish attorney, who attends the gaols to assist villains in evading justice.

To Nick. To win at dice, to hit the mark just in the nick of time, or at the critical moment.

Nick. Old Nick, the Devil.

Nick Name. A name given in ridicule or contempt; from the French *nom de nique*. N.que is a movement of the head to mark a contempt for any person or thing.

NICK NINNY. A simpleton.

NICKIN, NIKEY, or NIZEY. A soft simple fellow; also a diminutive of Isaac.

NICKNACKS. Toys, baubles, or curiosities.

NICKNACKATORY. A toy shop.

NICKUMPOOP, or NINCUMPOOP. A foolish fellow, also one who never saw his wife's ****.

NIFFYNAFFY FELLOW. A trifler.

NIG. The clippings of money. Nigging; clipping. Nigler; a clipper. *Cant*.

NIGGLING. Cutting aukwardly, trifling; also accompanying with a woman.

NIGHT MAGISTRATE. A constable.

NIGHTINGALE. A soldier who, as the term is, sings out at the halberts. It is a point of honour in some regiments, among the grenadiers, never to cry out, or become nightingales, whilst under the discipline of the cat of nine tails; to avoid which, they chew a bullet.

NIGHTMAN. One whose business it is to empty necessary houses in London, which is always done in the night the operation is called a wedding. See WEDDING.

NIGIT. A fool. seemingly a corruption and contraction of the words *an idiot*.

NIGMENOG. A very silly fellow.

To NIM. To steal, or pilfer. from the German *nemen*, to take. Nim a togeman; steal a cloak.

NIMGIMMER. A physician, or surgeon, particularly those who cure the venereal disease.

NINE LIVES. Cats are said to have nine lives, and women ten cats lives.

NINE SHILLINGS. Corruption of *nonchalance*.

NINNY, or NINNYHAMMER. A simpleton.

NIP. A cheat. Bung-nipper, a cut purse.

NIP CHEESE. A nick name for the purser of a ship. from those gentlemen being supposed sometimes to nip, or diminish, the allowance of the seamen, in that and every other article. It is also applied to stingy persons in general.

NIPPERKIN. A small measure.

NIPPS,

NIPPS. The sheers used in clipping money.

NIT SQUEEGER, i e. SQUEEZER. A hair dresser.

NO CATCHY NO HAVY. If I am not caught, I cannot be hurt. *Negro saying.*

NOB The head.

NOCK. The breech: from *nock*, a notch.

NOCKY BOY A dull simple fellow.

NOD He is gone to the land of nod, he is asleep.

NODDLE. The head.

NODDY. A simpleton or fool. Also a kind of buggy, or one-horse chaise, with a seat before it for a driver, used in and about Dublin in the manner of a hackney coach the fare is just half that of a coach, for the same distance; so that for six-pence one may have a set down, as it is called, of a mile and a half, and frequently a tumble down into the bargain. it is called a noddy from the nutation of its head. Knave noddy, the old-fashioned name for the knave of trumps.

NOKES. A ninny, or fool. John-a-Nokes and Tom-a-Stiles; two honest peaceable gentlemen, repeatedly set together by the ears by lawyers of different denominations: two fictitious names commonly used in law proceedings.

NOLL Old Noll, Oliver Cromwell

NON-CON. A nonconformist, presbyterian, or any other dissenter.

NONE-SUCH. One that is unequalled. frequently applied ironically

NOOZED Married, hanged.

NOPE A blow as, I took him a nope on the costard.

NORFOLK CAPON A red herring.

NORFOLK DUMPLING. A nick name, or term of jocular reproach to a Norfolk man, dumplings being a favourite food in that country.

NORTHUMBERLAND. Lord Northumberland's arms; a black eye so called in the last century

NORWAY NECKCLOTH. The pillory, usually made of Norway fir.

NOSE. As plain as the nose on your face, evidently to be seen. He is led by the nose, he is governed To follow one's nose, to go straight forward To put one's nose out of joint; to rival one in the favour of any person. To make a bridge of any one's nose, to pass by him in drinking. To nose a stink, to smell it. He cut off his nose to be revenged of his face; said of one who, to be revenged on his neighbour, has materially injured himself.

To NOSE. To bully.

NOSE BAG. A bag fastened to the horse's head, in which the soldiers of the cavalry put the oats given to their horses: whence the saying of, I see the nose bag in his face; i. e. he has been a private man, or rode private.

NOSE GENT. A nun.

NOSTRUM. A medicine prepared by particular persons only, a quack medicine.

NOTCH. The private parts of a woman.

NOTE. He changed his note; he told another sort of a story.

NOZZLE. The nose of a man or woman.

NUB. The neck; also coition.

NUBBING. Hanging. Nubbing cheat, the gallows. Nubbing cove; the hangman. Nubbing ken, the sessions house.

NUG. An endearing word. as, My dear nug; my dear love.

NUGGING DRESS. An out-of-the-way old-fashioned dress.

To NULL. To beat. as, He nulled him heartily.

NUMBERS. To consult the book of numbers, a term used in the House of Commons, when, instead of answering or confuting a pressing argument, the minister calls for a division, i. e. puts the matter to the vote.

NUMBSCULL. A stupid fellow.

NUMMS. A sham collar, to be worn over a dirty shirt.

NUNNERY. A bawdy house.

NUPSON. A cully, a fool.

To NURSE. To cheat. as, They nursed him out of it. An estate in the hands of trustees, for the payment of debts, is said to be at nurse.

NUTS. It was nuts for them; i. e. it was very agreeable to them.

NUTCRACKERS. The pillory. as, The cull peeped through the nutcrackers.

NUTMEGS. Testicles.

NYP, or NIP. A half pint, a nyp of ale. whence the nipperkin, a small vessel.

NYP SHOP. The Peacock in Gray's Inn Lane, where Burton ale is fold in nyps.

NYPPER A cut-purfe fo called by one Wotton, who in the year 1585 kept an academy for the education and perfection of pick-pockets and cut-purfes his fchool was near Billingfgate, London. As in the drefs of ancient times many people wore their purfes at their girdles, cutting them was a branch of the light-fingered art, which is now loft, though the name remains Maitland, from Stow, gives the following account of this Wotton. This man was a gentleman born, and fometime a merchant of good credit, but fallen by time into decay he kept an alehoufe near Smart's Key, near Billingfgate, afterwards for fome mifdemeanor put down He reared up a new trade of life, and in the fame houfe he procured all the cut-purfes about the city, to repair to his houfe, there was a fchool houfe fet up to learn young boys to cut purfes. two devices were hung up, one was a pocket, and another was a purfe, the pocket had in it certain counters, and was hung about with hawks bells, and over the top did hang a little facring bell The purfe had filver in it, and he that could take out a counter, without noife of any of the bells, was adjudged a judicial *nypper* according to their terms of art, a *foyfter* was a pick-pocket, a *nypper* was a pick-purfe, or cut-purfe

---

O.

O

O BE JOYFUL I'll make you fing O be joyful on the other fide of your mouth, a threat, implying the party threatened will be made to cry

OAF.

OLD

OAF. A silly fellow.

OAFISH. Simple

OAK. A rich man, a man of good substance and credit. To sport oak; to shut the outward door of a student's room at college. An oaken towel; an oaken cudgel. To rub a man down with an oaken towel, to beat him

OATS He has sowed his wild oats, he is staid, or sober, having left off his wild tricks.

OAR To put in one's oar, to intermeddle, or give an opinion unasked as, To be sure, you must put in your oar!

OBSTROPULOUS Vulgar misnomer of *obstreperous*, as, I was going my rounds, and found this here gemman very obstropulous.

OCCUPY. To occupy a woman; to have carnal knowledge of her.

OCTOGONIANS. This ancient and honourable order met, Nov. 16, 1750, at the Ship and Anchor, Temple Bar.

ODDS PLUT AND HER NAILS. A Welch oath, frequently mentioned in a jocular manner by persons, it is hoped, ignorant of its meaning, which is, By God's blood, and the nails with which he was nailed to the cross.

ODD-COME-SHORTLYS I'll do it one of these odd-come-shortlys; I will do it some time or another.

OGLES. Eyes. Rum ogles; fine eyes.

OIL OF BARLEY, or BARLEY BROTH. Strong beer

OIL OF GLADNESS. I will anoint you with the oil of gladness, ironically spoken for, I will beat you.

OIL OF STIRRUP. A dose the cobler gives his wife whenever she is obstropulous

OLD. Ugly. *Cant*

OLD DOG AT IT. Expert, accustomed.

OLD HAND Knowing or expert in any business.

OLD HARRY. A composition used by vintners to adulterate their wines. also a nick-name for the Devil.

OLD LING. See OLD HAT

OLD MR GORY A piece of gold.

OLD NICK. The Devil from *Neken*, the evil spirit of the north.

OLD ONE. The Devil.
OLD PEGG. Poor Yorkshire cheese.
OLD ROGER. The Devil.
OLD STAGER. One accustomed to business, one who knows mankind.
OLD TOAST. A brisk old fellow. *Cant.*
OLIVER'S SCULL. A chamber pot.
OLLI COMPOLLI. The name of one of the principal rogues of the canting crew. *Cant.*
OMNIUM GATHERUM. The whole together; jocular imitation of law Latin.
ONE IN TEN. A parson: an allusion to his tythes.
ONE OF US, or ONE OF MY COUSINS. A woman of the town, a harlot.
OPEN ARSE. A medlar. See MEDLAR.
ORGAN. A pipe. Will you cock your organ, i.e. smoke your pipe?
ORTHODOXY AND HETERODOXY. Somebody explained these terms by saying, the first was a man who had a doxy of his own, the second a person who made use of the doxy of another man.
OSCHIVES. Bone-handled knives. *Cant.*
OSMANIANS. A society held at Tunbridge Wells.
OSTLER. Oatstealer.
OTOMY. The vulgar word for a skeleton.
OTTOMISED. To be ottomised, to be dissected. You'll be scragged, ottomised, and grin in a glass case; you'll be hanged, anatomised, and your skeleton kept in a glass case at Surgeons Hall.
OVEN. A great mouth. The old woman would never have looked for her daughter in the oven, had she not been there herself.
OVERSEER. A man standing in the pillory, is, from his elevated situation, said to be made an overseer.
OUT AT HEELS, or OUT AT ELBOWS. In declining circumstances.
OUTRUN THE CONSTABLE. A man who has lived above his means, or income, is said to have outrun the constable.
OUTS. A gentleman of three outs. See GENTLEMAN.

OWL. To catch the owl, a trick practised upon ignorant country boobies, who are decoyed into a barn under pretence of catching an owl, where, after divers preliminaries, the joke ends in their having a pail of water poured upon their heads.

OWL IN AN IVY BUSH. He looks like an owl in an ivy bush; frequently said of a person with a large frizzled wig, or a woman whose hair is dressed a la-blowze.

OWLERS. Those who smuggle wool over to France.

OX HOUSE. He must go through the ox house to bed, a saying of an old fellow who marries a young girl.

OYSTER. A gob of thick phlegm, spit by a consumptive man, in law Latin, *unum viridum gobbum*.

P.

PAD

P's To mind one's P's and Q's; to be attentive to the main chance.

P. P. C. An inscription on the visiting cards of our modern fine gentlemen, signifying that they have called *pour prendre congé*, i. e. 'to take leave.' This has of late been ridiculed by cards inscribed D. I O i. e. 'Damme, I'm off.'

PACKET. A false report.

PACKTHREAD. To talk packthread, to use indecent language well wrapt up.

PAD The highway, or a robber thereon, also a bed. Foot pads; foot robbers. To go out upon the pad, to go out in order to commit a robbery.

PAD BORROWERS Horse stealers.

TO PAD THE HOOF. See TO BEAT THE HOOF.

PADDINGTON FAIR DAY. An execution day, Tyburn being in the parish or neighbourhood of Paddington. To dance the Paddington frisk, to be hanged.

PADDY.

PAR

PADDY. The general name for an Irishman; being the abbreviation of Patrick, the name of the tutelar saint of that island.

PAINTER. I'll cut your painter for you; I'll send you off: the painter being the rope that holds the boat fast to the ship. *Sea term.*

PAIR OF WINGS. Oars. *Cant*

To PALLAVER. To flatter: originally an African word for a treaty, talk, or conference.

PALLIARDS. Those whose fathers were clapperdogeons, or beggars born, and who themselves follow the same trade: the female sort beg with a number of children, borrowing them, if they have not a sufficient number of their own, and making them cry by pinching, in order to excite charity; the males make artificial sores on different parts of their bodies, to move compassion.

PAM. The knave of clubs.

PANNAM. Bread.

PANNY. A house. To do a panny, to rob a house. See the Sessions Papers. Probably, panny originally meant the butler's pantry, where the knives and forks, spoons, &c. are usually kept. *Cant*

PANTER. A hart: that animal is, in the Psalms, said to pant after the fresh water brooks. Also the human heart, which frequently pants in time of danger. *Cant*

PANTILE HOUSE. A presbyterian, or other dissenting meeting house, frequently covered with pantiles: called also a cock pit.

PANTLER. A butler.

PAP. Bread sauce; also the food of infants. His mouth is full of pap, he is still a baby.

PAPER SCULL. A thin-scull'd foolish fellow.

PAPLER. Milk pottage.

PARELL. Whites of eggs, bay salt, milk, and pump water, beat together, and poured into a vessel of wine to prevent its fretting.

PARENTHESIS. To put a man's nose into a parenthesis: to pull it, the fingers and thumb answering the hooks or crochets

PAU

The c[o]p[ulin]g of money. C[...]
[...] stockings are of two [...], [...]

[...] A jeering name for a militia man, from being frequently hired by the p[arish from w]hich [...]nabl[e...] is drawn.

A guide post, hand or finger post o[r...] rend [...]ng [tr]avellers compa[r]e[d t]o a parson, because [...] [...] people in the right w[ay]. See GUIDE POST [...]ou[l]d have luck in horse fle[sh], m[ust] kiss a par[son]

[...]ER [...] [a] jocul[a]r name, [of]te[r]m of reproach, [...] [...]he circ[ulat]ion of [the] g[ospe]l by preaching [...], [and] it is said w[h]o the h[...]pa[sto]r c[ie]d at [...]f[e]re[nce w]as under no p[...]p[...]

In[cli]ning more to one side [th]an t[o the] o[t]her, cook[...]
en[o]ugh

The pl[a]ce for pl[ayi]ng at p[al]l[ma]ge, cut into [...]m[...] [...] a rock [...] [...]ho[...] [r]ock or fund
[A] c[o]mp game with three [di]ce, [c]ou[nt]e[s], making [...]o[...]e, to [...]dd [or] win, an[d] o[...]e chances lose [...]e, or to [...]e purpo[se]

[...] C[...]ro[...] -pa[te]d, re[qu]i[t]ed

[...] [...]ER Co[...] The [of]f[...]c[e h]y[mn] of the [...]e, [...] [...]ing prie[s]ts [...] m[an]y peop[le un]der [...] g[os]pel or common pra[yer b]ook the couple [...]c[h] tw[o] of a dead bea[st], a[re] t[ie]d to [...] [to]ge[ther] [un]til them does part. [Al]so [...]al[ki]ng h[...]s, the wed[...]
[...] Also a [...] mini[s]ter or parson

[...] The m[...]rt[e]ring or pert repl[ie]s of [se]rvant[s]
[...] p[r]ayer in order to amuse one in[te]n[de]d [t]o [...] [R]e[ad]ing of prayer[s], the co[n]fu[s]ed found of a [...]fe[w p]e[r]sons pra[y]ing together.

[...]SHOP The [s]tree[t]

To conceal [i]n the h[an]d. To paum a die, to [hide in th]e palm of the hand. He paums, he cheats [...] to paum th[a]t upon me

T[h]e bell [...] some think Pa[u]nch was the original [...]hat face[t]ious prince of puppe[t]s, now called Mr. Punch,

PEE

Punch, as he is always represented with a very prominent belly, though the common opinion is, that both the name and character were taken from a celebrated Italian comedian, called Polichenello.

PAW. A hand or foot look at his dirty paws Fore paw; the hand Hind paw, the foot. To paw; to touch or handle clumsily

PAW PAW TRICKS. Forbidden tricks from the French prohibitory words *pas pas*.

TO PAY. To smear over To pay the bottom of a ship or boat, to smear it over with pitch. The devil to pay, and no pitch hot or ready *Sea term* — Also to beat: as, I will pay you as Paul paid the Ephesians, over the face and eyes, and all your d—d jaws To pay away, to fight manfully, also to eat voraciously To pay through the nose, to pay an extravagant price

TO PEACH To impeach called also to blow the gab, squeak, or turn stag.

PEAK Any kind of lace

PEAL. To ring a peal in a man's ears, to scold at him his wife rang him such a peal!

PECCAVI. To cry peccavi, to acknowledge oneself in an error, to own a fault. from the Latin *peccavi*, I have sinned

PECK Victuals Peck and booze; victuals and drink.

PECKISH Hungry

PECULIAR A mistress.

PED A basket *Cant*

PEDLAR'S FRENCH. The cant language. Pedlar's Pony; a walking stick.

TO PEEL. To strip allusion to the taking off the coat or rind of an orange or apple.

PEEPER. A spying-glass, also a looking-glass Track up the dancers, and pike with the peeper, whip up stairs, and run off with the looking-glass. *Cant*

PEEPERS. Eyes Single peeper, a one-eyed man.

PEEPING TOM A nick name for a curious prying fellow; derived from an old legendary tale, told of a taylor of Coventry, who, when Godiva countess of Chester rode at noon quite naked through that town, in order to procure certain immunities for the inhabitants (notwithstanding the rest of the people shut up their houses) slily peeped out of his window, for which he was miraculously struck blind. His figure, peeping out of the window, is still kept up in remembrance of the transaction.

PEEPY. Drowsy.

TO PEER. To look about, to be circumspect.

PEERY. Inquisitive, suspicious. The cull's peery; that fellow suspects something. There's a peery, 'tis snitch, we are observed, there's nothing to be done.

PEG. Old peg; poor hard Suffolk cheese. A peg is also a blow with a straight arm, a term used by the professors of gymnastic arts. A peg in the day-light, the victualling office, or the haltering-place, a blow in the eye, stomach, or under the ear.

PEG TRANTUM'S. Gone to Peg Trantum's, dead.

PEGO. The penis of man or beast.

PELL-MELL. Tumultuously, helter skelter, jumbled together.

PELT. A heat, chafe, or passion; as, What a pelt he was in! Pelt is also the skin of several beasts.

PENANCE BOARD. The pillory.

PENNY WISE AND POUND FOOLISH. Saving in small matters, and extravagant in great.

PENNYWORTH. An equivalent. A good pennyworth, a cheap bargain.

PENTHOUSE NAB. A broad-brimmed hat.

PEPPERED. Infected with the venereal disease.

PEPPERY. Warm, passionate.

PERKIN. Water cyder.

PERRIWINKLE. A wig.

PERSUADERS. Spurs.

PET. In a pet, in a passion or miff.

PETER. A portmanteau or cloke bag. Biter of peters, one that makes it a trade to steal boxes and trunks from behind stage coaches or out of waggons. To rob Peter to pay Paul, to borrow of one man to pay another; styled also manœuvring the apostles.

PETER GUNNER, will kill all the birds that died last summer. A piece of wit commonly thrown out at a person walking through a street or village near London, with a gun in his hand

PETER LAY The department of stealing portmanteaus, trunks, &c.

PETER LUG. Who is Peter Lug? who lets the glass stand at his door, or before him?

PETTICOAT HOLD. One who has an estate during his wife's life, called the apron string hold

PETTICOAT PENSIONER. One kept by a woman for secret services.

PETTISH. Passionate

PETTYFOGGER. A little dirty attorney, ready to undertake any litigious or bad cause it is derived from the French words *petit vogue*, of small credit, or little reputation

PHAROAH Strong malt liquor.

PHILISTINES Bailiffs, or officers of justice, also drunkards.

PHILO DRACO SANGUINARIANS, A club that met in London.

PHOENIX MEN Firemen belonging to an insurance office, which gave a badge charged with a phoenix these men were called likewise firedrakes

PHRASE OF PAPER Half a quarter of a sheet. See VESSEL.

PHIZ The face Rum phyz, an odd face or countenance.

PICAROON A pirate, also a sharper

PICKANINY. A young child, an infant *Negro term*

PICKING Pilfering, petty larceny.

PICKLE An arch waggish fellow In pickle, or in the pickling tub, in a salivation. There are rods in brine, or pickle, for him, a punishment awaits him, or is prepared for him. Pickle herring, the zany or merry Andrew of a mountebank. See JACK PUDDEN

PICKT HATCH. To go to the manor of pickt hatch, a cant name for some part of the town noted for bawdy houses in Shakespeare's time, and used by him in that sense

PICKTHANK A tale bearer, or mischief maker

PICTURE FRAME The sheriff's picture frame, the gallows or pillory

To PIDDLE. To make water. a childish expression; as, Mammy, I want to piddle. Piddling also means trifling, or doing any thing in a small degree perhaps from peddling

PIG. Sixpence, a sow's baby Pig-widgeon, a simpleton. To pig together; to lie or sleep together, two or more in a bed Cold pig, a jocular punishment inflicted by the maid servants, or other females of the house, on persons lying over long in bed it consists in pulling off all the bed clothes, and leaving them to pig or lie in the cold To buy a pig in a poke; to purchase any thing without seeing it. Pigs eyes; small eyes Pigsnyes, the same a vulgar term of endearment to a woman He can have boiled pig at home, a mark of being master of his own house an allusion to a well-known poem and story Brandy is Latin for pig and goose, an apology for drinking a dram after either.

PIG-HEADED Obstinate

PIG RUNNING. A piece of game frequently practised at fairs, wakes, &c A large pig, whose tail is cut short, and both soaped and greased, being turned out, is hunted by the young men and boys, and becomes the property of him who can catch and hold him by the tail, above the height of his head

PIGEON A weak silly fellow, easily imposed on. To pigeon; to cheat To milk the pigeon, to attempt impossibilities, to be put to shifts for want of money. To fly a blue pigeon, to steal lead off a church.

PIGEONS MILK. Boys and novices are frequently sent on the first of April to buy pigeons milk

To PIKE. To run away Pike off, run away

PILGRIM'S SALVE A sirreverence, human excrement

PILL, or PEELE GARLICK Said originally to mean one whose skin or hair had fallen off from some disease, chiefly the venereal one, but now commonly used by persons speaking of themselves. as, There stood poor pill garlick; i. e there stood I.

PILLALOO. The Irish cry or howl at funerals.

PIMP. A male procurer, or cock bawd, also a small faggot used about London for lighting fires, named from introducing the fire to the coals

PIMP WHISKIN. A top trader in pimping.

PIN In or to a merry pin; almost drunk: an allusion to a sort of tankard, formerly used in the north, having silver pegs or pins set at equal distances from the top to the bottom: by the rules of good fellowship, every person drinking out of one of these tankards, was to swallow the quantity contained between two pins; if he drank more or less, he was to continue drinking till he ended at a pin: by this means persons unaccustomed to measure their draughts were obliged to drink the whole tankard. Hence, when a person was a little elevated with liquor, he was said to have drank to a merry pin.

PIN BASKET. The youngest child.

PIN MONEY. An allowance settled on a married woman for her pocket expences.

PINCH At a pinch; on an exigency.

TO PINCH ON THE PARSON'S SIDE. To defraud the parson of his tythes.

PINCHERS Rogues who, in changing money, by dexterity of hand frequently secrete two or three shillings out of the change of a guinea. This species of roguery is called the pinch, or pinching lay.

TO PINK To stab or wound with a small sword: probably derived from the holes formerly cut in both men and women's clothes, called pinking. Pink of the fashion, the top of the mode. To pink and wink, frequently winking the eyes through a weakness in them.

PINKING-DINDEE. A sweater or monawk. *Irish*

PINNERIANS. A society formerly held at the Sun in Claremarket.

PINTLE SMITH, or PINTLE TAGGER. A surgeon.

PIPER A broken-winded horse.

PISCINARIANS A club or brotherhood, A. D. 1743.

PISS He will piss when he can't whistle, he will be hanged. He shall not piss my money against the wall, he shall not have my money to spend in liquor.

He who once a good name gets,
May piss a-bed, and say he sweats.

PISS-BURNED Discoloured: commonly applied to a discoloured grey wig.

PLA

PISS MAKER   A great drinker, one much given to liquor.

PISS POT HALL   A house at Clapton, near Hackney, built by a potter chiefly out of the profits of chamber pots, in the bottom of which the portrait of Dr Sacheverel was depicted

PISS PROPHET   A physician who judges of the diseases of his patients solely by the inspection of their urine

PISS-PROUD   Having a false erection. That old fellow thought he had an erection, but his ―― was only piss-proud; said of any old fellow who marries a young wife

PISSING DOWN ANY ONE'S BACK   Flattering him

PISSING PINS AND NEEDLES   To have a gonorrhea

PIT   To lay pit and boxes into one, an operation in midwifery, whereby the division between the anus and vagina is cut through and demolished a simile borrowed from the playhouse, when, for the benefit of some favourite player, the pit and boxes are laid together. The pit is also the hole under the gallows, where poor rogues unable to pay the fees are buried.

PIT'S PICTURE   A window stopt up on the inside, to save the tax imposed in that gentleman's administration *Party wit.*

PIT-A-PAT   The palpitation of the heart as, My heart went pit-a-pat Pintledy-pantledy; the same.

PITCH-KETTLED.   Stuck fast, confounded.

PITCHER   The miraculous pitcher, that holds water with the mouth downwards; a woman's commodity. She has cracked her pitcher or pipkin, she has lost her maidenhead

PIZZY CLUB   A society held, A. D 1744, at the sign of the Tower, on Tower-hill president, Don Pizzaro

PLAISTER OF WARM GUTS   One warm belly clapped to another a receipt frequently prescribed for different disorders

PLANT   The place in the house of the fence, where stolen goods are secreted

TO PLANT   To lay, place, or hide Plant your wids and flow them, be careful what you say, or let slip. Also to bury. as, He was planted by the parson

PLATE   Money, silver, prize He is in for the plate, he has won the *heat*, i e is infected with the venereal disorder a simile drawn from horse racing When the plate fleet comes in; when money comes to hand.

PLATTER-FACED.   Broad-faced.

PLAY

POK

PLAY To play booty, to play with an intention to lose. To play the whole game, to cheat. To play least in sight, to hide, or keep out of the way. To play the devil, to be guilty of some great irregularity or mismanagement.

PLUCK Courage. He wants pluck, he is a coward. Against the pluck; against the inclination. Pluck the ribbon, ring the bell. To pluck a crow with one, to settle a dispute, to reprove one for some past transgression. To pluck a rose, an expression said to be used by women for going to the necessary-house, which in the country usually stands in the garden. To pluck also signifies to deny a degree to a candidate at one of the Universities, on account of insufficiency.

PLUG TAIL A man's penis.

PLUMB An hundred thousand pounds.

PLUMP Fat, full, fleshy. Plump in the pocket, full in the pocket. To plump, to strike, or shoot. I'll give you a plump in the bread basket, or the victualling office, I'll give you a blow in the stomach. Plump his peepers, or day lights, give him a blow in the eyes. He pulled out his pops and plumped him, he drew out his pistols and shot him. A plumper, a single vote at an election. Plump also means directly, or exactly. as, It fell plump upon him, it fell directly upon him.

PLUMP CURRANT I am not plump currant, I am out of sorts.

PLUMPERS Contrivances said to be formerly worn by old maids, for filling out a pair of shrivelled cheeks.

PLIER. A crutch, also a trader.

POGY. Drunk.

POINT. To stretch a point; to exceed some usual limit, to take a great stride. Breeches were usually tied up with points, a kind of short laces, formerly given away by the churchwardens at Whitsuntide, under the denomination of tags. by taking a great stride these were stretched.

POISONED Big with child. that wench is poisoned, see how her belly is swelled. Poison-pated, red-haired.

POKE A blow with the fist. I'll lend you a poke. A poke likewise means a sack. whence, to buy a pig in a poke, i. e. to buy any thing without seeing or properly examining it.

POP

POKER. A sword. Fore pokers; aces and kings at cards.

POLE. He is like a rope dancer's pole, lead at both ends; saying of a stupid sluggish fellow.

POLISH. To polish the king's iron with one's eyebrows, to be in gaol, and look through the iron grated windows. To polish a bone, to eat a meal. Come and polish a bone with me, come and eat a dinner or supper with me.

POLL. The head, jolly nob, napper, or knowledge box, also a wig.

POLT. A blow. Lend him a polt in the muns, lend him a knock in the face.

TO POMMEL. To beat. originally confined to beating with the hilt of a sword, the nob being, from its similarity to a small apple, called *pomelle*, in Spanish it is still called the apple of the sword. As the clenched fist likewise somewhat resembles an apple, perhaps that might occasion the term pommelling to be applied to fistycuffs.

POMP. To save one's pomp at whist, is to score five before the adversaries are up, or win the game. originally derived from *pimp*, which is Welsh for five, and should be, I have saved my pimp.

POMPAGINIS. Aqua pompaginis, pump water. See AQUA.

POMPKIN. A man or woman of Boston in America. from the number of pompkins raised and eaten by the people of that country. Pompkinshire, Boston and its dependencies.

PONTIUS PILATE. A pawnbroker. Pontius Pilate's guards, the first regiment of foot, or royal Scots. so intitled from their supposed great antiquity. Pontius Pilate's counsellor; one who like him can say, *Non invenio causam*, I can find no cause.

POPE. A figure burned annually every fifth of November, in memory of the gunpowder plot, which is said to have been carried on by the papists.

POPE'S NOSE. The rump of a turkey.

POPS. Pistols. Pop shop, a pawnbroker's shop. To pop, to pawn, also to shoot. I popt my tatler, I pawned my watch. I popt the cull, I shot the man. His means are two pops and a galloper, that is, he is a highwayman.

POPLERS. Pottage. *Cant.*

PORK.

PORK. To cry pork, to give intelligence to the undertaker of a funeral; metaphor borrowed from the raven, whose note sounds like the word *pork*. Ravens are said to smell carrion at a distance.

PORKER. A hog; also a Jew.

PORRIDGE. Keep your breath to cool your porridge, i.e. hold your tongue.

PORRIDGE ISLAND. An alley leading from St. Martin's church-yard to Round-court, chiefly inhabited by cooks, who cut off ready-dressed meat of all sorts, and also sell soup.

POSEY, or POSES. A nosegay. I shall see you ride backwards up Holborn-hill, with a book in one hand, and a posey in t'other, i.e. I shall see you go to be hanged. Malefactors who piqued themselves on being properly equipped for that occasion, had always a nosegay to smell to, and a prayer book, although they could not read.

POSSE MOBILITATIS. The mob.

POST MASTER GENERAL. The prime minister, who has the patronage of all posts and places.

POST NOINTER. A house painter, who occasionally paints or anoints posts. Knight of the post, a false evidence, one ready to swear any thing for hire. From post to pillar, backwards and forwards.

POSTILION OF THE GOSPEL. A parson who hurries over the service.

POT. The pot calls the kettle black a—se, one rogue exclaims against another.

POT CONVERTS. Proselytes to the Romish church, made by the distribution of victuals and money.

POT HUNTER. One who hunts more for the sake of the prey than the sport. Pot valiant, courageous from drink. Pot wallopers, persons entitled to vote in certain boroughs by having boiled a pot there.

POTATO TRAP. The mouth. Shut your potato trap, and give your tongue a holiday, i.e. be silent. *Irish wit.*

POTHOOKS AND HANGERS. A scrawl, bad writing.

POULAIN. A bubo. *French.*

POUND. A prison. See LOB's POUND. Pounded; imprisoned. Shut up in the parson's pound; married

POWDER

P R I

PowDER Monkey. A boy on board a ship of war, whose business it is to fetch powder from the magazine.

POWDERING TUB. The same as pickling tub. See PICKLING TUB.

PRAD LAY. Cutting bags from behind horses. *Cant.*

PRANCER. A horse. Prancer's nab, a horse's head, used as a seal to a counterfeit pass. At the sign of the prancer's poll, i. e. the nag's head.

PRATE ROAST. A talkative boy. *Cant.*

PRATING CHEAT. The tongue.

PRATTS. Buttocks, also a tinder box. *Cant.*

PRATTLE BROTH. Tea. See CHATTER BROTH, SCANDAL BROTH, &c.

PRATTLING BOX. The pulpit.

PRAY. She prays with her knees upwards; said of a woman much given to gallantry and intrigue. At her last prayers; saying of an old maid.

PREADAMITE QUACKBITES. This great and laudable society (as they termed themselves) held their grand chapter at the Coal-hole.

PREY. Money.

PRICK. The virile member.

PRICK-EARED. A prick-eared fellow; one whose ears are longer than his hair; an appellation frequently given to puritans, who considered long hair as the mark of the Whore of Babylon.

PRICKLOUSE. A taylor.

PRIEST-CRAFT. The art of awing the laity, managing their consciences, and diving into their pockets.

PRIEST-LINKED. Married.

PRIEST-RIDDEN. Governed by a priest, or priests.

PRIG. A thief, a cheat; also a conceited coxcomical fellow.

PRIG NAPPER. A thief taker.

PRIGGERS. Thieves in general. Priggers of prancers; horse stealers. Priggers of cacklers, robbers of hen roosts.

PRIGGING. Riding, also lying with a woman.

PRIGSTAR. A rival in love.

PRIMINARY. I had like to be brought into a priminary, i. e. into trouble; from *premun re.*

PRINCE

PRY

PRINCE PRIG. A king of the gypsies; also the head thief or receiver general.

PRINCES When the majesty of the people was a favourite term in the House of Commons, a celebrated wit, seeing chimney sweepers dancing on a May day, styled them the young princes.

PRINCOD A pincushion. *Scotch* —Also a round plump man or woman

PRINCOX. A pert, lively, forward fellow.

PRINCUM PRANCUM Mrs. Princum Prancum; a nice, precise, formal madam

PRINKING. Dressing over nicely prinked up as if he came out of a bandbox, or fit to set upon a cupboard's head.

PRINT All in print; quite neat or exact, set, screwed up. Quite in print, set in a formal manner.

PRISCIAN. To break Priscian's head, to write or speak false grammar Priscian was a famous grammarian, who flourished at Constantinople in the year 525; and who was so devoted to his favourite study, that to speak false Latin in his company, was as disagreeable to him as to break his head.

PRITTLE PRATTLE Insignificant talk· generally applied to women and children

PROG. Provision. Rum prog, choice provision. To prog; to be on the hunt for provision called in the military term to forage.

PROPS Crutches

PROPERTY To make a property of any one, to make him a conveniency, tool, or cat's paw, to use him as one's own

PROUD. Desirous of copulation A proud bitch; a bitch at heat, or desirous of a dog.

PROVENDER He from whom any money is taken on the high-way perhaps providor, or provider *Cant*

PRUNELLA Mr Prunella; a parson. parsons gowns being frequently made of prunella

TO PRY To examine minutely into a matter or business. A prying fellow, a man of impertinent curiosity, apt to peep and enquire into other men's secrets

PUBLIC

P U M

PUBLIC LEDGER. A prostitute; because, like that paper, she is open to all parties.

PUCKER. All in a pucker, in a dishabille. Also in a fright: as, She was in a terrible pucker.

PUCKER WATER. Water impregnated with allum, or other astringents, used by old experienced traders to counterfeit virginity.

PUDDINGS. The guts. I'll let out your puddings.

PUDDING-HEADED FELLOW. A stupid fellow, one whose brains are all in confusion.

PUDDING SLEEVES. A parson.

PUDDING TIME. In good time, or at the beginning of a meal; pudding formerly making the first dish. To give the crows a pudding; to die. You must eat some cold pudding, to settle your love.

PUFF, or PUFFER. One who bids at auctions, not with an intent to buy, but only to raise the price of the lot, for which purpose many are hired by the proprietor of the goods on sale.

PUFF GUTS. A fat man.

PUFFING. Bidding at an auction, as above; also praising any thing above its merits, from interested motives. The art of puffing is, at present, greatly practised, and essentially necessary, in all trades, professions, and callings. To puff and blow; to be out of breath.

PUG. A Dutch pug, a kind of lap dog, formerly much in vogue; also a general name for a monkey.

PUG CARPENTER. An inferior carpenter, one employed only in small jobs.

PUG DRINK. Watered cyder.

PUGNOSED, or PUGIFIED. A person with a snub or turned up nose.

PULLY HAWLY. To have a game at pully hawly; to romp with women.

PUMP. A thin shoe. To pump; to endeavour to draw a secret from any one without his perceiving it. Your pump is good, but your sucker is dry; said by one to a person who is attempting to pump him. Pumping was also a punishment for bailiffs, who attempted to act in priviliged places,

P U Z

places, such as the Mint, Temple, &c. . it is also a piece of discipline administered to a pick-pocket caught in the fact, when there is no pond at hand To pump ship, to make water, and sometimes to vomit. *Sea phrase.*

PUMP-WATER. He was christened in pump-water; commonly said of a person that has a red face

PUNCH. A liquor called by foreigners Contradiction, from its being composed of spirits to make it strong, water to make it weak, lemon juice to make it sour, and sugar to make it sweet. Punch is also the name of the prince of puppets, the chief wit and support of a puppet-show. To punch it, is a cant term for running away Punchable; old passable money, anno 1695 A girl that is ripe for man, is called a punchable wench.

PUNK. A little whore, also a soldier's trull. See TRULL.

PUNY. Weak A puny child; a weak little child. A puny stomach, a weak stomach. Puny, or puisne judge; the last made judge.

PUPIL MONGERS. Persons at the universities who make it their business to instruct and superintend a number of pupils.

PUPPY. An affected or conceited coxcomb

PURBLIND. Dim-sighted.

PURE. A harlot, or lady of easy virtue.

PUREST PURE. A courtezan of high fashion

PURL. Ale in which wormwood has been infused.

PURL ROYAL. Canary wine, with a dash of tincture of wormwood.

PURSE PROUD. One that is vain of his riches.

PURSENETS. Goods taken up at thrice their value, by young spendthrifts, upon trust

PURSER'S PUMP. A bassoon from its likeness to a syphon, called a purser's pump.

PURSY, or PURSIVE. Short-breathed, or foggy, from being over fat.

PUSHING SCHOOL A fencing school, also a brothel

PUT. A country put, an ignorant awkward clown To put upon any one, to attempt to impose on him, or to make him the but of the company.

PUZZLE-CAUSE A lawyer who has a confused understanding.

PUZZLE-TEXT. An ignorant blundering parson.

Q.

QUE

QUACK. An ungraduated ignorant pretender to skill in physic, a vender of nostrums.

QUACK-SALVER. A mountebank, a seller of salves.

QUACKING CHEAT. A duck.

QUAG. Abbreviation of quagmire; marshy, moorish ground.

QUAIL-PIPE. A woman's tongue, also a device to take birds of that name, by imitating their call. Quail-pipe boots, boots resembling a quail-pipe, from the number of plaits; they were much worn in the reign of Charles II.

QUAKERS. A religious sect; so called from their agitations in preaching.

QUAKING CHEAT. A calf or sheep.

QUANDARY. To be in a quandary; to be puzzled. Also one so over-gorged, as to be doubtful which he should do first, sh—e or spew. Some derive the term quandary from the French phrase *qu'en d'raije?* what shall I say of it? others from an Italian word signifying a conjuror's circle.

QUARREL-PICKER. A glazier; from the small squares in casements, called *carreaux*, vulgarly quarrels.

QUARROMES, or QUARRON. A body. *Cant.*

QUARTERED. Divided into four parts. To be hanged, drawn, and quartered, is the sentence on traitors and rebels. Persons receiving part of the salary of an office from the holder of it, by virtue of an agreement with the donor, are said to be quartered on him. Soldiers billeted on a publican are likewise said to be quartered on him.

TO QUASH. To suppress, annul, or overthrow, vulgarly pronounced *squash*; they squashed the indictment.

QUEAN. A slut, a worthless woman, a strumpet.

QUEEN DICK. To the tune of the life and death of Queen Dick. That happened in the reign of Queen Dick, 1 0. never.

QUE

QUEEN STREET. A man governed by his wife, is said to live in Queen Street, or at the sign of the Queen's Head.

QUEER, or QUIRE. Base, roguish, bad, naught, or worthless. How queerly the cull touts; how roguishly the fellow looks. It also means odd, uncommon. *Cant.*

QUEER AS DICK'S HATBAND Out of order, without knowing one's disease.

QUEER BAIL. Insolvent sharpers, who make a profession of bailing persons arrested they are generally styled Jew bail, from that branch of business being chiefly carried on by the sons of Juda. The lowest sort of these, who borrow or hire clothes to appear in, are called Mounters, from their mounting particular dresses suitable to the occasion. *Cant.*

QUEER BIRDS. Rogues relieved from prison, and returned to their old trade.

QUEER BIT-MAKERS. Coiners. *Cant.*

QUEER BITCH An odd out-of-the-way fellow.

QUEER BLUFFER The master of a public-house the resort of rogues and sharpers, a cut-throat inn or alehouse keeper

QUEER BUNG An empty purse

QUEER CHECKERS Among strolling players, door keepers who defraud the company, by falsely checking the number of people in the house.

QUEER COLE FENCER. A putter off, or utterer, of bad money.

QUEER COLE MAKER A maker of bad money.

QUEER COVE A rogue *Cant*

QUEER CUFFIN A justice of the peace, also a churl.

QUEER DEGEN. An ordinary sword, brass or iron hilted.

QUEER KEN A prison *Cant.*

QUEER KICKS A bad pair of breeches.

QUEER MORT A diseased strumpet *Cant.*

QUEER NAB. A felt hat, or other bad hat.

QUEER PLUNGERS Cheats who throw themselves into the water, in order that they may be taken up by their accomplices, who carry them to one of the houses appointed by the Humane Society for the recovery of drowned persons, where they are rewarded by the society with a guinea each;

and the supposed drowned person, pretending he was driven to that extremity by great necessity, is also frequently sent away with a contribution in his pocket.

QUEER PRANCER. A bad, worn-out, foundered horse, also a cowardly or faint-hearted horse stealer.

QUEER ROOSTER. An informer that pretends to be sleeping, and thereby overhears the conversation of thieves in night cellars.

QUI TAM. A qui tam horse, one that will both carry and draw. *Law wit.*

To QUIBBLE. To make subtle distinctions, also to play upon words.

QUICK AND NIMBLE, more like a bear than a squirrel. Jeeringly said to any one moving sluggishly on a business or errand that requires dispatch.

QUID. The quantity of tobacco put into the mouth at one time. To quid tobacco, to chew tobacco. *Quid est hoc? hoc est quid.*

QUIDS. Cash, money. Can you tip me any quids? can you lend me some money?

QUIFFING. Rogering. See To ROGER.

QUIDNUNC. A politician; from a character of that name in the farce of the Upholsterer.

QUILL DRIVER. A clerk, scribe, or hackney writer.

QUIM. The private parts of a woman: perhaps from the Spanish *quemar*, to burn.

QUINSEY. Choaked by a hempen quinsey, hanged.

QUIPPS. Girds, taunts, jests.

QUIRE, or CHOIR BIRD. A complete rogue, one that has sung in different choirs or cages, i. e. gaols. *Cant.*

QUIRKS AND QUILLETS. Tricks and devices. Quirks in law, subtle distinctions and evasions.

QUIZ. A strange-looking fellow, an odd dog. *Oxford.*

QUOD. Newgate, or any other prison. The dab's in quod, the poor rogue is in prison.

QUOTA. Snack, share, part, proportion, or dividend. Tip me my quota; give me part of the winnings, booty, or plunder. *Cant.*

R.

RABBIT. A Welch rabbit, bread and cheese toasted, i. e. a Welsh rare bit. Rabbits were also a sort of wooden canns to drink out of, now out of use.

RABBIT CATCHER. A midwife.

RABBIT SUCKERS. Young spendthrifts, taking up goods on trust at great prices.

RACK RENT. Rent strained to the utmost value. To lie at rack and manger; to be in great disorder.

RACKABACK. A gormagon. See GORMAGON.

RAFFS. An appellation given by the gownsmen of the university of Oxford to the inhabitants of that place.

RAG. A farthing.

To RAG. To abuse, and tear to rags the characters of the persons abused. She gave him a good ragging, or ragged him off heartily.

RAG CARRIER. An ensign.

RAG FAIR. An inspection of the linen and necessaries of a company of soldiers, commonly made by their officers on Mondays or Saturdays.

RAG WATER. Gin, or any other common dram. these liquors seldom failing to reduce those that drink them to rags.

RAGAMUFFIN. A ragged fellow, one all in tatters, a tatterdemallion.

RAILS See HEAD RAILS. A dish of rails; a lecture, jobation, or scolding from a married woman to her husband.

RAINBOW. Knight of the rainbow; a footman. from being commonly clothed in garments of different colours. A meeting of gentlemen styled of the most ancient order of the rainbow, was advertised to be held at the Foppington's Head, Moorfields.

RAINY DAY. To lay up something for a rainy day; to provide against a time of necessity or distress.

RAKE, RAKEHELL, or RAKESHAME. A lewd, debauched fellow.

RALPH SPOONER. A fool.

RAM CAT. A he cat.

RAMMISH. Rank. Rammish woman, a sturdy virago.

RAMMER. The arm. The busnapper's kenchin seized my rammer, i. e. the watchman laid hold of my arm. *Cant.*

RAMSHACKLED. Out of repair. A ramshackled house; perhaps a corruption of *ransacked*, i. e. plundered.

RANDLE. A set of nonsensical verses, repeated in Ireland by school boys, and young people, who have been guilty of breaking wind backwards before any of their companions; if they neglect this apology, they are liable to certain kicks, pinches, and fillips, which are accompanied with diverse admonitory couplets.

RANDY. Obstreperous, unruly, rampant.

RANGING. Intriguing with a variety of women.

RANK. Stinking, rammish, ill-flavoured, also strong, great. A rank knave, a rank coward. perhaps the latter may allude to an ill favour caused by fear.

RANK RIDER. A highwayman.

RANTALLION. One whose scrotum is so relaxed as to be longer than his penis, i. e. whose shot pouch is longer than the barrel of his piece.

RANTIPOLE. A rude romping boy or girl; also a gadabout dissipated woman. To ride rantipole, the same as riding St George. See ST GEORGE.

RANTUM SCANTUM. Playing at rantum scantum, making the beast with two backs.

TO RAP. To take a false oath; also to curse. He rapped out a volley, i. e. he swore a whole volley of oaths. To rap, means also to exchange or barter. a rap is likewise an Irish halfpenny. Rap on the knuckles; a reprimand.

RAPPAREES. Irish robbers, or outlaws, who in the time of Oliver Cromwell were armed with short weapons, called in Irish *rapiers*, used for ripping persons up.

RAPPER. A swinging great lye.

RAREE SHEW MEN. Poor Savoyards, who subsist by shewing the magic lanthorn and marmots about London.

RASCAL. A rogue or villain: a term borrowed from the chase, a rascal originally meaning a lean shabby deer, at the time of changing his horns, penis, &c. whence, in the vulgar acceptation, rascal is conceived to signify a man without genitals: the regular vulgar answer to this reproach, if uttered by a woman, is the offer of an ocular demonstration of the virility of the party so defamed. Some derive it from *rascaglione*, an Italian word signifying a man without testicles, or an eunuch.

RAT. A drunken man or woman taken up by the watch, and confined in the watch-house. *Cant.*—To smell a rat; to suspect some intended trick, or unfair design.

RATS. Of these there are the following kinds: a black rat and a grey rat, a py-rat and a cu-rat.

RATTLE. A dice box. To rattle, to talk without consideration; also to move off or go away. To rattle one off, to rate or scold him.

RATTLE-PATE. A volatile, unsteady, or whimsical man or woman.

RATTLE-TRAPS. A contemptuous name for any curious portable piece of machinery, or philosophical apparatus.

RATTLER. A coach. Rattle and pad; a coach and horses.

RATTLING COVE. A coachman. *Cant.*

RATTLING MUMPERS. Beggars who ply coaches. *Cant.*

RAW HEAD AND BLOODY BONES. A bull-beggar, or scare-child, with which foolish nurses terrify crying brats.

READER. A pocket book. *Cant.*

READER MERCHANTS. Pickpockets, chiefly young Jews, who ply about the bank to steal the pocket books of persons who have just received their dividends there.

READY. The ready rhino, money. *Cant.*

REBUS. A riddle or pun on a man's name, expressed in sculpture or painting: thus a bolt or arrow, and a tun, for Bolton; death's head, and a ton, for Morton.

RECKON. To reckon without one's host, to make an erroneous judgment in one's own favour. To cast up one's reckoning or accounts; to vomit.

To RECRUIT To get a fresh supply of money
RED FUSTIAN Port wine.
RED LANE The throat. Gone down the red lane; swallowed.
RED LATTICE. A public house.
RED LETTER DAY. A saint's day or holiday, marked in the calendars with red letters. Red letter men; Roman Catholics. from their observation of the saints days marked in red letters.
RED RAG. The tongue. Shut your potatoe trap, and give your red rag a holiday, i e. shut your mouth, and let your tongue rest Too much of the red rag; too much tongue.
RED SAIL-YARD DOCKERS. Buyers of stores stolen out of the royal yards and docks.
RED SHANK. A duck. *Cant.*
RELIGIOUS HORSE. One much given to prayer, or apt to be down upon his knees.
RELIGIOUS PAINTER. One who does not break the commandment which prohibits the making of the likeness of any thing in heaven or earth, or in the waters under the earth.
REMEDY CRITCH. A chamber pot, or member mug
REMEMBER PARSON MELHAM. Drink about a Norfolk phrase
RENDEZVOUS. A place of meeting. The rendezvous of the beggars were, about the year 1638, according to the bell-man, St. Quinton's, the Three Crowns in the Vintry, St Tybs, and at Knapsbury. these were four barns within a mile of London In Middlesex were four other harbours, called Draw the Pudding out of the Fire, the Cross Keys in Craneford parish, St. Julian's in Isleworth parish, and the House of Pettie in Northall parish In Kent, the King's Barn near Dartford, and Ketbrooke near Blackheath.
REP. A woman of reputation
REPOSITORY. A lock-up or spunging house, a gaol Also livery stables, where horses and carriages are sold by auction.
RESCOUNTERS. The time of settlement between the bulls and bears of Exchange-alley, when the losers must pay

their

their differences, or become lame ducks, and waddle out of the Alley.

RESURRECTION MEN Persons employed by the students in anatomy to steal dead bodies out of church-yards.

REVERENCE An ancient custom, which obliges any person easing himself near the highway or foot path, on the word *reverence* being given him by a passenger, to take off his hat with his teeth, and without moving from his station to throw it over his head, by which it frequently falls into the excrement this was considered as a punishment for the breach of delicacy A person refusing to obey this law, might be pushed backwards Hence, perhaps, the term *sir-reverence*.

REVERSED. A man set by bullies on his head, that his money may fall out of his breeches, which they afterwards by accident pick up. See HOISTING

REVIEW OF THE BLACK CUIRASSIERS. A visitation of the clergy See CROW FAIR

RHINO Money *Cant*

RHINOCERICAL Rich the cull is rhinocerical. *Cant*

RIB. A wife an allusion to our common mother Eve, made out of Adam's rib. A crooked rib, a cross-grained wife.

RIBALDRY Vulgar abusive language, such as was spoken by ribalds. Ribalds were originally mercenary soldiers, who travelled about, serving any master for pay, but afterwards degenerated into a mere banditti

RIBBIN Money. The ribbin runs thick, i. e there is plenty of money *Cant*.

To RIBROAST. To beat I'll ribroast him to his heart's content.

RICH FACE, or NOSE A red pimpled face.

RICHARD SNARY. A dictionary. A country lad, having been reproved for calling persons by their christian names, being sent by his master to borrow a dictionary, thought to shew his breeding by asking for a Richard Snary.

RIDER. A person who receives part of the salary of a place or appointment from the ostensible occupier, by virtue of an agreement with the donor, or great man appointing The rider is said to be quartered upon the possessor, who

often

often has one or more perfons thus riding behind him. See QUARTERED

RIDGE A guinea. Ridge cully, a goldfmith. *Cant*

RIDING ST GEORGE The woman uppermoft in the amorous congrefs, that is, the dragon upon St. George. This is faid to be the way to get a bifhop

RIDING SKIMMINGTON A ludicrous cavalcade, in ridicule of a man beaten by his wife. It confifts of a man riding behind a woman, with his face to the horfe's tail, holding a diftaff in his hand, at which he feems to work, the woman all the while beating him with a ladle, a fmock difplayed on a ftaff is carried before them as an emblematical ftandard, denoting female fuperiority they are accompanied by what is called the *rough mufic*, that is, frying pans, bulls horns, marrow bones and cleavers, &c. A proceffion of this kind is admirably defcribed by Butler in his Hudibras He rode private, i e. was a private trooper

RIFF RAFF Low vulgar perfons, mob, tag-rag and bobtail.

RIG. Fun, game, diverfion, or trick To run one's rig upon any particular perfon, to make him a but. I am up to your rig, I am a match for your tricks

RIGGING Clothing. I'll unrig the blofs, I'll ftrip the wench. Rum rigging, fine clothes. The cull has rum rigging, let's ding him and mill him, and pike, the fellow has good clothes, let's knock him down, rob him, and fcour off, i e run away

RIGMAROLE. Roundabout, nonfenfical He told a long rigmarole ftory.

RING Money procured by begging beggars fo call it from its ringing when thrown to them Alfo a circle formed for boxers, wreftlers, and cudgel players, by a man ftyled Vinegar, who, with his hat before his eyes, goes round the circle, ftriking at random with his whip to prevent the populace from crowding in

TO RING A PEAL To fcold, chiefly applied to women. His wife rung him a fine peal!

RIP. A miferable rip, a poor, lean, worn-out horfe.

RIPPONS Spurs. Rippon is famous for a manufactory of fpurs, both for men and fighting cocks.

ROARATORIOS

ROARATORIOS AND UPROARS. Oratorios and operas.

ROARING BOY. A noisy, riotous fellow.

ROARING TRADE. A quick trade.

TO ROAST. To arrest. I'll roast the dab, I'll arrest the rascal.—Also to jeer, ridicule, or banter. He stood the roast, he was the butt.—Roast meat clothes, Sunday or holiday clothes. To cry roast meat, to boast of one's situation. To rule the roast, to be master or paramount.

ROAST AND BOILED. A nick name for the Life Guards, who are mostly substantial house-keepers, and eat daily of roast and boiled.

ROBERT'S MEN. The third old rank of the canting crew, mighty thieves, like Robin Hood.

ROBY DOUGLAS, with one eye and a stinking breath. The breech.

ROCHESTER PORTION. Two torn smocks, and what nature gave.

ROCKED. He was rocked in a stone kitchen, a saying meant to convey the idea that the person spoken of is a fool, his brains having been disordered by the jumbling of his cradle.

ROGER. A portmanteau, also a man's yard. *Cant*.

ROGER, or TIB OF THE BUTTERY. A goose. *Cant*. Jolly Roger; a flag hoisted by pirates.

TO ROGER. To bull, or lie with a woman. from the name of Roger being frequently given to a bull.

ROGUES. The fourth order of canters. A rogue in grain, a great rogue, also a corn chandler. A rogue in spirit, a distiller or brandy merchant.

ROMAN. A soldier in the foot guards, who gives up his pay to his captain for leave to work, serving, like an ancient Roman, for glory, and the love of his country.

ROMBOYLES. Watch and ward. Romboyled, sought after with a warrant.

ROME MORT. A queen.

ROMEVILLE. London. *Cant*.

ROMP. A forward wanton girl, a tomrig. Grey, in his notes to Shakespeare, derives it from arompo, an animal found in South Guinea, that is a man eater. See HOYDEN.

Rook. A cheat probably from the thievish disposition of the birds of that name. Also the cant name for a crow used in house-breaking.—To rook; to cheat, particularly at play.

Room. She lets out her fore room and lies backwards, saying of a woman suspected of prostitution.

Ropes. Upon the high ropes, elated, in high spirits, cock-a-whoop.

Rose. Under the rose; privately or secretly. The rose was, it is said, sacred to Harpocrates, the God of Silence, and therefore frequently placed in the ceilings of rooms destined for the receiving of guests; implying, that whatever was transacted there, should not be made public.

Rosy Gills. One with a sanguine or fresh-coloured countenance.

Rotan. A coach, cart, or other wheeled carriage.

Rot Gut. Small beer, called beer-a-bumble—will burst one's guts before 'twill make one tumble.

Rovers. Pirates, vagabonds.

Rough. To lie rough, to lie all night in one's clothes: called also roughing it. Likewise to sleep on the bare deck of a ship, when the person is commonly advised to chuse the softest plank.

Rough Music. Saucepans, frying-pans, poker and tongs, marrow bones and cleavers, bulls horns, &c. beaten upon and sounded in ludicrous processions.

Rouleau. A number of guineas, from twenty to fifty or more, wrapped up in paper, for the more ready circulation at gaming tables. sometimes they are inclosed in ivory boxes made to hold exactly 20, 50, or 100 guineas.

Round Dealing. Plain, honest dealing.

Round Heads. A term of reproach to the puritans and partizans of Oliver Cromwell, and the Rump Parliament, who it is said made use of a bowl as a guide to trim their hair.

Round Robin. A mode of signing remonstrances practised by sailors on board the king's ships, wherein their names are written in a circle, so that it cannot be discovered who first signed it, or was, in other words, the ringleader.

Round Sum. A considerable sum.

Rout

Rout. A modern card meeting at a private house, also an order from the Secretary at War, directing the march and quartering of soldiers.

Row. A disturbance a term used by the students at Cambridge.

Rowland. To give a Rowland for an Oliver, to give an equivalent. Rowland and Oliver were two knights famous in romance the wonderful achievements of the one could only be equalled by those of the other.

Rowlands. A fraternity, by the title of the ancient and honourable family of the Rowlands, held their annual meeting at the Prince and Princess of Orange, White Chapel Fields.

Royal Scamps Highwaymen who never rob any but rich persons, and that without ill treating them. See Scamp.

Royal Stag Society. Was held every Monday evening, at seven o'clock, at the Three Tuns, near the Hospital Gate, Newgate Street

Royster. A rude boisterous fellow; also a hound that opens on a false scent.

To Rub To run away Don't rub us to the whit, don't send us to Newgate *Cant* —To rub up, to refresh· to rub up one's memory A rub, an impediment. A rubber, the best two out of three To win a rubber, to win two games out of three

Ruby-faced. Red-faced.

Ruff. An ornament formerly worn by men and women round their necks Wooden ruff, the pillory.

Ruffian. The devil. *Cant*.—May the ruffian nab the cuffin queer, and let the harmanbeck trine with his kinchins about his colquarron, may the Devil take the justice, and let the constable be hanged with his children about his neck The ruffian cly thee, the Devil take thee Ruffian cook ruffian, who scalded the Devil in his feathers, a saying of a bad cook. Ruffian sometimes also means a justice.

Ruffles Handcuffs *Cant*.

Rufflers. The first rank of canters, also notorious rogues pretending to be maimed soldiers or sailors

Ruffmans. The woods, hedges, or bushes. *Cant*.

RUM

RUG. It is all rug; it is all right and safe, the game is secure. *Cant.*

RUM. Fine, good, valuable.

RUM BECK A justice of the peace. *Cant.*

RUM BITE A clever cheat, a clean trick

RUM BLEATING CHEAT. A fat wether sheep *Cant.*

RUM BLOWER A handsome wench *Cant*

RUM BLUFFER. A jolly host *Cant*

RUM BOB A young apprentice, also a sharp trick

RUM BOOZE. Wine, or any other good liquor Rum boozing welts, bunches of grapes *Cant*

RUM BUBBER A dexterous fellow at stealing silver tankards from inns and taverns

RUM BUGHER. A valuable dog. *Cant*

RUM BUNG A full purse *Cant*

RUM CHUB Among butchers, a customer easily imposed on, as to the quality and price of meat *Cant*

RUM CLOUT A fine silk, cambric, or holland handkerchief. *Cant*

RUM COD A good purse of gold. *Cant*

RUM COE. See COE.

RUM COLE. New money, or medals. *Cant.*

RUM COVE. A dexterous or clever rogue.

RUM CULL A rich fool, easily cheated, particularly by his mistress.

RUM DEGEN A handsome sword *Cant*

RUM DELL. See RUM DOXY

RUM DIVER A dexterous pickpocket *Cant.*

RUM DOXY. A fine wench. *Cant*

RUM DRAWERS. Silk, or other fine stockings *Cant.*

RUM DROPPER. A vintner. *Cant.*

RUM DUBBER. An expert picklock.

RUM DUKE. A jolly handsome fellow, also an odd excentric fellow, likewise the boldest and stoutest fellows lately among the Alsatians, Minters, Savoyards, and other inhabitants of privileged districts, sent to remove and guard the goods of such bankrupts as intended to take sanctuary in those places. *Cant.*

RUM FILE See RUM DIVER

RUM FUN. A sharp trick. *Cant.*

RUM

Rum Gaggers. Cheats who tell wonderful stories of their sufferings at sea, or when taken by the Algerines. *Cant.*

Rum Ghelt. See Rum Cole. *Cant.*

Rum Glymmer. King or chief of the link boys. *Cant.*

Rum Guttlers. Canary wine. *Cant.*

Rum Hopper. A drawer at a tavern. Rum hopper, tip us presently a boozing cheat of rum guttlers; drawer, bring us presently a bottle of the best canary. *Cant.*

Rum Kicks. Breeches of gold or silver brocade, or richly laced with gold or silver. *Cant.*

Rum Mawnd. One that counterfeits a fool. *Cant.*

Rum Mort. A queen, or great lady. *Cant.*

Rum Nab. A good hat.

Rum Nantz. Good French brandy. *Cant.*

Rum Ned. A very rich silly fellow. *Cant.*

Rum Pad. The highway. *Cant.*

Rum Padders. Highwaymen well mounted and armed. *Cant.*

Rum Peepers. Fine looking-glasses. *Cant.*

Rum Prancer. A fine horse. *Cant.*

Rum Quids. A great booty. *Cant.*

Rum Ruff Peck. Westphalia ham. *Cant.*

Rum Snitch. A smart fillip on the nose.

Rum Squeeze. Much wine, or good liquor, given among fidlers. *Cant.*

Rum Tilter. See Rum Degen.

Rum Tol. See Rum Degen.

Rum Topping. A rich commode, or woman's head dress.

Rum Ville. See Romeville.

Rum Wiper. See Rum Clout.

Rumbo. Rum, water, and sugar, also a prison.

Rumboyle. A ward or watch.

Rumbumptious. Obstreperous.

Rumford. To ride to Rumford to have one's backside new bottomed, i.e. to have a pair of new leather breeches. Rumford was formerly a famous place for leather breeches. A like saying is current in Norfolk and Suffolk, of Bungey, and for the same reason.—Rumford lion, a calf. See Essex Lion.

Rump.

RUMP. To rump any one, to turn the back to him an evolution sometimes used at court. Rump and dozen, a rump of beef and a dozen of claret, an Irish wager, called also buttock and trimmings. Rump and kidney men, fidlers that play at feasts, fairs, weddings, &c. and live chiefly on the remnants.

RUMPUS. A riot, quarrel, or confusion.

RUN GOODS. A maidenhead, being a commodity never entered.

RUNNING HORSE, or NAG. A clap, or gleet.

RUNNING SMOBBLE. Snatching goods off a counter, and throwing them to an accomplice, who brushes off with them.

RUNNING STATIONERS. Hawkers of newspapers, trials, and dying speeches.

RUNT. A short, squat man or woman; from the small cattle called Welsh runts.

RUSHERS. Thieves who knock at the doors of great houses, in London, in summer time, when the families are gone out of town, and on the door being opened by a woman, rush in and rob the house; also housebreakers who enter lone houses by force.

RUSSIAN COFFEE HOUSE. The Brown Bear in Bow-street, Covent Garden, a house of call for the thief-takers and runners of the Bow-street justices.

RUSTY. Out of use. To nab the rust; to be refractory: properly applied to a restive horse, and figuratively to the human species. To ride rusty; to be sullen: called also to ride grub.

RUSTY GUTS. A blunt surly fellow; a jocular misnomer of *rusticus*.

RUTTING. Copulating. Rutting time; the season when deer go to rut.

S.

S.

SAL

SACHEVEREL. The iron door, or blower, to the mouth of a stove. from a divine of that name, who made himself famous for blowing the coals of diffention in the latter end of the reign of Queen Ann.

SACK. A pocket. To buy the fack; to get drunk. To dive into the fack; to pick a pocket. To break a bottle in an empty fack; a bubble bet, a fack with a bottle in it not being an empty fack.

SAD DOG. A wicked debauched fellow: one of the ancient family of the fad dogs. Swift tranflates it into Latin by the words *triftis canis*.

SADDLE. To faddle the fpit; to give a dinner or fupper. To faddle one's nofe, to wear fpectacles. To faddle a place or penfion; to oblige the holder to pay a certain portion of his income to fome one nominated by the donor. Saddle fick; galled with riding, having loft leather.

SAINT. A piece of fpoilt timber in a coachmaker's fhop, like a faint, devoted to the flames.

SAINT GEOFFREY'S DAY. Never, there being no faint of that name tomorrow-come-never, when two Sundays come together.

SAINT LUKE'S BIRD. An ox. that evangelift being always reprefented with an ox.

SAINT MONDAY. A holiday moft religioufly obferved by journeymen fhoemakers, and other inferior mechanics. a profanation of that day, by working, is punifhable by a fine, particularly among the gentle craft An Irifhman obferved, that this faint's anniverfary happened every week.

SAINTONGE. A fociety formerly held at the Excife Coffee Houfe, Old Broad-ftreet.

SAL. An abbreviation of *falivation*. In a high fal; in the pickling tub, or under a falivation.

SALAMANDERS. The worthy Members of the Society of

B b Salamanders

Salamanders met at the Bull and Anchor, near Hammersmith.

SALESMAN's DOG. A barker. Vide BARKER.

SALMON-GUNDY. Apples, onions, veal or chicken and pickled herrings, minced fine and eaten with oil and vinegar. some derive the name of this mess from the French words *felon mon gouft*, because the proportions of the different ingredients are regulated by the palate of the maker, others say it bears the name of the inventor, who was a rich Dutch merchant. but the general and most probable opinion is, that it was invented by the countess of Salmagondi, one of the ladies of Mary de Medicis, wife of king Henry IV of France, and by her brought into France.

SALMON, or SALAMON. The beggars sacrament or oath.

SALT. Lecherous. A salt bitch, a bitch at heat, or proud bitch. Salt eel, a rope's end, used to correct boys, &c. at sea. you shall have a salt eel for supper.

SANDWICH. Ham, dried tongue, or some other salted meat, cut thin, and put between two slices of bread and butter. said to be a favourite morsel with the Earl of Sandwich.

SANDY PATE. A red-haired man or woman.

SANGAREE. Rack punch was formerly so called in bagnios.

SANK, SANKY, or CENTIPEE's. A taylor employed by clothiers in making soldiers clothing.

SAPSCULL. A simple fellow. Sappy, foolish.

SATYR. A libidinous fellow. those imaginary beings are by poets reported to be extremely salacious.

SAUCE BOX. A term of familiar raillery, signifying a bold or forward person.

SAVE-ALL. A kind of candlestick used by our frugal forefathers, to burn snuffs and ends of candles. Figuratively, boys running about gentlemen's houses in Ireland, who are fed on broken meats that would otherwise be wasted, also a miser.

SAUNTERER. An idle, lounging, fellow. by some derived from *sans terre*; applied to persons who, having no lands or home, lingered and loitered about. Some derive it from persons devoted to the Holy Land; *faint terre*, who loitered about, as waiting for company.

SAW.

SAW An old saw, an ancient proverbial saying.

SAWNY, or SANDY. A general nick-name for a Scotchman, as Paddy is for an Irishman, or Taffy for a Welchman; Sawny or Sandy being the familiar abbreviation or diminutive of Alexander, a very favourite name among the Scottish nation.

SCAB A worthless man or woman

SCALD MISERALLES A set of mock masons, who, A. D. 1744, made a ludicrous procession in ridicule of the Free Masons.

SCALY FISH An honest, rough, blunt sailor

SCAMP A highwayman Royal scamp, a highwayman who robs civilly Royal foot scamp, a footpad who behaves in like manner.

To SCAMPER. To run away hastily.

SCANDAL BROTH Tea

SCANDAL PROOF One who has eat shame and drank after it, or would blush at being ashamed.

SCANDALOUS A perriwig. Cant

SCAPEGALLOWS. One who deserves and has narrowly escaped the gallows, a slip-gibbet, one for whom the gallows is said to groan.

SCAPEGRACE. A wild dissolute fellow.

SCARCE. To make one's self scarce; to steal away

SCARLET HORSE A high-red, hired or hack horse: a pun on the word *hired*

SCAVEY Sense, knowledge "Massa, me no scavey," master, I dont know *(negros language)* perhaps from the French *scavoir*.

SCHEME A party of pleasure.

SCHISM MONGER. A dissenting teacher

SCHISM SHOP A dissenting meeting house.

SCHOOL OF VENUS A bawdy house

SCHOOL BUTTER. Cobbing, whipping

SCONCE. The head, probably as being the fort and citadel of a man. from *sconce*, an old name for a fort, derived from a Dutch word of the same signification To build a sconce; a military term for bilking one's quarters. To sconce or skonce, to impose a fine. *Academical phrase.*

SCOTCH BAIT. A halt and a resting on a stick, as practised by pedlars.

SCOTCH CHOCOLATE. Brimstone and milk.

SCOTCH FIDDLE. The itch.

SCOTCH MIST. A sober soaking rain: a Scotch mist will wet an Englishman to the skin.

SCOTCH WARMING PAN. A wench.

SCOUNDREL. A man void of every principle of honour.

SCOUR. To scour or score off; to run away. perhaps from *score*, i. e. full speed, or as fast as legs would carry one.— Also to wear. chiefly applied to irons, fetters, or handcuffs, because wearing scours them. He will scour the darbies; he will be in fetters. To scour the cramp ring, to wear bolts or fetters, from which, as well as from coffin hinges, rings supposed to prevent the cramp are made.

SCOURERS. Riotous bucks, who amuse themselves with breaking windows, beating the watch, and assaulting every person they meet. called scouring the streets.

SCOUT. A college errand boy at Oxford, called a gyp at Cambridge. Also a watchman or a watch. *Cant.*

SCRAGGED. Hanged.

SCRAGGY. Lean, bony.

SCRAN. Victuals.

SCRAP. A villanous scheme or plan. He whiddles the whole scrap; he discovers the whole plan or scheme.

SCRAPE. To get into a scrape, to be involved in a disagreeable business.

SCRAPER. A fidler, also one who scrapes plates for mezzotinto prints.

SCRAPING. A mode of expressing dislike to a person, or sermon, practised at Oxford by the students, in scraping their feet against the ground during the preachment, frequently done to testify their disapprobation of a proctor who has been, as they think, too rigorous.

SCRATCH. Old Scratch; the Devil: probably from the long and sharp claws with which he is frequently delineated.

SCRATCH LAND. Scotland.

SCRATCH PLATTER, or TAYLORS RAGOUT. Bread sopt

in the oil and vinegar in which cucumbers have been sliced.

To Screw. To copulate. A female screw; a common prostitute. To screw one up, to exact upon one in a bargain or reckoning.

Screw Jaws. A wry-mouthed man or woman.

Scrip. A scrap or slip of paper. The cully freely blotted the scrip, and tipt me forty hogs; the man freely signed the bond, and gave me forty shillings.—Scrip is also a Change Alley phrase for the last loan or subscription. What does scrip go at for the next rescounters? what does scrip fell for delivered at the next day of settling?

Scroby. To be tipt the scroby, to be whipt before the justices.

Scrope. A farthing. *Cant.*

Scrub. A low mean fellow, employed in all forts of dirty work

Scrubbado. The itch

Scull. A head of a house, or master of a college, at the universities.

Scull, or Sculler. A boat rowed by one man with a light kind of oar, called a scull, also a one-horse chaise or buggy

Scull Thatcher. A peruke maker

Scum. The riff raff, tag-rag and bobtail, or lowest order of the people.

Scut. The tail of a hare or rabbit; also that of a woman

Scuttle. To scuttle off; to run away. To scuttle a ship, to make a hole in her bottom, in order to sink her.

Sea Crab. A sailor.

Sealer, or Squeeze Wax. One ready to give bond and judgment for goods or money.

Secret. He has been let into the secret; he has been cheated at gaming or horse-racing. He or she is in the grand secret, i. e. dead.

Seedy. Poor, pennyless, stiver-cramped, exhausted.

Sees. The eyes. See Daylights.

Seraglio. A bawdy house, the name of that part of the Great Turk's palace where the women are kept.

SHA

SET. A dead set, a concerted scheme to defraud a person by gaming.

SETTER A bailiff's follower, who, like a setting dog, follows and points out the game for his master. Also sometimes an exciseman

To SETTLE. To knock down or stun any one. We settled the cull by a stoter on his nob, we stunned the fellow by a blow on the head

SEVEN-SIDED ANIMAL A one-eyed man or woman, each having a right side and a left side, a fore side and a back side, an outside, an inside, and a blind side.

SHABBAROON. An ill-dressed shabby fellow, also a mean-spirited person.

SHAFTSBURY. A gallon pot full of wine, with a cock.

To SHAG. To copulate He is but bad shag, he is no able woman's man.

SHAG-BAG, or SHAKE-BAG. A poor sneaking fellow, a man of no spirit. a term borrowed from the cock-pit.

SHAKE To shake one's elbow, to game with dice To shake a cloth in the wind; to be hanged in chains.

SHALLOW PATE A simple fellow.

SHAM. A cheat, or trick. To cut a sham, to cheat or deceive. Shams, false sleeves to put on over a dirty shirt, or false sleeves with ruffles to put over a plain one.

SHARP. Subtle, acute, quick-witted; also a sharper or cheat, in opposition to a flat, dupe, or gull. Sharp's the word and quick's the motion with him, said of any one very attentive to his own interest, and apt to take all advantages. Sharp set, hungry.

SHARPER. A cheat, one that lives by his wits. Sharpers tools; a fool and false dice.

SHAVER. A cunning shaver, a subtle fellow, one who trims close, an acute cheat. A young shaver, a boy. *Sea term.*

SHAVINGS. The clippings of money.

SHE HOUSE. A house where the wife rules, or, as the term is, wears the breeches.

SHE LION. A shilling.

SHE NAPPER. A woman thief-catcher; also a bawd or pimp.

SHEEP'S HEAD. Like a sheep's head, all jaw, saying of a talkative man or woman.

SHEEPISH. Bashful. A sheepish fellow, a bashful or shame-faced fellow. To cast a sheep's eye at any thing; to look wishfully at it.

SHERIFF'S BALL. An execution. To dance at the sheriff's ball, and loll out one's tongue at the company, to be hanged, or go to rest in a horse's night cap, i. e. a halter.

SHERIFF'S BRACELETS. Handcuffs.

SCOTCH BAIT. A halt and a resting on a stick, as practised by pedlars.

SCOTCH CHOCOLATE. Brimstone and milk.

SCOTCH FIDDLE. The itch.

SCOTCH MIST. A sober soaking rain: a Scotch mist will wet an Englishman to the skin.

SCOTCH WARMING PAN. A wench.

SCOUNDREL. A man void of every principle of honour.

SCOUR. To scour or score off, to run away: perhaps from *score*, i.e. full speed, or as fast as legs would carry one.— Also to wear: chiefly applied to irons, fetters, or handcuffs, because wearing scours them. He will scour the darbies; he will be in fetters. To scour the cramp ring; to wear bolts or fetters, from which, as well as from coffin hinges, rings supposed to prevent the cramp are made.

SCOURERS. Riotous bucks, who amuse themselves with breaking windows, beating the watch, and assaulting every person they meet: called scouring the streets.

SCOUT. A college errand boy at Oxford, called a gyp at Cambridge. Also a watchman or a watch. *Cant.*

SCRAGGED. Hanged.

SCRAGGY. Lean, bony.

SCRAN. Victuals.

SCRAP. A villanous scheme or plan. He whiddles the whole scrap; he discovers the whole plan or scheme.

SCRAPE. To get into a scrape, to be involved in a disagreeable business.

SCRAPER. A fidler, also one who scrapes plates for mezzotinto prints.

SCRAPING. A mode of expressing dislike to a person, or sermon, practised at Oxford by the students, in scraping their feet against the ground during the preachment, frequently done to testify their disapprobation of a proctor who has been, as they think, too rigorous.

SCRATCH. Old Scratch; the Devil, probably from the long and sharp claws with which he is frequently delineated.

SCRATCH LAND. Scotland.

SCRATCH PLATTER, or TAYLORS RAGOUT. Bread sopt

in the oil and vinegar in which cucumbers have been sliced.

To Screw. To copulate. A female screw; a common prostitute. To screw one up; to exact upon one in a bargain or reckoning.

Screw Jaws. A wry-mouthed man or woman.

Scrip. A scrap or slip of paper. The cully freely blotted the scrip, and tipt me forty hogs; the man freely signed the bond, and gave me forty shillings.—Scrip is also a Change Alley phrase for the last loan or subscription. What does scrip go at for the next rescounters? what does scrip sell for delivered at the next day of settling?

Scroby. To be tipt the scroby, to be whipt before the justices.

Scrope. A farthing. *Cant.*

Scrub. A low mean fellow, employed in all sorts of dirty work.

Scrubbado. The itch.

Scull. A head of a house, or master of a college, at the universities.

Scull, or Sculler. A boat rowed by one man with a light kind of oar, called a scull, also a one-horse chaise or buggy.

Scull Thatcher. A peruke maker.

Scum. The riff raff, tag-rag and bobtail, or lowest order of the people.

Scut. The tail of a hare or rabbit; also that of a woman.

Scuttle. To scuttle off; to run away. To scuttle a ship, to make a hole in her bottom, in order to sink her.

Sea Crab. A sailor.

Sealer, or Squeeze Wax. One ready to give bond and judgment for goods or money.

Secret. He has been let into the secret; he has been cheated at gaming or horse-racing. He or she is in the grand secret, i. e. dead.

Seedy. Poor, pennyless, stiver-cramped, exhausted.

Sees. The eyes. See Daylights.

Seraglio. A bawdy house; the name of that part of the Great Turk's palace where the women are kept.

SET. A dead set, a concerted scheme to defraud a person by gaming.

SETTER. A bailiff's follower, who, like a setting dog, follows and points out the game for his master. Also sometimes an exciseman.

TO SETTLE. To knock down or stun any one. We settled the cull by a stoter on his nob; we stunned the fellow by a blow on the head.

SEVEN-SIDED ANIMAL. A one-eyed man or woman, each having a right side and a left side, a fore side and a back side, an outside, an inside, and a blind side.

SHABBAROON. An ill-dressed shabby fellow; also a mean-spirited person.

SHAFTSBURY. A gallon pot full of wine, with a cock.

TO SHAG. To copulate. He is but bad shag, he is no able woman's man.

SHAG-BAG, or SHAKE-BAG. A poor sneaking fellow, a man of no spirit. a term borrowed from the cock-pit.

SHAKE. To shake one's elbow, to game with dice. To shake a cloth in the wind; to be hanged in chains.

SHALLOW PATE. A simple fellow.

SHAM. A cheat, or trick. To cut a sham, to cheat or deceive. Shams, false sleeves to put on over a dirty shirt, or false sleeves with ruffles to put over a plain one. To sham abram, to counterfeit sickness.

TO SHAMBLE. To walk awkwardly. Shamble-legged, one that walks wide, and shuffles about his feet.

SHANKER. A venereal wart.

SHANKS. Legs, or gams.

SHANKS NAGGY. To ride shanks naggy; to travel on foot. *Scotch.*

SHANNON. A river in Ireland. persons dipped in that river are perfectly and for ever cured of bashfulness.

SHAPES. To shew one's shapes, to be stript, or made peel, at the whipping post.

SHAPPO, or SHAP. A hat. corruption of *chapeau. Cant.*

SHARK. A sharper. perhaps from his preying upon any one he can lay hold of. Also a custom-house officer, or tide-waiter. Sharks, the first order of pickpockets. *Bow-street term,* A. D. 1785.

SHARP.

SHARP. Subtle, acute, quick-witted; also a sharper or cheat, in opposition to a flat, dupe, or gull. Sharp's the word and quick's the motion with him, said of any one very attentive to his own interest, and apt to take all advantages. Sharp set, hungry.

SHARPER. A cheat, one that lives by his wits. Sharpers tools, a fool and false dice.

SHAVER. A cunning shaver, a subtle fellow, one who trims close, an acute cheat. A young shaver, a boy. *Sea term.*

SHAVINGS. The clippings of money.

SHE HOUSE. A house where the wife rules, or, as the term is, wears the breeches.

SHE LION. A shilling.

SHE NAPPER. A woman thief-catcher, also a bawd or pimp.

SHEEP'S HEAD. Like a sheep's head, all jaw, saying of a talkative man or woman.

SHEEPISH. Bashful. A sheepish fellow, a bashful or shame-faced fellow. To cast a sheep's eye at any thing, to look wishfully at it.

SHERIFF'S BALL. An execution. To dance at the sheriff's ball, and loll out one's tongue at the company, to be hanged, or go to rest in a horse's night cap, i. e. a halter.

SHERIFF'S BRACELETS. Handcuffs.

SHERIFF'S HOTEL. A prison.

SHERIFF'S PICTURE FRAME. The gallows.

To SHERK. To evade or disappoint. to sherk one's duty.

To SHERRY. To run away. sherry off.

SHIFTING BALLAST. A term used by sailors, to signify soldiers, passengers, or any landsmen on board.

SHILLALEY. An oaken sapling, or cudgel. from a wood of that name famous for its oaks. *Irish.*

SHILLY SHALLY. Irresolute. To stand shilly-shally, to hesitate, or stand in doubt.

SHINE. It shines like a shitten barn door.

SHIP SHAPE. Proper, as it ought to be. *Sea phrase.*

SH-T SACK. A dastardly fellow, also a non-conformist. This appellation is said to have originated from the following story ftory.—After the reftoration, the laws againft the non-conformifts were extremely fevere. They fometimes met in very obfcure places and there is a tradition that one of their congregations were affembled in a barn, the rendezvous of beggars and other vagrants, where the preacher, for want of a ladder or tub, was fufpended in a fack fixed to the beam. His difcourfe that day being on the laft judgment, he particularly attempted to defcribe the terrors of the wicked at the founding of the trumpet; on which a trumpeter to a puppet fhow, who had taken refuge in that barn and lay hid under the ftraw, founded a charge. The congregation, ftruck with the utmoft confternation, fled in an inftant from the place, leaving their affrighted teacher to fhift for himfelf. The effects of his terror are faid to have appeared at the bottom of the fack, and to have occafioned that opprobrious appellation by which the nonconformifts were vulgarly diftinguifhed.

SH-T-NG THROUGH THE TEETH. Vomiting. Hark ye, friend, have you got a padlock on your a-fe, that you fh-te through your teeth? vulgar addrefs to one vomiting.

SHOD ALL ROUND. A parfon who attends a funeral is faid to be fhod all round, when he receives a hat-band, gloves, and fcarf: many fhoeings being only partial.

SHOEMAKER'S STOCKS. New, or ftrait fhoes. I was in the fhoemaker's ftocks; i. e. had on a new pair of fhoes that were too fmall for me.

TO SHOOLE. To go fkulking about.

TO SHOOT THE CAT. To vomit from excefs of liquor: called alfo catting.

SHOP. A prifon. Shopped; confined, imprifoned.

SHOPLIFTER. One that fteals whilft pretending to purchafe goods in a fhop.

SHORT-HEELED WENCH. A girl apt to fall on her back.

SHOT. To pay one's fhot; to pay one's fhare of a reckoning. Shot betwixt wind and water, poxed or clapped.

SHOTTEN HERRING. A thin meagre fellow.

TO SHOVE THE TUMBLER. To be whipped at the cart's tail.

SHOVEL. To be put to bed with a fhovel; to be buried.

SIM

He or she was fed with a fire-shovel; a saying of a person with a large mouth.

SHOULDER CLAPPER. A bailiff, or member of the catch club. Shoulder clapped, arrested.

SHOULDER SHAM A partner to a file. See FILE

SHRED. A taylor

SHRIMP. A little diminutive person.

TO SHUFFLE. To make use of false pretences, or unfair shifts. A shuffling fellow; a slippery shifting fellow

SHY COCK One who keeps within doors for fear of bailiffs.

SICE Sixpence

SICK AS A HORSE Horses are said to be extremely sick at their stomachs, from being unable to relieve themselves by vomiting Bracken, indeed, in his Farriery, gives an instance of that evacuation being procured, but by a means which he says would make the Devil vomit Such as may have occasion to administer an emetic either to the animal or the fiend, may consult his book for the recipe.

SIDE POCKET He has as much need of a wife as a dog of a side pocket; said of a weak old debilitated man He wants it as much as a dog does a side pocket; a simile used for one who desires any thing by no means necessary

SIDLEDYWRY. Crooked.

SIGN OF A HOUSE TO LET A widow's weeds

SIGN OF THE { FIVE SHILLINGS The crown.
TEN SHILLINGS. The two crowns.
FIFTEEN SHILLINGS The three crowns

SILENCE To silence a man, to knock him down, or stun him. Silence in the court, the cat is pissing; a gird upon any one requiring silence unnecessarily

SILENT FLUTE See PEGO, SUGAR STICK, &c

SILK SNATCHERS. Thieves who snatch hoods or bonnets from persons walking in the streets.

SIMKIN. A foolish fellow.

SIMON. Sixpence. Simple Simon; a natural, a silly fellow Simon Suck-egg, sold his wife for an addle duck egg.

TO SIMPER To smile to simper like a furmity kettle.

SIMPLETON Abbreviation of simple Tony or Anthony, a foolish fellow

SIMPLES. Physical herbs; also follies. He must go to Battersea, to be cut for the simples—Battersea is a place famous for its garden grounds, some of which were formerly appropriated to the growing of simples for apothecaries, who at a certain season used to go down to select their stock for the ensuing year, at which time the gardners were said to cut their simples; whence it became a popular joke to advise young people to go to Battersea, at that time, to have their simples cut, or to be cut for the simples.

TO SING SMALL. To be humbled, confounded, or abashed, to have little or nothing to say for one's self.

SINGLE PEEPER. A person having but one eye.

SINGLETEN. A very foolish fellow; also a particular kind of nails.

SINGLETON. A cork screw, made by a famous cutler of that name, who lived in a place called Hell, in Dublin; his screws are remarkable for their excellent temper.

SIR JOHN. The old title for a country parson: as Sir John of Wrotham, mentioned by Shakespeare.

SIR JOHN BARLEYCORN. Strong beer.

SIR LOIN. The sur, or upper loin

SIR REVERENCE. Human excrement, a t—d.

SIR TIMOTHY. One who, from a desire of being the head of the company, pays the reckoning, or, as the term is, stands squire. See SQUIRE.

SITTING BREECHES One who stays late in company, is said to have his sitting breeches on, or that he will sit longer than a hen.

SIX AND EIGHT PENCE. An attorney, whose fee on several occasions is fixed at that sum.

SIX AND TIPS. Whisky and small beer. *Irish*

SIX POUNDER. A servant maid, from the wages formerly given to maid servants, which was commonly six pounds.

SIXES. Small beer, formerly sold at six shillings the barrel.

SIXES AND SEVENS. Left at sixes and sevens, i. e. in confusion: commonly said of a room where the furniture, &c. is scattered about, or of a business left unsettled.

SIZE OF ALE. Half a pint. Size of bread and cheese, a certain

SLA

tain quantity. Sizings; Cambridge term for the college allowance from the buttery, called at Oxford battles.

SIZER. A poor or inferior student on the college establishment at Cambridge, called at Oxford a servitor.

SKEW. A cup, or beggar's wooden dish

SKEWVOW, or ALL ASKEW. Crooked, inclining to one side.

SKIN. In a bad skin, out of temper, in an ill humour. Thin-skinned, touchy, peevish.

SKIN FLINT An avaritious man or woman.

SKINK. To skink, is to wait on the company, ring the bell, stir the fire, and snuff the candles, the duty of the youngest officer in a military mess. See BOOTS.

SKINS. A tanner.

SKIP JACKS. Youngsters that ride horses on sale, horse dealers boys.

SKIP KENNEL A footman.

SKIPPER. A barn, also a Dutch seaman. *Cant.*

To SKIT. To wheedle. *Cant.*

SKRIP See SCRIP.

SKULKER. A soldier who by feigned sickness, or other pretences, evades his duty, a sailor who keeps below in time of danger, in the civil line, one who keeps out of the way, when any work is to be done. To skulk, to hide one's self, to avoid labour or duty

SKY FARMERS. Cheats who pretend they were farmers in the isle of Sky, or some other remote place, and were ruined by a flood, hurricane, or some such public calamity; or else called sky farmers from their farms being *in nubibus*, ' in the clouds.'

SKY PARLOUR. The garret, or upper story.

SLABBERING BIB A parson or lawyer's band.

SLAG. A slack-mettled fellow, one not ready to resent an affront.

SLAM. A trick, also a game at whist lost without scoring one. To flam to a door, to shut it with violence.

SLAMMAKIN. A female sloven, one whose clothes seem hung on with a pitch-fork, a careless trapes.

SLANG Cant language

SLAP-BANG SHOP. A petty cook's shop where there is no

credit given, but what is had must be paid *down with the ready slap-barg*, i. e. immediately. This is a common appellation for a night cellar frequented by thieves, and sometimes for a stage coach or caravan.

SLAPDASH Immediately, instantly, suddenly.

SLASHER. A bullying riotous fellow. *Irish*.

SLAT. Half a crown. *Cant*.

SLATE A sheet. *Cant*.

SLATER's PAN. The gaol at Kingston in Jamaica Slater is the deputy provost martial.

SLATTERN A woman sluttishly negligent in her dress.

SLEEPING PARTNER. A partner in a trade, or shop, who lends his name and money, for which he receives a share of the profit, without doing any part of the business.

SLEEPY. Much worn. the cloth of your coat must be extremely sleepy, for it has not had a nap this long time

SLEEVELESS ERRAND. A fool's errand, in search of what it is impossible to find

SLICE To take a slice; to intrigue, particularly with a married woman, because a slice of a cut loaf is not missed

SLIPGIBBET See SCAPEGALLOWS.

SLIPPERY CHAP. One on whom there can be no dependance, a shuffling fellow.

SLIPSLOPS Tea, water gruel, or any innocent beverage taken medicinally.

SLIPSLOPPING. Misnaming and misapplying any hard word: from the character of Mrs Slipslop, in Fielding's Joseph Andrews

SLOPS Wearing apparel and bedding used by seamen.

SLOP SELLER. A dealer in those articles, who keeps a slop shop

SLOUCH A stooping gate, a negligent slovenly fellow. To slouch, to hang down one's head A slouched hat, a hat whose brims are let down.

SLUBBER DE GULLION. A dirty nasty fellow.

SLUG A piece of lead of any shape, to be fired from a blunderbuss. To fire a slug; to drink a dram

SLUG-A-BED. A drone, one that cannot rise in the morning

SLUICE YOUR GOB. Take a hearty drink.

SLUR.

SLUR. To slur, is a method of cheating at dice, also to cast a reflection on any one's character, to scandalize.

SLUSH Greasy dish water, or the skimmings of a pot where fat meat has been boiled.

SLUSH BUCKET A foul feeder, one that eats much greasy food

SLY BOOTS. A cunning fellow, under the mask of simplicity.

SMABBLED, or SNABBLED. Killed in battle.

TO SMACK. To kiss I had a smack at her muns; I kissed her mouth To smack calves skin; to kiss the book, i. e. to take an oath The queer cuffin bid me smack calves skin, but I only bussed my thumb, the justice bid me kiss the book, but I only kissed my thumb

SMACK SMOOTH Level with the surface, every thing cut away

SMACKING COVE. A coachman.

SMALL CLOTHES. Breeches a gird at the affected delicacy of the present age, a suit being called, coat, waistcoat, and articles, or small clothes.

SMART Spruce, fine as smart as a carrot new scraped.

SMART MONEY. Money allowed to soldiers or sailors for the loss of a limb, or other hurt received in the service.

SMASH Leg of mutton and smash, a leg of mutton and mashed turnips. *Sea term.*

TO SMASH. To break; also to kick down stairs. *Cant.*

SMEAR A plaisterer.

SMEAR GELT. A bribe. *German.*

SMELLER. A nose. Smellers, a cat's whiskers.

SMELLING CHEAT. An orchard, or garden, also a nosegay. *Cant.*

SMELTS. Half guineas. *Cant.*

SMICKET. A smock, or woman's shift

SMIRK. A finical spruce fellow To smirk, to smile, or look pleasantly.

SMITER An arm To smite one's tutor, to get money from him. *Academic term*

SMITHFIELD BARGAIN A bargain whereby the purchaser is taken in. This is likewise frequently used to express

matches

matches or marriages contracted solely on the score of interest, on one or both sides, where the fair sex are bought and sold like cattle in Smithfield.

SMOCK-FACED. Fair-faced.

To SMOKE. To observe, to suspect.

SMOKER. A tobacconist.

SMOKY. Curious, suspicious, inquisitive.

SMOUCH. Dried leaves of the ash tree, used by the smugglers for adulterating the black or bohea teas.

SMOUS. A German Jew.

SMUG. A nick-name for a blacksmith; also neat and spruce.

SMUGGLING KEN. A bawdy house.

To SMUSH. To snatch, or seize suddenly.

SMUT. Bawdy. Smutty story; an indecent story.

SNACK. A share. To go snacks; to be partners.

To SNABBLE. To rifle or plunder; also to kill.

SNAFFLER. A highwayman. Snaffler of prancers; a horse stealer.

To SNAFFLE. To steal. To snaffle any one's poll; to steal his wig.

SNAGGS. Large teeth, also snails.

SNAKESMAN. See LITTLE SNAKESMAN.

SNAP DRAGON. A christmas gambol: raisins and almonds being put into a bowl of brandy, and the candles extinguished, the spirit is set on fire, and the company scramble for the raisins.

To SNAP THE GLAZE. To break shop windows, or show glasses.

SNAPPERS. Pistols.

SNAPT. Taken, caught.

SNATCH CLY. A thief who snatches women's pockets.

SNEAK. A pilferer. Morning sneak; one who pilfers early in the morning, before it is light. Evening sneak; an evening pilferer. Upright sneak; one who steals pewter pots from the alehouse boys employed to collect them. To go upon the sneak, to steal into houses whose doors are carelessly left open. *Cant.*

SNEAKER. A small bowl.

SNEAKING BUDGE. One that robs alone.

SNEAKSBY. A mean-spirited fellow, a sneaking cur.

SNEERING.

SOL

SNEERING. Jeering, flickering, laughing in scorn.

SNICKER. A glandered horse.

To SNICKER, or SNIGGER. To laugh privately, or in one's sleeve.

To SNILCH. To eye, or look at any thing attentively: the cull snilches. *Cant.*

SNIP. A taylor.

SNITCH. To turn snitch, or snitcher; to turn informer.

To SNITE. To wipe, or flap. Snite his snitch; wipe his nose, i e give him a good knock.

To SNIVEL. To cry, to throw the snot or snivel about. Snivelling, crying A snivelling fellow, one that whines or complains.

To SNOACH. To speak through the nose, to snuffle.

SNOB. A nick-name for a shoemaker.

To SNOOZE, or SNOODGE. To sleep. To snooze with a mort; to sleep with a wench. *Cant.*

SNOUT. A hogshead. *Cant*

SNOWBALL. A jeering appellation for a negroe.

To SNUB. To check, or rebuke.

SNUB DEVIL. A parson.

SNUB NOSE. A short nose turned up at the end.

SNUDGE. A thief who hides himself under a bed, in order to rob the house.

SNUFF. To take snuff; to be offended.

To SNUFFLE. To speak through the nose.

SNUFFLES. A cold in the head, attended with a running at the nose.

SNUG. All's snug, all's quiet.

To SOAK. To drink An old soaker, a drunkard, one that moistens his clay to make it stick together.

SOCKET MONEY. A whore's fee, or hire, also money paid for a treat, by a married man caught in an intrigue.

SOLDIERS BOTTLE. A large one.

SOLDIERS MAWND. A pretended soldier, begging with a counterfeit wound, which he pretends to have received at some famous siege or battle.

SOLDIERS POMATUM. A piece of tallow candle.

SOLFA. A parish clerk.

SOLO

matches or marriages contracted solely on the score of interest, on one or both sides, where the fair sex are bought and sold like cattle in Smithfield.

SMOCK-FACED. Fair-faced.

To SMOKE. To observe, to suspect.

SMOKER. A tobacconist.

SMOKY. Curious, suspicious, inquisitive.

SMOUCH. Dried leaves of the ash tree, used by the smugglers for adulterating the black or bohea teas.

SMOUS. A German Jew.

SMUG. A nick-name for a blacksmith; also neat and spruce.

SMUGGLING KEN. A bawdy house.

To SMUSH. To snatch, or seize suddenly.

SMUT. Bawdy Smutty story; an indecent story.

SNACK. A share. To go snacks; to be partners.

To SNABBLE. To rifle or plunder; also to kill.

SNAFFLER. A highwayman. Snaffler of prancers; a horse stealer.

To SNAFFLE. To steal. To snaffle any one's poll; to steal his wig.

SNAGGS. Large teeth; also snails.

SNAKESMAN. See LITTLE SNAKESMAN.

SNAP DRAGON. A christmas gambol raisins and almonds being put into a bowl of brandy, and the candles extinguished, the spirit is set on fire, and the company scramble for the raisins.

To SNAP THE GLAZE. To break shop windows, or show glasses.

SNAPPERS. Pistols.

SNAPT. Taken, caught.

SNATCH CLY. A thief who snatches women's pockets.

SNEAK. A pilferer. Morning sneak; one who pilfers early in the morning, before it is light. Evening sneak, an evening pilferer. Upright sneak, one who steals pewter pots from the alehouse boys employed to collect them. To go upon the sneak, to steal into houses whose doors are carelessly left open. *Cant.*

SNEAKER. A small bowl.

SNEAKING BUDGE. One that robs alone.

SNEAKSBY. A mean-spirited fellow, a sneaking cur.

SNEERING.

SOL

SNEERING. Jeering, flickering, laughing in scorn.

SNICKER. A glandered horse.

To SNICKER, or SNIGGER. To laugh privately, or in one's sleeve

To SNILCH. To eye, or look at any thing attentively: the cull snilches. *Cant*.

SNIP. A taylor.

SNITCH. To turn snitch, or snitcher; to turn informer.

To SNITE. To wipe, or slap. Snite his snitch, wipe his nose, i. e. give him a good knock.

To SNIVEL. To cry, to throw the snot or snivel about. Snivelling; crying A snivelling fellow; one that whines or complains

To SNOACH To speak through the nose, to snuffle.

SNOB. A nick-name for a shoemaker.

To SNOOZE, or SNOODGE. To sleep. To snooze with a mort; to sleep with a wench *Cant*

SNOUT. A hogshead. *Cant*.

SNOWBALL A jeering appellation for a negroe.

To SNUB. To check, or rebuke.

SNUB DEVIL. A parson.

SNUB NOSE. A short nose turned up at the end.

SNUDGE. A thief who hides himself under a bed, in order to rob the house

SNUFF To take snuff; to be offended

To SNUFFLE. To speak through the nose.

SNUFFLES. A cold in the head, attended with a running at the nose.

SNUG All's snug; all's quiet.

To SOAK. To drink. An old soaker; a drunkard, one that moistens his clay to make it stick together.

SOCKET MONEY. A whore's fee, or hire, also money paid for a treat, by a married man caught in an intrigue.

SOLDIERS BOTTLE. A large one.

SOLDIERS MAWND A pretended soldier, begging with a counterfeit wound, which he pretends to have received at some famous siege or battle.

SOLDIERS POMATUM. A piece of tallow candle.

SOLFA. A parish clerk.

SOLO

SOLO PLAYER. A miserable performer on any instrument; who always plays alone, because no one will stay in the room to hear him.

SOLOMON. The mass. *Cant.*

SON OF PRATTLEMENT. A lawyer.

SONG He changed his song; he altered his account or evidence. It was bought for an old song, i. e. very cheap. His morning and his evening song do not agree, he tells a different story.

SOOTERKIN. A joke upon the Dutch women, supposing that, by their constant use of stoves, which they place under their petticoats, they breed a kind of small animal in their bodies, called a sooterkin, of the size of a mouse, which when mature slips out.

SOP A bribe. A sop for Cerberus; a bribe for a porter, turnkey, or gaoler.

SORREL A yellowish red. Sorrel pate, one having red hair.

SORROW SHALL BE HIS SOPS. He shall repent this. Sorrow go by me, a common expletive used by the presbyterians in Ireland.

SORRY. Vile, mean, worthless. A sorry fellow, or hussey; a worthless man or woman.

SOSS BRANGLE. A slatternly wench.

SOT WEED Tobacco

SOUL DOCTOR, or DRIVER. A parson.

SOUNDERS. A herd of swine.

SOUSE Not a souse, not a penny. *French.*

SOUSE CROWN. A silly fellow.

SOUTH SEA. Mountain, gin

Sow. A fat woman. He has got the wrong sow by the ear; he mistakes his man Drunk as David's sow; see DAVID'S SOW.

Sow's BABY. A sucking pig.

Sow CHILD. A female child.

SPADO. A sword. *Spanish*

SPANISH. The Spanish, ready money

SPANISH COIN. Fair words, and compliments.

SPANISH FAGGOT. The sun.

SPANISH GOUT. The pox.

SPANISH PADLOCK. A kind of girdle contrived by jealous
husbands

husbands of that nation, to secure the chastity of their wives.

SPANISH, or KING OF SPAIN'S, TRUMPETER. An ass when braying.

SPANISH WORM. A nail so called by carpenters when they meet with one in a board they are sawing.

SPANKS, or SPANKERS. Money; also blows with the open hand.

SPANKING. Large.

SPARK. A spruce, trim, or smart fellow. A man that is always thirsty, is said to have a spark in his throat.

SPARKISH. Fine, gay.

SPARRING BLOWS. Blows given by cocks before they close, or, as the term is, mouth it: used figuratively for words previous to a quarrel.

SPARROW. Mumbling a sparrow; a cruel sport frequently practised at wakes and fairs: for a small premium, a booby having his hands tied behind him, has the wing of a cock sparrow put into his mouth: with this hold, without any other assistance than the motions of his lips, he is to get the sparrow's head into his mouth: on attempting to do it, the bird defends itself surprisingly, frequently pecking the mumbler till his lips are covered with blood, and he is obliged to desist: to prevent the bird from getting away, he is fastened by a string to a button of the booby's coat.

SPARROW-MOUTHED. Wide-mouthed, like the mouth of a sparrow: it is said of such persons, that they do not hold their mouths by lease, but have it from year to year; i. e. from ear to ear. One whose mouth cannot be enlarged without removing their ears, and who when they yawn have their heads half off.

SPATCH COCK. [Abbreviation of *dispatch cock*.] A hen just killed from the roost, or yard, and immediately skinned, split, and broiled: an Irish dish upon any sudden occasion.

To SPEAK WITH. To rob. I spoke with the cull on the cherry-coloured prancer, I robbed the man on the black horse. *Cant*.

SPECKED WIPER. A coloured handkerchief. *Cant*.

SPIDER-SHANKED. Thin-legged.

TO SPIFLICATE. To confound, silence, or dumbfound.

SPILL. A small reward, or gift of money.

SPILT. Thrown from a horse, or overturned in a carriage: pray, coachee, don't spill us.

SPINDLE SHANKS. Slender legs.

TO SPIRIT AWAY. To kidnap, or inveigle away.

SPIRITUAL FLESH BROKER. A parson.

SPIT. He is as like his father as if he was spit out of his mouth; said of a child much resembling his father.

SPIT. A sword.

SPIT FIRE. A violent, pettish, or passionate person.

SPLICED. Married: an allusion to joining two ropes ends by splicing. *Sea term.*

SPLIT CROW. The sign of the spread eagle, which being represented with two heads on one neck, gives it somewhat the appearance of being split.

SPLIT CAUSE. A lawyer.

SPLIT FIG. A grocer.

SPOIL IRON. The nick-name for a smith.

SPOIL PUDDING. A parson who preaches long sermons, keeping his congregation in church till the puddings are over done.

TO SPORT. To exhibit: as, Jack Jehu sported a new gig yesterday; I shall sport a new suit next week. To sport or flash one's ivory; to shew one's teeth. To sport timber, to keep one's outside door shut: this term is used in the inns of court to signify denying one's self. N. B. The word *sport* was in great vogue ann. 1783 and 1784.

SPUNGE. A thirsty fellow, a great drinker. To spunge; to eat and drink at another's cost. Spunging-house, a bailiff's lock-up-house, or repository, to which persons arrested are taken, till they find bail, or have spent all their money: a house where every species of fraud and extortion is practised, under the protection of the law.

SPUNK. Rotten touchwood, or a kind of fungus prepared for tinder; figuratively, spirit, courage.

SPOON HAND. The right hand.

TO SPOUT. To rehearse theatrically.

SQU

SPOUTERS CLUB. A meeting of apprentices and mechanics to rehearse different characters in plays: thus forming recruits for the strolling companies.

SPOUTING. Theatrical declamation.

SPREAD EAGLE. A soldier tied to the halberts in order to be whipped. his attitude bearing some likeness to that figure, as painted on signs.

SPRING-ANKLE WAREHOUSE. Newgate, or any other gaol. *Irish*

SQUAB. A fat man or woman; from their likeness to a well stuffed couch, called also a squab. A new-hatched chicken.

SQUARE TOES. An old man. square-toed shoes were anciently worn in common, and long retained by old men.

SQUEAK. A narrow escape, a chance; he had a squeak for his life. To squeak; to confess, peach, or turn stag. They squeak beef upon us; they cry out thieves after us. *Cant*

SQUEAKER. A bar boy; also a bastard or any other child. To stifle the squeaker, to murder a bastard, or throw it into the necessary house.—Organ pipes are likewise called squeakers. The squeakers are meltable, the small pipes are silver. *Cant.*

SQUEEZE CRAB. A sour-looking, shrivelled, diminutive fellow.

SQUEEZE WAX. A good-natured foolish fellow, ready to become security for another, under hand and seal.

SQUELCH. A fall. Formerly a bailiff caught in a barrack-yard in Ireland, was liable by custom to have three tosses in a blanket, and a squelch, the squelch was given by letting go the corners of the blanket, and suffering him to fall to the ground. Squelch-gutted, fat, having a prominent belly.

SQUIB. A small satirical or political temporary jeu d'esprit, which, like the firework of that denomination, sparkles, bounces, stinks, and vanishes.

SQUINT-A-PIPES. A squinting man or woman: said to be born in the middle of the week, and looking both ways for Sunday, or born in a hackney coach, and looking out of both windows, fit for a cook, one eye in the pot, and the other up the chimney; looking nine ways at once.

SQUIRE OF ALSATIA. A weak profligate spendthrift, the squire of the company; one who pays the whole reckoning, or treats the company, called standing squire.

SQUIRISH. Foolish.

SQUIRREL. A prostitute. because she, like that animal, covers her back with her tail. *Meretrix corpore corpus alit.* Menagiana, ii. 128.

SQUIRREL HUNTING. See HUNTING.

STAG. To turn stag; to impeach one's confederates: from a herd of deer, who are said to turn their horns against any of their number who is hunted

STAGGERING BOB, WITH HIS YELLOW PUMPS. A calf just dropped, and unable to stand, killed for veal in Scotland: the hoofs of a young calf are yellow.

STALL WHIMPER. A bastard. *Cant.*

STALLING. Making or ordaining. Stalling to the rogue, an ancient ceremony of instituting a candidate into the society of rogues, somewhat similar to the creation of a herald at arms. It is thus described by Harman, The upright man taking a gage of bowse, i. e. a pot of strong drink, pours it on the head of the rogue to be admitted, saying—I, A. B., do stall thee B. C. to the rogue; and from henceforth it shall be lawful for thee to cant for thy living in all places.

STALLING KEN. A broker's shop, or that of a receiver of stolen goods.

STALLION. A man kept by an old lady for secret services.

STAM FLESH To cant *Cant.*

STAMMEL, or STRAMMEL A coarse brawny wench.

STAMP. A particular manner of throwing the dice out of the box, by striking it with violence against the table.

STAMPS. Legs

STAMPERS. Shoes.

STAND-STILL. He was run to a stand-still; i. e. till he could no longer move.

STAR GAZER. A horse who throws up his head; also a hedge whore.

TO STAR THE GLAZE. To break and rob a jeweller's show glass. *Cant.*

STARCHED. Stiff, prim, formal, affected.

STARING QUARTER. An ox cheek.

START, or THE OLD START. Newgate; he is gone to the start, or the old start, *Cant.*

STARTER. One who leaves a jolly company, a milksop; he is no starter, he will sit longer than a hen.

STARVE'EM, ROB'EM, AND CHEAT'EM. Stroud, Rochester, and Chatham. so called by soldiers and sailors, and not without good reason.

STATE To lie in state, to be in bed with three harlots.

STAYTAPE. A taylor. from that article, and its coadjutor buckram, which make no small figure in the bills of those knights of the needle.

STEEL BAR. A needle. A steel bar flinger; a taylor, staymaker, or any other person using a needle.

STEENKIRK. A muslin neckcloth carelessly put on, as at the battle of Steenkirk.

STEEPLE HOUSE. A name given to the church by Dissenters.

STEPNEY. A decoction of raisins of the sun and lemons in conduit water, sweetened with sugar and bottled up.

STEWED QUAKER. Burnt rum, with a piece of butter: an American remedy for a cold.

STICKS Pops or pistols. Stow your sticks; hide you pistols. *Cant.* See Pops.

STICK FLAMS A pair of gloves.

STIFF-RUMPED. Proud, stately.

STINGBUM. A niggard.

STINGO Strong beer, or other liquor.

STIRRUP CUP. A parting cup or glass, drank on horseback by the person taking leave.

STITCH. A nickname for a taylor; also a term for lying with a woman.

STITCHBACK Strong ale.

STIVER-CRAMPED. Needy, wanting money. A stiver is a Dutch coin, worth somewhat more than a penny sterling.

STOCK A good stock, i. e. of impudence. Stock and block, the whole he has lost stock and block.

STOCK DRAWERS Stockings *Cant.*

STOCK JOBBERS. Persons who gamble in Exchange Alley, by pretending to buy and sell the public funds, but in reality

reality only bet·ing that they will be at a certain price, at a particular time; poffeffing neither the ftock pretended to be fold, nor money fufficient to make good the payments for which they contract: thefe gentlemen are known under the different appellations of bulls, bears, and lame ducks.

STOMACH WORM The ftomach worm gnaws, I am hungry.

STONE. Two ftone under weight, or wanting, an eunuch. Stone doublet, a prifon Stone dead, dead as a ftone.

STOOP-NAPPERS, or overfeers of the new pavement. Perfons fet in the pillory *Cant*

STOP HOLE ABBEY The nick-name of the chief rendezvous of the canting crew of beggars, gypfies, cheats, thieves, &c. &c.

STOTER A great blow. Tip him a ftoter in the haltering place; give him a blow under the left ear.

STOUP. A veffel to hold liquor: a veffel containing a fize, or half a pint, is fo called at Cambridge.

STOW. Stow you; be filent, or hold your peace. Stow your whidds and plant 'em, for the cove of the ken can cant 'em; you have faid enough, the man of the houfe underftands you

STRAIT-LACED Precife, over nice, puritanical

STRAIT WAISTCOAT. A tight waiftcoat, with long fleeves coming over the hands, having ftrings for binding them behind the back of the wearer: thefe waiftcoats are ufed in madhoufes for the management of lunatics when outrageous.

STRAMMEL. See STAMMEL.

STRANGER. A guinea.

STRANGLE GOOSE. A poulterer.

STRAPPER. A large man or woman.

STRAPPING. Lying with a woman. *Cant.*

STRAW. The good woman in the ftraw; a lying-in woman. His eyes draw ftraw; his eyes are almoft fhut, or he is almoft afleep one eye draws ftraw, and t'other ferves the thatcher.

STRETCHING. Hanging. He'll ftretch for it, he will be hanged for it Alfo telling a great lye: he ftretched ftoutly

STRIKE Twenty fhillings. *Cant.*

STROKE.

STROKE. To take a stroke, to take a bout with a woman.

STROLLERS. Itinerants of different kinds. Strolling morts; beggars or pedlars pretending to be widows.

STROMMEL Straw. *Cant.*

STRONG MAN. To play the part of the strong man, i e to push the cart and horses too; to be whipt at the cart's tail.

STROUD GREEN. The aldermen and corporation formerly met at the Castle in Fleet-lane.

STRUM A perriwig Rum strum, a fine large wig. *Cant.*

To STRUM. To have carnal knowledge of a woman, also to play badly on the harpsichord, or any other stringed instrument. A strummer of wire, a player on any instrument strung with wire

STRUMPET. A harlot.

STUB-FACED. Pitted with the small-pox. the devil run over his face with horse stubbs (horse nails) in his shoes.

STUBBLE IT. Hold your tongue *Cant.*

STULING KEN. See STALLING KEN *Cant*

STUM. The flower of fermenting wine, used by vintners to adulterate their wines.

STURDY BEGGARS The fifth and last of the most ancient order of canters, beggars that rather demand than ask. *Cant.*

SUCCESSFULLY Used by the vulgar for *successively*. as, Three or four landlords of this house have been ruined successfully by the number of soldiers quartered on them. *Irish.*

SUCH A REASON PIST MY GOOSE, OR MY GOOSE PIST. Said when any one offers an absurd reason.

SUCK Strong liquor of any sort. To suck the monkey; see MONKEY Sucky, drunk

SUCKING CHICKEN. A young chicken.

SUDS. In the suds, in trouble, in a disagreeable situation, or involved in some difficulty.

SUGAR STICK The virile member.

SUGAR SOPS. Toasted bread soaked in ale, sweetened with sugar, and grated nutmeg it is eaten with cheese.

SUIT AND CLOAK. Good store of brandy, or other strong liquor, let down gutter lane

SULKY.

SULKY. A one-horse chaise, or carriage, capable of holding but one person: called by the French a *disobligeant*.

SUN. To have been in the sun; said of one that is drunk.

SUNBURNT. Clapped; also having many male children.

SUNDAY MAN. One who goes abroad on that day only, for fear of arrests

SUNNY BANK. A good fire in winter.

SUNSHINE. Prosperity.

SUPERNACULUM. Good liquor, of which there is not even a drop left sufficient to wet one's nail.

SUPOUCH A landlady of an inn, or hostess.

SURVEYOR OF THE HIGHWAYS One reeling drunk.

SURVEYOR OF THE PAVEMENT. One standing in the pillory.

SUS. PER COLL. Hanged: persons who have been hanged are thus entered in the jailer's books.

SUSPENCE. One in a deadly suspence, a man just turned off at the gallows.

SUTLER. A camp publican; also one that pilfers gloves, tobacco boxes, and such small moveables.

SWABBERS The ace of hearts, knave of clubs, ace and deuce of trumps, at whist; also the lubberly seamen, put to swab and clean the ship.

SWAD, or SWADKIN. A soldier. *Cant*.

To SWADDLE. To beat with a stick.

SWADLERS. The tenth order of the canting tribe, who not only rob, but beat, and often murder passengers *Cant.*—Swaddlers is also the Irish name for methodists

SWAG A shop Rum swag; a shop full of rich goods. *Cant*.

SWAGGER. To bully, brag, or boast, also to strut.

SWANNERY. He keeps a swannery; i. e. all his geese are swans.

SWEATING. A mode of diminishing the gold coin, practised chiefly by the Jews, who corrode it with aqua regia. Sweating was also a diversion practised by the bloods of the last century, who styled themselves Mohocks these gentlemen lay in wait to surprise some person late in the night, when surrounding him, they with their swords
pricked

pricked him in the posteriors, which obliged him to be constantly turning round, this they continued till they thought him sufficiently sweated.

SWEET. Easy to be imposed on, or taken in; also expert, dexterous, clever. Sweet's your hand; said of one dexterous at stealing.

SWEET HEART. A term applicable to either the masculine or feminine gender, signifying a girl's lover, or a man's mistress. derived from a sweet cake in the shape of a heart.

SWEETNERS. Guinea droppers, cheats, sharpers. To sweeten; to decoy, or draw in. To be sweet upon, to coax, wheedle, court, or allure. He seemed sweet upon that wench, he seemed to court that girl

SWELLED HEAD. A disorder to which horses are extremely liable, particularly those of the subalterns of the army. This disorder is generally occasioned by remaining too long in one livery stable or inn, and often arises to that height that it prevents their coming out of the stable door. The most certain cure is the *unguentum aureum*—not applied to the horse, but to the palm of the master of the inn or stable. N B Neither this disorder, nor its remedy, is mentioned by either Bracken, Bartlet, or any of the modern writers on farriery

SWIG. A hearty draught of liquor.

SWIGMEN Thieves who travel the country under colour of buying old shoes, old clothes, &c. or selling brooms, mops, &c. *Cant.*

TO SWILL To drink greedily.

SWILL TUB. A drunkard, a sot.

SWIMMER. A counterfeit old coin.

TO SWING. To be hanged He will swing for it; he will be hanged for it.

SWING TAIL A hog

TO SWINGE To beat stoutly

SWINGING. A great swinging fellow, a great stout fellow A swinging lye; a lusty lye.

SWINDLER. One who obtains goods on credit by false pretences, and sells them for ready money at any price, in order to make up a purse. This name is derived from the

German word *schwindlen*, to totter, to be ready to fall; these arts being generally practised by persons on the totter, or just ready to break. The term *swindler* has since been used to signify cheats of every kind.

SWIPES. Purser's swipes, small beer so termed on board the King's ships, where it is furnished by the purser.

TO SWIVE. To copulate.

SWIVEL-EYED. Squinting.

SWIZZLE. Drink, or any brisk or windy liquor. In North America, a mixture of spruce beer, rum, and sugar, was so called. The 17th regiment had a society called the Swizzle Club, at Ticonderoga, A. D. 1760.

SWOP. An exchange.

SYEBUCK. Sixpence.

SYNTAX. A schoolmaster.

T.

TABBY. An old maid; either from Tabitha, a formal antiquated name, or else from a tabby cat, old maids being often compared to cats. To drive Tab, to go out on a party of pleasure with a wife and family.

TACE. Silence, hold your tongue. *Tace* is Latin for a candle; a jocular admonition to be silent on any subject.

TACKLE. A mistress; also good clothes. The cull has tipt his tackle rum rigging, the fellow has given his mistress good clothes. A man's tackle, the genitals.

TAFFY i e Davy. A general name for a Welchman, St. David being the tutelar saint of Wales. Taffy's day; the first of March, St. David's day.

TAG-RAG AND BOBTAIL. An expression meaning an assemblage of low people, the mobility of all sorts. To tag after one like a tantony pig, to follow one wherever one goes, just as St Anthony is followed by his pig.

TAIL A sword

TAKEN IN Imposed on, cheated.

TALE TELLERS. Persons said to have been formerly hired to tell wonderful stories of giants and fairies, to lull their hearers to sleep Talesman; the author of a story or report I'll tell you my tale, and my talesman. Tale bearers, mischief makers, incendiaries in families.

TALL BOY. A bottle, or two-quart pot.

TAILY MEN. Brokers that let out clothes to the women of the town. See RABBIT SUCKERS.

TALLYWAGS, or TARRYWAGS. A man's testicles.

TAME To run tame about a house, to live familiarly in a family with which one is upon a visit. Tame army; the city trained bands

TANDEM A two-wheeled chaise, buggy, or noddy, drawn by two horses, one before the other, that is, *at length.*

TANGIER A room in Newgate where debtors were confined, hence called Tangierines.

TANTADLIN TART A sirreverence, human excrement.

TANTRUMS. Pet, or passion Madam was in her tantrums.

TANTWIVY. Away they went tantwivy, away they went full speed. Tantwivy was the sound of the hunting horn in full cry, or that of a post horn.

TAP A gentle blow A tap on the shoulder; an arrest To tap a girl; to be the first seducer. To tap a guinea; to get it changed.

TAPPERS Shoulder tappers, bailiffs.

TAPE Red, white, or blue tape, gin, or any other spirituous liquor

TAPLASH. Thick and bad beer

TAPTOO A beat of the drum, or signal for soldiers to go to their quarters, and a direction to the sutlers to close the tap, and draw no more liquor for them. It is generally beat at nine in summer and eight in winter. The devil's taptoo, beating the foot against the ground, as done by persons in low spirits.

TAR. Don't lose a sheep for an halfpennyworth of tar: tar is used to mark sheep. A jack tar; a sailor.

TARADIDDLE. A fib, or falsity.

TARPAWLIN. A coarse cloth tarred over; also, figuratively, a sailor.

TARRING AND FEATHERING. A punishment lately inflicted by the good people of Boston on any person convicted, or suspected, of loyalty such delinquents being stripped naked, were daubed all over with tar, and afterwards put into a hogshead of feathers.

TART. Sour, sharp, quick, pert.

TARTAR. To catch a tartar; to attack one of superior strength or abilities. This saying originated from a story of an Irish soldier in the imperial service, who, in a battle against the Turks, called out to his comrade that he had caught a Tartar. 'Bring him along then,' said he. 'He 'won't come,' answered Paddy.' 'Then come along your-'self,' replied his comrade 'Arrah,' cried he, 'but he 'won't let me '—A tartar is also an adept at any feat, or game: he is quite a tartar at cricket, or billiards.

TAT Tit for tat; an equivalent.

TATS. False dice.

TATLER. A watch.

TATMONGER One that uses false dice.

TATTERDEMALLION. A ragged fellow, whose clothes hang all in tatters.

TAW. A school boy's game, played with small round balls made of stone dust, called marbles. I'll be one upon your taw presently, a species of threat.

TAWDRY Garish, gawdy with lace or staring and discordant colours: a term said to be derived from the shrine and altar of St Audrey (an Isle of Ely saintess), which for finery exceeded all others thereabouts, so as to become proverbial; whence any fine-dressed man or woman was said to be all St. Audrey, and by contraction all tawdry.

TAWED. Beaten.

TAYLE. See TAIL.

TAYLE DRAWERS. Thieves who snatch gentlemen's swords from their sides. He drew the cull's tail rumly; he snatched away the gentleman's sword cleverly.

TAYLOR. Nine taylors make a man; an ancient and common saying, originating from the effeminacy of their employment, or, as some have it, from nine taylors having been robbed by one man; according to others, from the speech of a woollen-draper, meaning that the custom of nine taylors would make or enrich one man.—A London taylor, rated to furnish half a man to the trained bands, asking how that could possibly be done? was answered, By sending four journeymen and an apprentice.—Put a taylor, a weaver, and a miller into a sack, shake them well, and the first that puts out his head is certainly a thief.—A taylor is frequently styled pricklouse, from their assaults on those vermin with their needles.

TAYLOR'S GOOSE. An iron with which, when heated, they press down the seams of clothes.

TEA VOIDER. A chamber pot.

TEAGUELAND. Ireland. Teaguelanders; Irishmen.

TEARS OF THE TANKARD. The drippings of liquor on a man's waistcoat.

TEDDY MY GODSON. An address to a supposed simple fellow, or nysey.

TEIZE. To nap the teize; to receive a private whipping. *Cant.*

TEMPLE PICKLING. Pumping a bailiff: a punishment formerly administered to any of that fraternity caught exercising their functions within the limits of the Temple.

TEN TOES. See BAYARD OF TEN TOES.

TEN IN THE HUNDRED. An usurer: more than five in the hundred being deemed usurious interest.

TENANT AT WILL. One whose wife usually fetches him from the alehouse.

TENDER PARNELL. A tender creature, fearful of the least puff of wind or drop of rain. As tender as Parnell, who broke her finger in a posset drink.

TERCEL GENTLE. A rich man.

TERMAGANT.

TERMAGANT. An outrageous scold: from Termagantes, a cruel Pagan, formerly represented in diverse shows and entertainments, where being dressed *a la Turque*, in long clothes, he was mistaken for a furious woman.

TERRA FIRMA An estate in land.

TESTER. A sixpence: from *teston*, a coin with a head on it.

TETBURY PORTION. A **** and a clap.

THAMES. He will not find out a way to set the Thames on fire, he will not make any wonderful discoveries, he is no conjurer

THATCH-GALLOWS. A rogue, or man of bad character.

THICK. Intimate. They are as thick as two inkle weavers.

THIFF. You are a thief and a murderer, you have killed a baboon and stole his face, vulgar abuse

THIEF IN A CANDLE Part of the wick or snuff, which falling on the tallow, burns and melts it, and causing it to gutter, thus steals it away.

THIEF TAKERS Fellows who associate with all kinds of villains, in order to betray them, when they have committed any of those crimes which entitle the persons taking them to a handsome reward, called blood money. It is the business of these thief takers to furnish subjects for a handsome execution, at the end of every sessions.

THINGSTABLE. Mr. Thingstable, Mr Constable a ludicrous affectation of delicacy in avoiding the pronunciation of the first syllable in the title of that officer, which in sound has some similarity to an indecent monosyllable

THINGUMBOB. Mr. Thingumbob, a vulgar address or nomination to any person whose name is unknown, the same as Mr. What-d'ye-call'em. Thingumbobs; testicles.

THIRDING. A custom practised at the universities, where two thirds of the original price is allowed by the upholsterers to the students for household goods returned to them within the year.

THIRTEENER A shilling in Ireland, which there passes for thirteen-pence.

THOMAND. Like Lord Thomand's cocks, all on one side.
Lord

Lord Thomand's cock-feeder, an Irishman, being entrusted with some cocks which were matched for a considerable sum, the night before the battle, shut them altogether in one room, concluding that, as they were all on the same side, they would not disagree: the consequence was, they were most of them either killed or lamed before the morning.

THOMAS. Man Thomas, a man's penis.

THORNS. To be or sit upon thorns; to be uneasy, impatient, anxious for an event.

THORNBACK. An old maid.

THOROUGH CHURCHMAN. A person who goes in at one door of a church, and out at the other, without stopping.

THOROUGH GOOD-NATURED WENCH. One who being asked to sit down, will lie down.

THOROUGH GO NIMBLE. A looseness, a violent purging.

THOROUGH COUGH. Coughing and breaking wind backwards at the same time.

THOROUGH STITCH. To go thorough stitch, to stick at nothing, over shoes, over boots.

THOUGHT. What did thought do? lay in bed and besh-t himself, and thought he was up; reproof to any one who excuses himself for any breach of positive orders, by pleading that he thought to the contrary.

THREE TO ONE. He is playing three to one, though sure to lose; said of one engaged in the amorous congress.

THREE-PENNY UPRIGHT. A retailer of love, who, for the sum mentioned, dispenses her favours standing against a wall.

THREE-LEGGED MARE, or STOOL. The gallows, formerly consisting of three posts, over which were laid three transverse beams. This clumsy machine has lately given place to an elegant contrivance, called the *new drop*, by which the use of that vulgar vehicle a cart, or mechanical instrument a ladder, is also avoided; the patients being left suspended, by the dropping down of that part of the floor on which they stand. This invention was first made use of for a Peer. See DROP.

THREE THREADS. Half common ale, mixed with stale and double beer.

THREPS. Threepence.

THROTTLE.

THROTTLE. The throat, or gullet.

TO THRUM. To play on any inſtrument ſtringed with wire. A thrummer of wire; a player on the ſpinet, harpſichord, or guitar.

THRUMS. Threepence.

THUMB. By rule of thumb; to do any thing by dint of practice. To kiſs one's thumb inſtead of the book; a vulgar expedient to avoid perjury in taking a falſe oath.

THUMBKINS. An inſtrument formerly uſed in Scotland, like a vice, to pinch the thumbs of perſons accuſed of different crimes, in order to extort confeſſion.

THUMP. A blow. This is better than a thump on the back with a ſtone; ſaid on giving any one a drink of good liquor on a cold morning. Thatch, thiſtle, thunder, and thump; words to the Iriſh, like the Shibboleth of the Hebrews.

THUMPING. Great a thumping boy.

THWACK. A great blow with a ſtick acroſs the ſhoulders.

TIB. A young laſs.

TIB OF THE BUTTERY. A gooſe. *Cant*—Saint Tibb's evening; the evening of the laſt day, or day of judgment: he will pay you on St. Tibb's eve. *Iriſh*.

TICK. To run o'tick, to take up goods upon truſt, to run in debt. Tick; a watch. See *Seſſions Papers*.

TICKLE TEXT. A parſon.

TICKLE PITCHER. A thirſty fellow, a ſot.

TICKLE TAIL. A rod, or ſchoolmaſter.

TICKRUM. A licence.

TIDY. Neat.

TIFFING. Eating or drinking out of meal time, diſputing or falling out; alſo lying with a wench. A tiff of punch, a ſmall bowl of punch.

TILT. To tilt; to fight with a ſword. To run full tilt againſt one; alluſion to the ancient tilting with the lance.

TILTER. A ſword.

TIM WHISKY. A light one-horſe chaiſe without a head.

TIMBER TOE. A man with a wooden leg.

TINY. Little.

TO TIP. To give or lend. Tip me your daddle; give me
your

your hand. Tip me a hog; give me a shilling. To tip the lion, to flatten a man's nose with the thumb, and at the same time to extend his mouth with the fingers, thereby giving him a sort of lion-like countenance. To tip the velvet, tonguing a woman. To tip all nine; to knock down all the nine pins at once, at the game of bowls, or skittles. tipping, at these games, is slightly touching the tops of the pins with the bowl. Tip; a draught. don't spoil his tip.

TIP-TOP. The best perhaps from fruit, that growing at the top of the tree being generally the best, as partaking most of the sun. A tip-top workman; the best, or most excellent workman.

TIPPERARY FORTUNE. Two town lands, stream's town, and ballinocack; said of Irish women without fortune.

TIPPLE. Liquor.

TIPPLERS. Sots who are continually sipping.

TIPSEY Almost drunk.

TIRING. Dressing. perhaps abbreviation of *attiring*. Tiring women, or tire women, women that used to cut ladies hair, and dress them.

TIT. A horse. A pretty little tit; a smart little girl. A tit, or tid bit; a delicate morsel. Tommy tit; a smart lively little fellow

TIT FOR TAT. An equivalent.

TO TITTER To suppress a laugh.

TITTER-TATTER. One reeling, and ready to fall at the least touch, also the childish amusement of riding upon the two ends of a plank, poised upon a prop underneath its center, called also see-saw. Pernaps tatter is a rustic pronunciation of totter

TITTLE-TATTLE. Idle discourse, scandal, women's talk, or small talk

TITTUP. A gentle hand gallop, or canter

TOAD EATER A poor female relation, an humble companion, or reduced gentlewoman, in a great family, the standing butt on whom all kinds of practical jokes are played off, and all ill humours vented This appellation is derived from a mountebank's servant, on whom all experiments

periments used to be made in public by the doctor, his master; among which was the eating of toads, formerly supposed poisonous. Swallowing toads is here figuratively meant for swallowing or putting up with insults, as disagreeable to a person of feeling, as toads to the stomach.

TOAD. Toad in a hole; meat baked or boiled in pye crust. He or she sits like a toad on a chopping block; a saying of any one who sits ill on horseback. As much need of it as a toad of a side pocket; said of a person who desires any thing for which he has no real occasion. As full of money as a toad is of feathers.

TOAST. A health; also a beautiful woman whose health is often drank by men. The origin of this term (as it is said) was this: A beautiful lady bathing in a cold bath, one of her admirers out of gallantry drank some of the water; whereupon another of her lovers observed, he never drank in the morning but he would kiss the toast, and immediately saluted the lady.

TOASTING IRON, or CHEESE TOASTER. A sword.

TOBACCO. A plant, once in great estimation as a medicine:
Tobacco hic
Will make you well if you be sick,
Tobacco hic
If you be well will make you sick.

TODDY. Originally the juice of the cocoa tree, and afterwards rum, water, sugar, and nutmeg.

TODGE. Beat all to a todge; said of any thing beat to mash

TOGE. A coat. *Cant.*

TOGEMANS. A cloak. *Cant.*

TOKEN. The plague; also the venereal disease. She tipped him the token; she gave him a clap or pox.

TOL, or TOLEDO. A sword from Spanish swords made at Toledo, which place was famous for sword blades of an extraordinary temper

TOL TAWDRUM. To talk toll tawdrum; a term used by ladies to signify talking a little loosely, making use of double entendres.

TOLLIBAN RIG. A species of cheat carried on by a woman, assuming the character of a dumb and deaf conjuror.

T O P

Tom T—dman. A night man, one who empties necessary houses.

Tom Boy. A romping girl, who prefers the amusements used by boys, to those of her own sex.

Tom of Bedlam. The same as abram man.

Tom Cony. A simple fellow.

Tom Long. A tiresome story teller. It is coming by Tom Long, the carrier; said of any thing that has been long expected.

Tom Thumb. A dwarf, a little hop-o'-my-thumb.

Tommy. Soft Tommy; bread is so called by sailors, to distinguish it from biscuit.

To-Morrow come never. When two Sundays come together; never.

Tongue. Tongue enough for two sets of teeth; saying of a talkative person. As old as my tongue, and a little older than my teeth, a dovetail in answer to the question, How old are you? Tongue pad; a scold, or nimble-tongued person.

Tony. A silly fellow, or ninny. A mere tony, a simpleton.

Tool. The instrument of any person or faction, a cat's paw. See Cat's Paw.

Tooth Music. Chewing.

To Top. To cheat, or trick; also to insult he thought to have topped upon me. Top, the signal among taylors for snuffing the candles he who last pronounces that word, is obliged to get up and perform the operation.

Top Diver. A lover of women. An old top diver; one who has loved old hat in his time.

Top Heavy. Drunk.

Top Lights The eyes. Blast your top lights. See Curse.

Top Sail. He paid his debts at Portsmouth with the topsail; i e. he went to sea and left them unpaid. So soldiers are said to pay off their scores with the drum; that is, by marching away.

Toper One that loves his bottle, a soaker. See To Soak.

Topping Fellow. One at the top or head of his profession.

Topping Cheat The gallows. *Cant.*

Topping Cove. The hangman. *Cant.*

Topsy-Turvy. The top side the other way; i. e. the

TRA

wrong side upwards: some explain it, the top side turf ways, turf being always laid the wrong side upwards.

TORCHECUL. Bumfodder.

TORMENTOR OF CATGUT. A fidler.

TORY. An advocate for absolute monarchy and church power; also an Irish vagabond, robber, or rapparee.

TOSS POT. A drunkard.

TOSS OFF. Manual pollution.

TOTTY-HEADED. Giddy hair-brained.

TOUCH. To touch, to get money from any one, also to arrest. Touched in the wind; broken-winded. Touched in the head; insane, crazy. To touch up a woman, to have carnal knowledge of her. Touch bone and whistle; any one having broken wind backwards, according to the vulgar law, may be pinched by any of the company till he has touched bone (i. e. his teeth) and whistled.

TOUCH BUN FOR LUCK. See BUN.

TOUT. A look-out house, or eminence.

TOUTING. [From *tueri*, to look about.] Publicans forestalling guests, or meeting them on the road, and begging their custom; also thieves or smugglers looking out to see that the coast is clear. Touting ken, the bar of a public house.

TOW ROW. A grenadier. The tow row club, a club or society of the grenadier officers of the line.

TOWEL. An oaken towel, a cudgel. To rub one down with an oaken towel, to beat or cudgel him.

TOWER. Clipped money; they have been round the tower with it. *Cant.*

TO TOWER. To overlook, to rise aloft as in a high tower.

TOWER HILL PLAY. A slap on the face, and a kick on the breech.

TOWN. A woman of the town; a prostitute. To be on the town, to live by prostitution.

TOWN BULL. A common whoremaster. To roar like a town bull; to cry or bellow aloud.

TO TRACK. To go. Track up the dancers, go up stairs. *Cant.*

TRADING JUSTICES. Broken mechanics, discharged footmen, and other low fellows, smuggled into the commission of the peace, who subsist by fomenting disputes, granting

warrants,

warrants, and otherwise retailing justice to the honour of the present times, these nuisances are by no means so common as formerly.

TRANSLATORS Sellers of old mended shoes and boots, between coblers and shoemakers.

To TRANSMOGRAPHY, or TRANSMIGRIFY. To patch up, vamp, or alter

To TRANSNEAR To come up with any body.

TRANTER See CROCKER.

TRAP. To understand trap, to know one's own interest.

TRAP STICKS Thin legs, gambs. from the sticks with which boys play at trap-ball.

TRAPS Constables and thief takers. *Cant.*

To TRAPAN. To inveigle, or ensnare.

TRAPES A slatternly woman, a careless sluttish woman.

TRAVELLER To tip the traveller, to tell wonderful stories, to romance

TRAY TRIP An ancient game like Scotch hop, played on a pavement marked out with chalk into different compartments.

TRENCHER CAP The square cap worn by the collegians, at the universities of Oxford and Cambridge

TRENCHER MAN A stout trencher man, one who has a good appetite, or, as the term is, plays a good knife and fork.

TRESWINS. Threepence

TRIB A prison. perhaps from tribulation

TRICKUM LEGIS A quirk or quibble in the law

TRIG. The point at which school boys stand to shoot their marbles at taw; also the spot whence bowlers deliver the bowl

To TRIG IT. To play truant. To lay a man trigging, to knock him down.

TRIGRYMATE An idle female companion.

TRIM. State, dress In a sad trim, dirty.—Also spruce or fine a trim fellow

TRIM TRAM. Like master, like man.

TRIMMING. Cheating, changing side, or beating. I'll trim his jacket, I'll thresh him. To be trimmed; to be shaved. I'll just step and get trimmed.

TRINE.

TRINE. To hang; also Tyburn.
TRINGUM TRANGUM. A whim, or maggot.
TRINING. Hanging.
TRINKETS. Toys, bawbles, or nicknacks.
TRIP. A short voyage or journey, a false step or stumble, an error in the tongue, a bastard. She has made a trip; she has had a bastard.
TRIPE. The belly, or guts. Mr. Double Tripe; a fat man. Tripes and trullibubs, the entrails: also a jeering appellation for a fat man.
To TROLL. To loiter or saunter about.
TROLLY LOLLY. Coarse lace once much in fashion.
TROLLOP. A lusty coarse sluttish woman.
TROOPER. Half-a-crown. You will die the death of a trooper's horse, that is, with your shoes on; a jocular method of telling any one he will be hanged.
TROT. An old trot, a decrepit old woman. A dog trot; a gentle pace.
TROTTERS. Feet. To shake one's trotters at Bilby's ball, where the sheriff pays the fidlers, perhaps the Bilboes ball, i. e. the ball of fetters fetters and stocks were anciently called the bilboes.
To TROUNCE. To punish by course of law.
TRUCK. To exchange, swop, or barter, also a wheel such as ships guns are placed upon.
TRUE BRITONS. This honourable corporation held their annual feast at the Three Kings, in the Minories, Oct. 29, 1743, being lord mayor's day.
TRUG. A dirty puzzle, an ordinary sorry woman.
TRULL. A soldier or a tinker's trull; a soldier or tinker's female companion.—*Guteli*, or *trulli*, are spirits like women, which shew great kindness to men, and hereof it is that we call light women Trulls. *Randle Holms's Academy of Armory.*
TRUMPERY. An old whore, or goods of no value; rubbish.
TRUMPET. To sound one's own trumpet; to praise one's self.
TRUMPETER. The King of Spain's trumpeter, a braying ass. His trumpeter is dead, he is therefore forced to sound his

own trumpet. He would make an excellent trumpeter, for he has a strong breath; said of one having a fœtid breath.

TRUMPS To be put to one's trumps; to be in difficulties, or put to one's shifts. Something may turn up trumps; something lucky may happen. All his cards are trumps; he is extremely fortunate.

TRUNDLERS. Pease.

TRUNK. A nose. How fares your old trunk? does your nose still stand fast? an allusion to the proboscis or trunk of an elephant. To shove a trunk, to introduce one's self unasked into any place or company. Trunk-maker like; more noise than work.

TRUSTY TROJAN, or TRUSTY TROUT. A true friend.

TRYNING See TRINING.

TU QUOQUE. The mother of all saints.

TUB THUMPER A presbyterian parson.

TUCKED UP. Hanged. A tucker up to an old batchelor or widower; a supposed mistress.

TUFT HUNTER. An university parasite, one who courts the acquaintance of nobility whose caps are adorned with a gold tuft.

TUMBLER. A cart; also a sharper employed to draw in pigeons to game; likewise a posture master, or rope dancer. To shove the tumbler, or perhaps tumbril, to be whipt at the cart's tail.

To TUNE. To beat. his father tuned him delightfully perhaps from fetching a tune out of the person beaten, or from a comparison with the disagreeable sounds of instruments when tuning.

TUP. A ram, figuratively, a cuckold.

TUP RUNNING. A rural sport practised at wakes and fairs in Derbyshire a ram, whose tail is well soaped and greased, is turned out to the multitude; any one that can take him by the tail, and hold him fast, is to have him for his own.

T—D. There were four t—ds for dinner; stir t—d, hold t—d, tread t—d, and must—t—d; to wit, a hogs face, feet, and chitterlings, with mustard. He will never sh—e a seaman's t—d; i. e. he will never make a good seaman.

TURF.

T W O

TURF. On the turf; persons who keep running horses, or attend and bet at horse-races, are said to be on the turf.

TURK. A cruel hard-hearted man. Turkish treatment; barbarous usage. Turkish shore; Lambeth, Southwark, and Rotherithe side of the Thames.

TURKEY MERCHANT. A poulterer.

TURNCOAT. One who has changed his party from interested motives.

TURNIP-PATED. White or fair haired.

TURNPIKE MAN. A parson; because the clergy collect their tolls at our entrance into and exit from the world.

TUSKIN. A country carter or ploughman.

TUZZY-MUZZY. The monosyllable.

TWADDLE. Perplexity, confusion, or any thing else; a fashionable term that for a while succeeded that of *bore* See BORE.

TWANGEY, or STANGEY. A north country name for a taylor.

TWEAGUE. In a great tweague; in a great passion. Tweaguey; peevish, passionate.

To TWEAK. To pull to tweak any one's nose

TWELVER. A shilling

TWIDDLE-DIDDLES. Testicles

TWIDDLE-POOP. An effeminate looking fellow.

To TWIG. To observe. Twig the cull, he is peery; observe the fellow, he is watching us Also to disengage, snap asunder, or break off. To twig the darbies; to knock off the irons.

TWIST. A mixture of half tea and half coffee, likewise brandy, beer, and eggs. A good twist; a good appetite. To twist it down apace; to eat heartily.

TWISTED. Executed, hanged.

To TWIT. To reproach a person, or remind him of favours conferred.

TWITTER. All in a twitter, in a fright. Twittering is also the note of some small birds, such as the robin, &c.

TWITTOC. Two *Cant.*

TWO HANDED PUT The amorous congress.

Two-

Two Thieves beating a Rogue. A man beating his hands againſt his ſides to warm himſelf in cold weather; called alſo Beating the Booby, and Cuffing Jonas.

Two to One Shop. A pawn-broker's: alluding to the three blue balls, the ſign of that trade, or perhaps to its being two to one that the goods pledged are never redeemed.

Two-handed, Great. A two-handed fellow or wench; a great ſtrapping man or woman. Two-handed put, the amorous congreſs.

Tye. A neckcloth.

Tyburn Blossom. A young thief or pick-pocket, who in time will ripen into fruit borne by the deadly nevergreen.

Tyburn Tippet. A halter: ſee Latimer's ſermon before Edward VI. A D 1549.

Tyburn Top, or Foretop. A wig with the foretop combed over the eyes in a knowing ſtyle ſuch being much worn by the gentlemen pads, ſcamps, divers, and other knowing hands.

Tyke. A dog, alſo a clown. a Yorkſhire tyke.

Tyney. See Tiney.

V.

V A L

VAGARIES Frolics, wild rambles.

Vain-glorious, or Ostentatious Man. One who boaſts without reaſon, or, as the canters ſay, piſſes more than he drinks.

Valentine. The firſt woman ſeen by a man, or man ſeen by a woman, on St. Valentine's day, the 14th of February, when it is ſaid every bird chuſes his mate for the enſuing year.

To VAMP. To pawn any thing. I'll vamp it, and tip you the cole; I'll pawn it, and give you the money. Also to refit, new dress, or rub up old hats, shoes, or other wearing apparel, likewise to put new feet to old boots.

VAMPERS. Stockings.

VAN Madam Van; see MADAM.

VAN-NECK. Miss or Mrs. Van-Neck; a woman with large breasts, a bushel bubby

VARDY. To give one's Vardy, i. e. verdict or opinion.

VARLETS. Now rogues and rascals, formerly yeomen's servants.

VAULTING SCHOOL A bawdy house; also an academy where vaulting and other manly exercises are taught.

VELVET. To tip the velvet; to put one's tongue into a woman's mouth. To be upon velvet; to have the best of a bet or match. To the little gentleman in velvet, i. e. the mole that threw up the hill that caused Crop (King William's horse) to stumble; a toast frequently drank by the tories and catholics in Ireland.

VENERABLE MONOSYLLABLE. *Pudendum muliebre.*

VERNONIANS. The gentlemen belonging to this honourable society held their meeting at the Rose Tavern, in Cheapside.

VESSEL OF PAPER. Half a quarter of a sheet.

VICAR OF BRAY. See BRAY —

VICE ADMIRAL OF THE NARROW SEAS A drunken man that pisses under the table into his companions shoes.

VICTUALLING OFFICE. The stomach.

VINCENT'S LAW. The art of cheating at cards, composed of the following associates: bankers, those who play booty, the gripe, he that betteth, and the person cheated, who is styled the vincent; the gains acquired, termage

VINEGAR. A name given to the person who with a whip in his hand, and a hat held before his eyes, keeps the ring clear at boxing matches and cudgel playings, also, in cant terms, a cloak.

VIXEN A termagant, also a she fox, who, when she has cubs, is remarkably fierce

To VOWEL. A gamester who does not immediately pay

his

his losings, is said to vowel the winner, by repeating the vowels I. O. U., or perhaps from giving his note for the money according to the Irish form, where the acknowledgment of the debt is expressed by the letters I. O. U. which, the sum and name of the debtor being added, is deemed a sufficient security among gentlemen.

UNCLE. Mine uncle's; a necessary house. He is gone to visit his uncle, saying of one who leaves his wife soon after marriage. It likewise means a pawnbroker's; goods pawned are frequently said to be at mine uncle's, or laid up in lavender.

UNDERSTRAPPER. An inferior in any office, or department.

UNFORTUNATE GENTLEMEN. The horse guards, who thus named themselves in Germany, where a general officer seeing them very aukward in bundling up their forage, asked what the devil they were; to which some of them answered, unfortunate gentlemen.

UNGRATEFUL MAN. A parson, who at least once a week abuses his best benefactor, i. e. the devil.

UNGUENTUM AUREUM. A bribe.

UNICORN. A coach drawn by three horses.

UNLICKED CUB. A rude uncouth young fellow.

UNRIGGED. Undressed, or stripped. Unrig the drab, strip the wench.

UNTRUSS. To untruss a point; to let down one's breeches in order to ease one's self. Breeches were formerly tied with points, which till lately were distributed to the boys every Whit Monday by the churchwardens of most of the parishes in London, under the denomination of tags these tags were worsteds of different colours twisted up to a size somewhat thicker than packthread, and tagged at both ends with tin. Laces were at the same time given to the girls.

UNTWISTED. Undone, ruined, done up.

UNWASHED BAWDRY. Rank bawdry.

UP TO THEIR GOSSIP. To be a match for one who attempts to cheat or deceive; to be on a footing, or in the secret. I'll be up with him; I will repay him in kind.

UPHILLS. False dice that run high.

UPPER BENJAMIN. A great coat. *Cant.*

UPPER STORY, or GARRET. Figuratively used to signify the head. His upper story or garrets are unfurnished, i. e. he is an empty or foolish fellow.

UPPING BLOCK. [Called in some counties a leaping stock, in others a jossing block.] Steps for mounting a horse. He sits like a toad on a jossing block, said of one who sits ungracefully on horseback.

UPPISH. Testy, apt to take offence.

UPRIGHT. Go upright; a word used by shoemakers, taylors, and their servants, when any money is given to make them drink, and signifies, Bring it all out in liquor, though the donor intended less, and expects change, or some of his money, to be returned. Three-penny upright; see THREE-PENNY UPRIGHT.

UPRIGHT MAN. An upright man signifies the chief or principal of a crew. The vilest, stoutest rogue in the pack is generally chosen to this post, and has the sole right to the first night's lodging with the dells, who afterwards are used in common among the whole fraternity. He carries a short truncheon in his hand, which he calls his filchman, and has a larger share than ordinary in whatsoever is gotten in the society. He often travels in company with thirty or forty males and females, abram men, and others, over whom he presides arbitrarily. Sometimes the women and children who are unable to travel, or fatigued, are by turns carried in panniers by an ass or two, or by some poor jades procured for that purpose.

UPSTARTS. Persons lately raised to honours and riches from mean stations.

URCHIN. A child, a little fellow, also a hedgehog.

URINAL OF THE PLANETS. Ireland; so called from the frequent rains in that island.

USED UP. Killed: a military saying, originating from a message sent by the late General Guise, on the expedition at Carthagena, where he desired the commander in chief to order him some more grenadiers, for those he had were all used up.

W.

W.

WAL.

WABLER. Foot wabler; a contemptuous term for a foot soldier, frequently used by those of the cavalry.

WACUT. The brethren of this society held their meetings at the Bell, in Mincing-lane.

To WADDLE. To go like a duck. To waddle out of Change Alley as a lame duck, a term for one who has not been able to pay his gaming debts, called his differences, on the Stock Exchange, and therefore absents himself from it.

WAG. An arch frolicsome fellow

WAGGISH. Arch, gamesome, frolicsome

WAGGON LAY. Waiting in the street to rob waggons going out or coming into town, both commonly happening in the dark

WAGTAIL A lewd woman.

WAITS Musicians of the lower order, who in most towns play under the windows of the chief inhabitants at midnight, a short time before Christmas, for which they collect a christmas-box from house to house. They are said to derive their name of waits, from being always in waiting to celebrate weddings and other joyous events happening within their district

WAKE A country feast, commonly on the anniversary of the tutelar saint of the village, that is, the saint to whom the parish church is dedicated Also a custom of watching the dead, called Late Wake, in use both in Ireland and Wales, where the corps being deposited under a table, with a plate of salt on its breast, the table is covered with liquor of all sorts, and the guests, particularly the younger part of them, amuse themselves with all sorts of pastimes and recreations the consequence is generally more than replacing the departed friend

WALKING CORNET An ensign of foot.

WALKING POULTERER One who steals fowls, and hawks them from door to door.

WALKING

WALKING STATIONER. A hawker of pamphlets, &c.

WALKING THE PLANK. A mode of destroying devoted persons or officers in a mutiny on ship-board, by blindfolding them, and obliging them to walk on a plank laid over the ship's side, by this means, as the mutineers suppose, avoiding the penalty of murder.

WALKING UP AGAINST THE WALL. To run up a score, which in alehouses is commonly recorded with chalk on the walls of the bar.

WALL. To walk or crawl up the wall; to be scored up at a public house. Wall-eyed; having an eye with little or no sight, all white like a plaistered wall.

WALLOWISH. Maukish, ill-tasted.

TO WAP. To copulate. If she won't wap for a winne, let her trine for a make, if she won't lie with a man for a penny, let her hang for a halfpenny. Mort wap-apace, a woman of experience, or very expert at the sport.

WAPPER-EYED. Sore-eyed.

WARE. A woman's ware, her commodity.

WARM. Rich, in good circumstances. To warm, or give a man a warming; to beat him. See CHAFED.

WARMING-PAN. A large old-fashioned watch. A Scotch warming-pan; a female bedfellow.

WARREN. One that is security for goods taken up on credit by extravagant young gentlemen. Cunny warren; a girls boarding-school, also a bawdy house.

WASH. Paint for the face, or cosmetic water. Hog wash; thick and bad beer.

WASP. An infected prostitute, who like wasp carries a sting in her tail.

WASPISH. Peevish, spiteful.

WASTE. House of waste; a tavern or alehouse where idle people waste both their time and money.

WATER. His chops watered at it; he longed earnestly for it. To watch his waters; to keep a strict watch on any one's actions. In hot water; in trouble, engaged in disputes.

WATER BEWITCHED. Very weak punch or beer.

WATERPAD. One that robs ships in the river Thames.

WHE

WATERY-HEADED. Apt to shed tears.

WATTLES. Ears. *Cant*

WEAR A-SE. A one-horse chaise.

WEDPING. The emptying of a necessary-house, particularly in London. You have been at an Irish wedding, where black eyes are given instead of favours; saying to one who has a black eye.

WEDGE. Silver plate, because melted by the receivers of stolen goods into wedges. *Cant*

WEEPING CROSS. To come home by weeping cross; to repent.

WEEZLE-FACED. Thin, meagre-faced. Weezle-gutted; thin-bodied a weezle is a thin long slender animal, with a sharp face.

WELCH COMB. The thumb and four fingers.

WELCH FIDDLE. The itch See SCOTCH FIDDLE

WELCH MILE Like a Welch mile, long and narrow. His story is like a Welch mile, long and tedious.

WELCH RABBIT. [i. e. a Welch rare bit.] Bread and cheese toasted. See RABBIT.—The Welch are said to be so remarkably fond of cheese, that in cases of difficulty their midwives apply a piece of toasted cheese to the *janua vitæ*, to attract and entice the young Taffy, who on smelling it makes most vigorous efforts to come forth.

WESTMINSTER WEDDING. A match between a whore and a rogue

WET PARSON. One who moistens his clay freely, in order to make it stick together.

WET QUAKER One of that sect who has no objection to the spirit derived from wine

WHACK. A share of a booty obtained by fraud A paddy whack; a stout brawny Irishman

WHAPPER. A large man or woman.

WHEEDLE. A sharper To cut a wheedle, to decoy by fawning or insinuation *Cant*

WHEELBAND IN THE NICK. Regular drinking over the left thumb.

WHELP An impudent whelp; a saucy boy

WHEREAS, To follow a whereas, to become a bankrupt,

to

to figure among princes and potentates: the notice given in the Gazette that a commission of bankruptcy is issued out against any trader, always beginning with the word whereas. He will soon march in the rear of a whereas.

WHET. A morning's draught, commonly white wine, supposed to whet or sharpen the appetite

WHETSTONE'S PARK. A lane between Holborn and Lincoln's-inn Fields, formerly famed for being the resort of women of the town.

WHIDS Words. *Cant.*

To WHIDDLE To tell or discover He whiddles; he peaches, He whiddles the whole scrap, he discovers all he knows. The cull whiddled because they would not tip him a snack, the fellow peached because they would not give him a share. They whiddle beef, and we must brush; they cry out thieves, and we must make off *Cant*

WHIDDLER. An informer, or one that betrays the secrets of the gang.

WHIFFLES. A relaxation of the scrotum.

WHIFFLERS. Ancient name for fifers, also persons at the universities who examine candidates for degrees. A whiffling cur, a small yelping cur.

WHIGLAND Scotland

WHIMPER, or WHINDLE. A low cry.

To WHINE To complain.

WHINYARD. A sword.

To WHIP THE COCK. A piece of sport practised at wakes, horse races, and fairs in Leicestershire a cock being tied or fastened into a hat or basket, half a dozen carters blindfolded, and armed with their cart whips, are placed round it, and, after being turned thrice about, begin to whip the cock, which if any one strikes so as to make it cry out, it becomes his property, the joke is, that instead of whipping the cock they flog each other heartily

WHIP JACKS The tenth order of the canting crew, rogues who having learned a few sea terms, beg with counterfeit passes, pretending to be sailors shipwrecked on the neighbouring coast, and on their way to the port from whence they sailed.

To

WHI

To WHIP OFF. To run away, to drink off greedily, to snatch. He whipped away from home, went to the alehouse, where he whipped off a full tankard, and coming back whipped off a fellow's hat from his head.

WHIP-BELLY VENGEANCE, or pinch gut vengeance, of which he that gets the most has the worst share. Weak or four beer.

WHIPPER-SNAPPER. A diminutive fellow.

WHIPSHIRE. Yorkshire.

WHIPSTER. A sharp or subtle fellow.

WHIPT SYLLABUB. A flimsy, frothy discourse or treatise, without solidity.

WHIRLYGIGS Testicles.

WHISK. A little inconsiderable impertinent fellow.

WHISKER. A great lye.

WHISKER SPLITTER. A man of intrigue.

WHISKIN. A shallow brown drinking bowl

WHISKY A malt spirit much drank in Ireland; also a one-horse chaise. See TIM WHISKY.

WHISTLE. The throat. To wet one's whistle; to drink.

WHISTLING SHOP. Rooms in the King's Bench prison where drams are privately sold.

WHIT. [i. e. Whittington's] Newgate *Cant.*—Five rumpadders are rubbed in the darkmans out of the whit, and are piked into the deuseaville, five highwaymen broke out of Newgate in the night, and are gone into the country

WHITE FEATHER. He has a white feather; he is a coward; an allusion to a game cock, where having a white feather is a proof he is not of the true game breed.

WHITE-LIVERED. Cowardly, malicious.

WHITE LYE A harmless lye, one not told with a malicious intent, a lye told to reconcile people at variance.

WHITE SERJEANT A man fetched from the tavern or alehouse by his wife, is said to be arrested by the white serjeant.

WHITE SWELLING. A woman big with child is said to have a white swelling.

WHITE TAPE. Geneva.

WHITE WOOL. Geneva.

WHITECHAPEL. Whitechapel portion; two smocks, and what nature gave. Whitechapel breed; fat, ragged, and saucy: see ST GILES's BREED. Whitechapel beau; one who dresses with a needle and thread, and undresses with a knife. To play at whist Whitechapel fashion; i. e. aces and kings first.

WHITECHAPEL PROVINCE. A club or brotherhood under the government of a prætor.

WHITEWASHED. One who has taken the benefit of an act of insolvency, to defraud his creditors, is said to have been whitewashed

WHITFIELITE. A follower of George Whitfield, a methodist

WHITHER-GO-YE. A wife: wives being sometimes apt to question their husbands whither they are going.

WHITTINGTON'S COLLEGE. Newgate built or repaired by the famous Lord Mayor of that name.

WHORE'S BIRD A debauched fellow, the largest of all birds. He sings more like a whore's bird than a canary bird, said of one who has a strong manly voice.

WHORE'S CURSE A piece of gold coin, value five shillings and three-pence, frequently given to women of the town by such as professed always to give gold, and who before the introduction of those pieces always gave half a guinea.

WHORE'S KITLING, or WHORE'S SON. A bastard.

WHORE-MONGER. A man that keeps more than one mistress A country gentleman, who kept a female friend, being reproved by the parson of the parish, and styled a whore-monger, asked the parson whether he had a cheese in his house; and being answered in the affirmative, 'Pray,' says he, 'does that one cheese make you a cheese-
'monger?'

WHORE-PIPE The penis.

WHOW BALL. A milk-maid. from their frequent use of the word *whow*, to make the cow stand still in milking, Ball is the supposed name of the cow.

WIBBLE Bad drink.

WIBLING'S WITCH. The four of clubs from one James Wibling, who in the reign of King James I. grew rich by private gaming, and was commonly observed to have
that

that card, and never to lose a game but when he had it not.

WICKET. A casement; also a little door.

WIDOW'S WEEDS. Mourning clothes of a peculiar fashion, denoting her state. A grass widow, a discarded mistress. A widow bewitched; a woman whose husband is abroad, and said, but not certainly known, to be dead.

WIFE IN WATER COLOURS. A mistress, or concubine. water colours being, like their engagements, easily effaced or dissolved.

WIGANNOWNS A man wearing a large wig.

WIGSBY. Mr. Wigsby, a man wearing a wig.

WILD ROGUES. Rogues trained up to stealing from their cradles.

WILD SQUIRT. A looseness.

WILD-GOOSE CHASE A tedious uncertain pursuit, like the following a flock of wild geese, who are remarkably shy

WILLING TIT. A free horse, or a coming girl.

WILLOW. Poor, and of no reputation. To wear the willow; to be abandoned by a lover or mistress.

WIN. A penny

To WIN. To steal. The cull has won a couple of rum glimsticks, the fellow has stolen a pair of fine candlesticks.

WIND. To raise the wind; to procure money.

WINDFALL. A legacy, or any accidental accession of property.

WINDMILLS IN THE HEAD. Foolish projects.

WINDOW PEEPER. A collector of the window tax.

WINDWARD PASSAGE. One who uses or navigates the windward passage, a sodomite.

WINDY. Foolish. A windy fellow, a simple fellow.

WINK. To tip one the wink; to give a signal by winking the eye.

WINNINGS. Plunder, goods, or money acquired by theft.

WINTER CRICKET. A taylor.

WINTER'S DAY. He is like a winter's day, short and dirty.

WIPE A blow, or reproach. I'll give you a wipe on the chops. That story gave him a fine wipe.

WIPER. A handkerchief. *Cant.*

WIPER DRAWER. A pickpocket, one who steals handkerchiefs. He drew a broad, narrow, cam, or specked wiper, he picked a pocket of a broad, narrow, cambrick, or coloured handkerchief.

To WIREDRAW To lengthen out or extend any book, letter, or discourse

WISE As wise as Waltham's calf, that ran nine miles to suck a bull.

WISE MEN OF GOTHAM. Gotham is a village in Nottinghamshire. its magistrates are said to have attempted to hedge in a cuckow: a bush, called the cuckow's bush, is still shewn in support of the tradition. A thousand other ridiculous stories are told of the men of Gotham.

WISEACRE. A foolish conceited fellow.

WISEACRE'S HALL Gresham college.

WIT. He has as much wit as three folks, two fools and a madman.

WITCHER. Silver Witcher bubber; a silver bowl Witcher tilter, a silver-hilted sword Witcher cully, a silversmith.

To WOBBLE. To boil. Pot wobbler; one who boils a pot.

WOLF IN THE BREAST. An extraordinary mode of imposition, sometimes practised in the country by strolling women, who have the knack of counterfeiting extreme pain, pretending to have a small animal called a wolf in their breasts, which is continually gnawing them.

WOLF IN THE STOMACH. A monstrous or canine appetite.

WOOD In a wood, bewildered, in a maze, in a peck of troubles, puzzled, or at a loss what course to take in any business. To look over the wood; to ascend the pulpit, to preach I shall look over the wood at St. James's on Sunday next To look through the wood; to stand in the pillory

WOOD PECKER. A bystander, who bets whilst another plays.

WOODCOCK A taylor with a long bill.

WOODEN HABEAS A coffin A man who dies in prison is said to go out with a wooden habeas. He went out with a wooden habeas, i. e. his coffin.

WOODEN

WOR

WOODEN HORSE. To ride the wooden horse, was a military punishment formerly in use. This horse consisted of two or more planks about eight feet long, fixed together so as to form a sharp ridge or angle, which answered to the body of the horse. It was supported by four posts, about six feet long, for legs. A head, neck, and tail, rudely cut in wood, were added, which completed the appearance of a horse. On this sharp ridge delinquents were mounted, with their hands tied behind them, and to steady them (as it was said), and least the horse should kick them off, one or more firelocks were tied to each leg. In this situation they were sometimes condemned to sit an hour or two; but at length it having been found to injure the soldiers materially, and sometimes to rupture them, it was left off about the time of the accession of King George I. A wooden horse was standing in the Parade at Portsmouth as late as the year 1750.

WOODEN RUFF. The pillory. See NORWAY NECKCLOTH.

WOODEN SURTOUT. A coffin.

WOMAN OF THE TOWN, or WOMAN OF PLEASURE. A prostitute.

WOMAN AND HER HUSBAND. A married couple, where the woman is bigger than her husband.

WOMAN'S CONSCIENCE. Never satisfied.

WOMAN OF ALL WORK. Sometimes applied to a female servant, who refuses none of her master's commands.

WOMBLETY CROPT. The indisposition of a drunkard after a debauch. See CROPSICK.

WOOLBIRD. A sheep. *Cant*

WOOL GATHERING. Your wits are gone a wool gathering; saying to an absent man, one in a reverie, or absorbed in thought.

WOOLLEY CROWN. A soft-headed fellow.

WORD GRUBBERS. Verbal critics, and also persons who use hard words in common discourse.

WORD PECKER. A punster, one who plays upon words.

WORD OF MOUTH. To drink by word of mouth, i. e. out of the bowl or bottle instead of a glass.

WORLD.

WORLD. All the world and his wife; every body, a great company.

WORM. To worm out; to obtain the knowledge of a secret by craft, also to undermine or supplant He is gone to the diet of worms, he is dead and buried, or gone to Rot-his-bone.

WRAP RASCAL. A red cloak, called also a roquelaire.

WRAPT UP IN WARM FLANNEL. Drunk with spirituous liquors. He was wrapt up in the tail of his mother's smock; saying of any one remarkable for his success with the ladies. To be wrapt up in any one, to have a good opinion of him, or to be under his influence.

WRINKLE. A wrinkle-bellied whore; one who has had a number of bastards. child-bearing leaves wrinkles in a woman's belly. To take the wrinkles out of any one's belly; to fill it out by a hearty meal. You have one wrinkle more in your a-se; i. e. you have one piece of knowledge more than you had, every fresh piece of knowledge being supposed by the vulgar naturalists to add a wrinkle to that part.

WRY MOUTH AND A PISSEN PAIR OF BREECHES. Hanging.

WRY NECK DAY. Hanging day.

WYN. See WIN.

X.

X A N

XANTIPPE. The name of Socrates's wife: now used to signify a shrew or scolding wife.

Y.

Y.

YOW

YAFFLING. Eating. *Cant.*

TO YAM. To eat or stuff heartily.

YANKEY, or YANKEY DOODLE. A booby, or country lout: a name given to the New England men in North America.

YARMOUTH CAPON. A red herring: Yarmouth is a famous place for curing herrings.

YARMOUTH COACH. A kind of low two-wheeled cart drawn by one horse, not much unlike an Irish car

YARMOUTH PYE. A pye made of herrings highly spiced, which the city of Norwich is by charter bound to present annually to the king

YARUM. Milk. *Cant.*

YEA AND NAY MAN. A quaker, a simple fellow, one who can only answer yes or no.

YELLOW To look yellow; to be jealous. I happened to call on Mr. Green, who was out: on coming home, and finding me with his wife, he began to look confounded blue, and was, I thought, a little yellow.

YELLOW BELLY. A native of the Fens of Lincolnshire: an allusion to the eels caught there

YELLOW BOYS Guineas

YELLOW CAT. The golden lion, a noted brothel in the Strand, so named by the ladies who frequented it.

TO YELP To cry out Yelper, a town cryer, also one apt to make great complaints on trifling occasions.

YEST A contraction of yesterday.

YOKED Married A yoke, the quantum of labour performed at one spell by husbandmen, the day's work being divided in summer into three yokes. *Kentish term.*

YORKSHIRE TYKE A Yorkshire clown. To come Yorkshire over any one, to cheat him

TO YOWL. To cry aloud, or howl.

Z.

Z.

Zad. Crooked like the letter Z. He is a mere zad, or perhaps zed, a description of a very crooked or deformed person.

Zany. The jester, Jack Pudden, or merry Andrew, to a mountebank

Zedland. Great part of the west country, where the letter Z. is substituted for S, as zee for see, zun for sun, &c. &c. This prevails through the counties of Devonshire, Dorsetshire, and Somersetshire.

Znees Frost or frozen Zneesy weather; frosty weather.

Znuz. The same as znees

Zoc, or Soc. A blow. I gid him a zoc; I gave him a blow. *West country.*

Zouch, or Slouch A slovenly ungenteel man, one who has a stoop in his gait. A slouched hat, a hat with its brims let down, or uncocked.

Zounds An exclamation, an abbreviation of *God's wounds.*

Zucks. A withered stump of a tree.

FINIS

New Publications printed for S. HOOPER.

A GUIDE TO HEALTH, BEAUTY, RICHES, AND HONOUR.

Price 1s. 6d.

Printed the same size as the large and small editions of the Antiquities of England and Wales, and illustrated with 10 beautiful Views, from original drawings taken on the spot by F. Grose, Esquire; the Plan from an actual survey made by an Engineer, THE

HISTORY OF DOVER CASTLE,

By the Rev. William Darrell, Chaplain to Queen Elizabeth.—The original Latin MS. from which this work was transcribed, is in the library of the College of Arms.

THE MANOEUVERER,
OR SKILFUL SEAMAN.

Being an Essay on the Theory and Practice of the various Movements of a Ship at Sea, as well as of Naval Evolutions in general. Translated from the French of Mr. Bourdé de Villehuet, by the Chevalier de Sauseuil, Knight of the most Noble Order of St. Philip; Captain of Infantry in the French Service; late Captain and Major-Adjutant of the Legion

New Publications printed for S. HOOPER.

of Tonnere, and Member of the English Society for the Encouragement of Arts, Manufactures, and Commerce. Illustrated with 13 Copper-plates; five of which, with many interesting Observations interspersed through the work by way of Notes, are the production of an English Officer.

Dedicated to his Royal Highness PRINCE WILLIAM HENRY.—Price in Boards 18s.

THE
ART OF WAR AT SEA;
Or, NAVAL TACTICS, reduced to New Principles.

With a New Order of Battle.

Translated from the French of Viscount de Grenier, Rear Admiral in the French service, by the Chevalier de Sauseuil, Knight of the most Noble Order of St. Philip, Captain of Infantry in the French service, and late Captain and Major-Adjutant of the Legion of Tonnêre.

With Copper-plates to illustrate the Evolutions.

AN ESSAY ON

DAY AND NIGHT SIGNALS.

With 16 Copper-plates to illustrate the Subjects. The Battle and Flag Signals are neatly coloured. Price in boards 5s.

NEW PUBLICATIONS,

By F. GROSE, Efq. F. R. S.

Printed for S. HOOPER, No. 212, High Holborn, facing Bloomfbury Square.

Elegantly printed on a fine Imperial Paper, in 8 vols octavo, containing upwards of 700 Views, &c. finely engraved by eminent Artifts, and a Portrait of the Author by Bartolozzi,

THE ANTIQUITIES OF ENGLAND AND WALES.

Being a Collection of Views of the moft remarkable Ruins and Ancient Buildings, accurately drawn on the fpot. To each View is added, an Hiftorical Account of its fituation, when and by whom built (tracing its poffeffors from its foundation to the prefent time), with every interefting circumftance relating thereto. And to render this work a complete introduction to the ftudy of every fpecies of our national antiquities, a defcription is given of fonts, and the feveral kinds of fepulchral and druidical monuments.

A PROVINCIAL GLOSSARY,

With a Collection of local Proverbs and popular Superftitions, octavo, price in boards 5s.

New Publications printed for S. HOOPER.

Elegantly printed on a fine Medium Paper, in 2 vols. quarto,

MILITARY ANTIQUITIES.

Being a History of the English Army from the Conquest to the present time; under the articles of raising, paying, quartering, clothing, and exercise; regulations respecting prisoners of war, and administration of justice; with an account of the ancient projectile machines the whole compiled from authentic manuscripts, public records, and other approved authorities; illustrated with 80 Copper-plate Prints, neatly engraved.

Also, printed the same size, with like elegance, with 51 Copper-plates, containing upwards of 200 subjects, beautifully engraved by Mr. Hamilton (price 2l. 2s)

A TREATISE

ON

ANCIENT ARMOUR AND WEAPONS.

Illustrated by Plates, taken from the original Armour in the Tower of London, and other arsenals, museums, and cabinets.

RULES FOR DRAWING CARICATURES,
With an Essay on Comic Painting.

2s.

Lightning Source UK Ltd.
Milton Keynes UK
UKHW030952051118
331794UK00005B/330/P